an evening with

NATIONAL REVIEW

some
memorable
articles
from
the
first
five
years

Pg. 70
"John Keynes:
2+2= Anything
you like"

NATIONAL REVIEW, INC.
150 East 35th Street
New York 16, New York

Contents

CARTOONS *by C. D. Batchelor and John D. Kreuttner*

DRAWINGS *by A. Derso and Rosamond Horton*

Printed in the United States of America

FEDERAL PROJECTS, UNLIMITED

BASIC ECONOMY PREVENTION AND MOON MONEY

AID TO OVERSTAFFED COMMISSIONS APPOINTED
TO IGNORE THE HOOVER REPORT

OFFICE OF EVENTUALLY-WHY-NOT-NOW BANKRUPTCY

AID TO UNBORN INDONESIANS FROM UNBORN
AMERICANS

FARM SUBSIDIES FOR RURAL-MINDED FOLKS
WHO DON'T LIKE CITY WAYS

AID FOR INDEPENDENCE OF ANTI-WESTERN
TREE-DWELLERS, IN INVERSE RATIO TO THEIR
CAPACITY FOR SELF-GOVERNMENT

CULTURAL EXCHANGES WITH OUTER SPACE
AND UNCOMMITTED PLANETS

BUREAU OF UNTAPPED, UNDREAMED OF, AND
WE'VE ONLY BEGUN, SOURCES

COUNCIL FOR THE DEPRESSED, DISTRESSED, OB-
SESSED AND REPRESSED, GOLF COURSE
MAINTENANCE AS A DEFENSE ITEM, AND
QUADRUPLICATION

REVIVIFICATION OF U.S. MUTUAL ASSISTANCE PACT
WITH THE REPUBLIC OF SAN MARINO, TO SAVE NATO

HARD LUCK RELIEF FOR OUSTED BUREAUCRATS
WHO SOMETIMES GO TOO FAR

AGENCY FOR REMOVING THE STIGMA FROM
BITING THE HAND THAT FEEDS

DEPARTMENT OF LEAKS, TRIAL BALLOONS, MIS-
QUOTATIONS, DENIALS AND GOOFS

CRACKDOWN ON MONOPOLISTIC PRACTICES OUT-
SIDE OF GOVERNMENT, SUB-STANDARD VICUNA
AND LUKE-WARM REACTIONS TO THE BOLSHOI BALLET

FEDERAL COMMISSION FOR DEFINING A BLIGHTED
AREA AS CHICKENS IN THE BED ROOM WITH OR
WITHOUT THREE TV SETS

SPECIAL WHITE HOUSE TASK FORCE TO STUDY,
THROUGH GROUP DYNAMICS, THE ADVISABILITY
OF RESTORING THE 1933 DOLLAR BY DEVALU-
ATING WEIGHTS AND MEASURES, TO RELIEVE
TENSIONS

ADVISORY COMMITTEE ON NEEDED EXPENDI-
TURES, FREE ENTERPRISE MUST GO, AND UN-
THINKABLE OMISSIONS

DEPARTMENT OF TAX INEQUALITIES, DOLLAR
REDEMPTION IN GOLD TO ANYBODY EXCEPT U.S.
CITIZENS, INITIATIVE PENALTIES, SELF-PER-
PETUATION IN OFFICE AND TOGETHERNESS

BUREAU OF REASONS FOR ALWAYS INCREASING
AND NEVER DECREASING

COMMITTEE FOR POOH-POOHING INFLATION, THE 280
BILLION DOLLAR DEBT AND OTHER FRINGE BENEFITS

CATCH-ALL RELIEF FOR ANYBODY NOT OTHERWISE
COVERED DUE TO TECHNICALITIES RESORTED TO BY
VINDICTIVE FASCISTS IN PIVOTAL POSITIONS

*"How does it go? 'Government
should do everything that the
people can't do themselves.'
Now how can anybody argue
with that?"*

The New Journalism: 'National Review'

JOHN CHAMBERLAIN

Mr. Chamberlain, one of America's most distinguished literary critics, surveys the first years of National Review

The Eightieth Congress—the one which passed the Taft-Hartley Act—lives in retrospect as a gosh-awful nightmare to Liberals of the statist persuasion. It is not so much that Bob Taft finally managed to make his impression in the Eightieth; nor is it that taxes were cut back a bit, or that public housing received a slight rebuff, or that price controls were rejected, or that social security was left precisely where it was. No, the thing which really annoys the latter-day Liberals about the Eightieth Congress is that it symbolizes the resurgence, ever so faint, of an intellectual opposition to trends which they had considered operative for eternity. The true reason for the Liberals' wrath is accurately reported by historian Eric Goldman. Quoting columnist T.R.B. of the *New Republic,* Goldman says with an air of horror too anguished to be restrained: "Everything was debatable again."

That is it: the fear of debate. Although Voltaire ("I wholly disapprove of what you have to say but will defend to the death your right to say it") is still quoted by latter-day Liberals, they don't really believe in Voltaire. They have a birth-controller attitude toward any sentiment which offends the statist canon. It is not that they want to murder an opposing idea; it is just that they don't want it to be born.

Ideas, however, persist in eluding the birth-controller. Since 1947 when "everything was debatable again," there have been many parturitions. Where once the *Nation* and the *New Republic* lorded it over the world of intellectual politics, there is now a whole new journalism of ideas. It is a journalism which has had to struggle into being. But the new journalism has no reason to complain: struggle is the law of life. The new journalism is the more finely tempered for having had to deal with the machinations of the Liberal birth-controllers.

NATIONAL REVIEW is the latest—and, to my mind, the most comprehensive and solidly rooted—manifestation of the new journalism of ideas. Because it is eloquent and effective it has received the full treatment of denigration from the latter-day Liberals. In the beginning, just a few years ago, it was the object of the Averted Gaze. But when the Averted Gaze didn't keep it from being born, NATIONAL REVIEW got the next—or the We-need-a-good-conservative-magazine-but-this-isn't-it—phase of the treatment. That is still the standard criticism of it in Liberal circles. The common element is most of the latter-day Liberal screeds on the subject of conservatism and/or libertarianism is a refusal to argue about anything that is basic. The Liberal will never confront an uncomfortable idea.

When Liberals Are Intolerant

The latter-day Liberal is a Fabian. He believes in a mild, constitutional movement toward more and more statism, toward more and more cradle-to-grave social security, toward an ever-increasing increment of government controls, supports and ownership. To him, a "good" conservatism consists in a willingness to "conserve" whatever "advances" have already been achieved under the New and Fair Deals, plus a willingness to follow the Liberal lead toward socialist goals, though at a slower, more sedate pace. What the latter-day Liberal rejects as "bad" conservatism is any manifestation of a Fabianism-in-the-opposite-direction, a Fabianism which aspires to restore voluntary methods in place of the state compulsion advocated by the Liberals.

When the conservative—or libertarian—opposition to Liberal Fabianism was a mere matter of esoteric books, the Liberal was a more or less tolerant fellow. He could take an Albert Jay Nock, author of *Our Enemy the State,* as a crotchety manifestation of a queer, vestigial point of view. He could write off Hilaire Belloc's *The Servile State* or the works of Lord Acton or Burckhardt or de Tocqueville as a collection of shrewd insights which somehow did not apply when one's friends were rising to power. But when the conservatism, or libertarianism, of the books became journalism—*i.e.,* applied to living trends and tissues—the mask of toleration was off.

Anything the modern Liberal can't take over, or manipulate by remote control, he hates. He will accept the point of view of self-proclaimed "conservatives" such as Peter Viereck or Clinton Rossiter, for these conservatives stem from a Tory socialist tradition which believes in a considerable range of governmental interference in the affairs of men. The modern Liberal doesn't quarrel particularly with the doctrine currently known as the New Republicanism, for the programmatic outline of "progressive moderation" hardly differs save as a matter of degree from what has gone before it under the name of the New Deal. But when a *Freeman* or a NATIONAL REVIEW comes along to propose a Fabianism-in-reverse, the hatred flashes.

The Liberal's refusal to accept opposing ideas as arguable propositions makes for a predominantly sullen intellectual atmosphere. When I first came to New York, in the mid-twenties, the controversies raged quite as they do now. But intellectual warfare in those days was waged gaily. Reporters were not treated as untouchables for insisting on strict standards of reporting: a Paul Anderson could produce the most startling and damaging stories for Villard's *Nation* and still mingle with

1

his opposites in police society. The sectarian impulse had not yet triumphed, and parties were stimulating gatherings instead of meetings of mutual admiration societies. But today there is always a "line" of affairs which must not be crossed. If a John T. Flynn, for example, steps over the line in pursuit of his journalistic duty to ferret out the facts on Pearl Harbor he will get no credit for a scoop. He will be lucky indeed if the treatment he receives stops short with the Averted Gaze.

"Unquenchable Insouciance"

In the contemporary climate it would scarcely be cause for wonder if the image of the Happy Warrior were completely to disappear from the intellectual life. The strange thing about it, however, is that this hasn't happened. It hasn't happened mainly because of the phenomenon of NATIONAL REVIEW. Some time ago John Fischer, the editor of *Harper's*, found the contributors to NATIONAL REVIEW a "dreadfully earnest" lot. Their tone, he said, was one of "humorless indignation." But if Mr. Fischer had indeed gone to the trouble of reading successive issues of NATIONAL REVIEW he must have been suffering from myopia. For the truly distinguishing thing about NATIONAL REVIEW writers is the gaiety with which they accept their mission of confounding the Liberals and making all things "debatable again."

I have been a steady reader of NATIONAL REVIEW from the first issue. At times I have had a feeling that the articles fall short of the fresh contemporary reference that is achieved by hard digging. At other times I have thought the departments were all too contemporary. Reading the issues' over again for anthologizing purposes, however, I was surprised by the long-term timeliness of the articles. I was also gratified to discover that the departments, though they are often unavoidably devoted to issues that die within the month, have the same long-term value.

Beyond all this, what stands up about the magazine is its unquenchable insouciance. Take the spoof involved in the tongue-in-cheek theory that there is actual staff work involved in coordinating or "gleich-

schalting," what goes into the New York *Post*, the *Nation*, the Washington *Post*, the *Reporter* and what-not. Now everyone knows, or should know if he has a spark of humor, that there is no Liberal high command handing out the weekly line on the "McCarthy Era" or anything involving Nehru. There doesn't have to be. The truly horrifying thing is that the Liberal publications all come out with the same sentiments at precisely the same moment simply because their responses have become automatic. Hence the justification in treating them on an "as if" basis.

The departmental contributors to NATIONAL REVIEW write out of backgrounds that combine immense learning with a distinctly worldly experience of their subjects. They, too, have the moral passion which Editor Fischer of *Harper's* thinks is so "dreadfully earnest." But they also have firmness and a quality of urbanity which is the very antithesis of "dreadful." Contributors such as Burnham, Meyer and Kirk have been so tempered in controversy that they do not easily lose their good manners. But the general good humor with which they conduct their departments does not weaken the ability of any one of them to cut through to conclusions that are inexorable. Nobody reading Burnham's reports from the battlefront of the Third World War would ever be deceived into thinking peaceful coexistence possible with someone who has taken an unholy vow to cut his enemy's throat. And nobody reading Meyer and Kirk would ever suppose that the diseases of American pedagogy can be cured with a poultice.

The overseas letter writers—Lejeune from England, Kuehnelt-Leddihn from the European continent—are unbluffable men with firm roots in the older liberalism of the nineteenth century. The editorials, even down to the smallest paragraph, make the most of the humorous, sometimes tragically humorous, circumstances provided by Liberal double-standards, and Liberal doublethink. They give nothing to the easy pragmatism of politics as it is practiced among a people which regards the state as a proper dispenser of bargain counter notions. But they are not so "dreadfully earnest" as to suppose that the political mores of a people can be

changed by fiat. They are written by fighters who know they are in for a war that will still be raging when the torch—and the weapon—have passed to other hands. The quality of combativeness in the editorial columns of NATIONAL REVIEW is canalized by patience. Thus there can be no easy anger directed at NATIONAL REVIEW for its objection to the Liberals' idea that the mores of the American South can be legislated out of existence overnight by a sociological dictum of the Supreme Court. In their decent respect for the organic quality of society NATIONAL REVIEW editors neither expect to have things both ways nor do they propose to let the Liberals get away with the two-way standard.

The Man Behind

When Emerson said an institution is but the lengthened shadow of a man, he had something. The trouble with most institutions, including a majority of the big foundations, is the moral insubstantiality of the men behind them. Thus we have shadows of shadows. The institutional framework of NATIONAL REVIEW, however, is something quite different. A magazine with a single director naturally takes color from the character of its editor, and the editor in this instance is a man of honor in the Ortega y Gasset definition.

The man behind NATIONAL REVIEW, William F. Buckley Jr., is a young man who chose deliberately to buck a tide. Neither he nor Mr. Brent Bozell, who made the choice with him when they were both still in college, could have expected anything but contumely for such brazen effrontery. And contumely is what they got. The remarkable thing is that amid blows neither Mr. Buckley nor Mr. Bozell has lost a fundamental sweetness of temper.

"Dreadfully earnest"? "Humorless indignation"? No, the Liberal critics of NATIONAL REVIEW must have had some other magazine in mind when they trotted forth these stereotyped responses. Their picture of a conservative has apparently been formed by Peter Arno's *New York* cartoon of the elderly clubman. They don't know that the radical zest has passed from the Liberals and found a new home across the lines.

A Fable

Clearly the President of the United States had gone crazy; he had promised a new and dynamic foreign policy and he had come up with . . .

PETER CRUMPET

The message was handed to Ambassador Ronald Hagan at breakfast. He signed the receipt, broke the seal and read it.

Putting the paper down on the table, beside his plate, he grasped both arms of his chair and mumbled,

"My God. He has lost his senses."

"Who's lost his senses, dear?" asked his wife, who was interested in all such things.

The Ambassador regarded her with mouth sprung open.

"Dear," she repeated, "who's lost his senses?"

He swallowed. "The President."

The Ambassador rose and strode out of the room, leaving his wife to her shrunken heads, collected while at their last post in Peru, with which she habitually played at the breakfast table. He ordered coat, hat, cane and Cadillac, and left immediately for the residence of the Prime Minister of France. There he delivered the message.

The Prime Minister got up from his desk, went trance-like to the window, and poked his head out to see if the sun was still there. It was. He returned to his desk and said, "What!"

Ambassador Hagan repeated the message.

The Prime Minister refused to allow himself the luxury of screaming. He stated simply:

"The man is crazee. One never *heard* of the United States doing such a thing." In spite of himself, his voice began to rise. "One never *heard* of it, I say!"

Ambassador Hagan stood in rocky silence. The Prime Minister, whose complexion was changing like a traffic light on the blink, punched a bell on his desk.

"Arnaud, be so good as to get me a whiskey glass and a bottle of cognac."

"A whiskey glass?" said Arnaud.

"Idiot, do as you are told!"

Then he addressed the Ambassador.

"Mr. Hagan, can you explain how this incredible decision came about? What kind of man have you foolish, foolish people elected? Who *is* this Willmoore Wheeler?" shouted the Prime Minister, banging his fist on the table. "Where did he come from?"

"From nowhere," answered the Ambassador. "A quiet professor at a small liberal arts college. I suppose the fact that he was a nobody seemed as good a recommendation as any to the deadlocked Convention. He was picked by the Democrats in a dark horse, surprise nomination. It had narrowed down to a battle between Kefauver and Kennedy, which many Democrats considered a fate no worse, after all, than death. I suppose because Mr. Wheeler was an intellectual, the liberals assumed he'd be on the right side. He campaigned on the basis of the Eisenhower Mess, which seemed sound to everybody. He called for monetary reform, lower taxes, reduced national debt, armed strength against Russia and a flexible foreign policy. It seemed innocuous enough."

"I know, I know," said the Prime Minister, shaking his head. He swept off his pince-nez, rubbing his eyes and temples as if he could rub away reality. The cognac arrived, and he took of it greedily. "Over here we thought he was only another . . . I mean, another Truman or Eisenhower or Stevenson."

"Evidently, he is not," said the Ambassador. "He vetoed the latest Congressional porkbarrel bill on the grounds that this was the stave which broke the barrel's back. He has proposed an immediate tax cut, inversely progressive. He has stated, you must admit, over and over again that it was time Europe faced up to her responsibilities."

"I know all that," said the Prime Minister. Without the glasses his eyes looked as red as a skinned rat. "But

I never thought—who *could* have thought!—it would come to *this*."

"Nobody," said the Ambassador. "Least of all the Diplomatic Service. Nobody thought that when he said he was tired of hearing neutrality and anti-American propaganda coming out of nations which were accepting American funds and surviving by grace of America's might—nobody thought he would actually take such measures as to regretfully inform you, your Excellency, of his decision to withdraw troops, equipment and funds from France."

The Prime Minister hurled the photograph of his mother-in-law across the room and burst into sobs.

The Blow Falls

The announcement stunned Europe. There followed immediately a barrage of hate-America editorials and riots, which were duly followed by a Russian diplomatic offensive. But anxiety had fallen across the bland brow of Europe. The joviality, the outstretched vodka of Soviet consular staffs—a performance previously praised by Europeans, who prefer any kind of theater to reality—were now greeted with disquietude. Journalists by the hundreds from Paris, London, Brussels, Munich, Copenhagen and Geneva, crowded Le Havre to watch the first embarkation of America's NATO forces stationed in France. Overhead the skies groaned under the lashes of departing jet aircraft, and in the distance loomed a great convoy of troop carriers. The Chamber of Deputies resounded with imprecations, but not a few men raised their voices in despair, and even the Socialists wondered out loud whether the Russian lamb might not now become more fearsome a beast than the materialist American wolf. Businessmen who for years had been agitating against the Ameri-

3

can embargo on goods to Russia did not respond to the flood of Soviet orders that came without hard cash; and the government, realizing that national defense was now left in its own hands, proclaimed a strict embargo on military and industrial goods to Russia. (Harold Stassen committed suicide.) The Prime Minister of France shook the Soviet Ambassador's hand rather limply when the Russian came to inform him that his country was prepared to protect France from further American atrocities—indeed, Russia was willing to take over the airfields Americans were deserting. Prices everywhere skyrocketed, and many industries, including the great government industry of subsidization, were paralyzed.

Why, why, why? came the chorus, and the detailed Presidential message which was broadcast over every station in Europe fell upon fear-deafened ears.

"France's instransigent neutrality . . . the outcry against nuclear weapons and missile bases . . . the inability of the government to govern, the unstable situation perilous to American investment in arms and money . . . the rankly socialist aims to which American funds have been sacrificed with conscienceless prodigality . . ."

The message was an hour long, and during the entire hour of its broadcast, people shuddered and asked their neighbors how it could have come to this. One sage quoted an old French proverb: "Nobody recognizes the court fool out of uniform."

The People Speak

At first there was hope in the American Congress, whose record for apathy, utopianism and gullibility had been one of the constants of European politics since the war. There were still many friends of the Western Community there, and no lack of savants like Kefauver, who opined that if the whole world would only be good, it would be a very good thing indeed. Such stalwarts as Bowles and Kennan, Adlai Stevenson and the now somewhat crotchety Dean Acheson, had not tired of calling for a *new* American policy of give and take-it-on-the-chin for doing so, known by them as the Policy of Wag-

ing Peace, and by others as the pluperfect tense of greatness. But their lamentations, like those of a lost chorus, fell upon an empty chamber, and they felt that they were speaking against vast, blank silences. The People—that perverse entity that constantly interfered with the wonderful designs these good men contrived for them—somehow seemed to believe President Wheeler's policy was newer than just about anything being prepared. Congress did censure the President, and several members called for measures leading to the limitation of his powers (the Brick Amendment). The American people, however, reacted to such proposals with undreamed-of violence. Henry Luce was tarred and feathered. Molasses was poured into the linotype machines of the *Washington Post*. Harry Truman and Eleanor Roosevelt were sent two huge gold keys locking two toothy bear traps, with the names of four million, three hundred thousand, four hundred and thirty-two people inscribed on the gift cards. To the dismay of Rockefeller, Fulbright, Gallup, Conant and Soapy Williams, the people obviously approved of President Wheeler's measures.

In France, the government reversed the order of things by *not* rocking: nobody except the Communists wanted to pick up the reins, and there was an almost universal determination that this should not happen. Homegrown Marxists within, and Soviets without—the prospect chilled even the proverbially warm hearts of the citizens of Paris. Russia played it cool, and this was even more fearful. A proposal for federation of the "two great democracies" advanced by Dmitri Karamazov—the newly elected Premier—incited a rash of student riots and greatly increased sheet music sales of the *Marseillaise* (which was the only bright spot in a gloomy economic picture).

On the Putting Green

Pride was finally swallowed at the insistence of Britain and Italy and the Scandinavian countries. A delegation of European politicians, including the Prime Minister of France, flew to Washington to treat with President Willmoore Wheeler.

President Wheeler greeted them at

the putting green his predecessor had installed on the White House lawn. He was dressed in a jersey and flannels, and his glistening white beard gave him a homely appearance. He did not look like an ogre.

"Ah, hello," he said, smiling easily and extending his hand.

"Do you play golf?" hopefully asked the British Secretary.

"Heavens no. Don't have the time."

A groan escaped the delegation.

"Perhaps you are a historian, like Mr. Truman?" suggested Italy.

"A historian, yes," beamed President Wheeler, whose first forty years had been spent studying the Constitution, and admiring it. "But unlike Mr. Truman. My years in the cloisters have left me with a respect for verisimilitude."

Another groan from the delegation.

"But perhaps," said the Secretary-General of the United Nations, who had muscled in on the delegation at the last moment, "you enjoy travelling to foreign places for pleasurable conferences with the leaders of other lands, like Mr. Roosevelt?"

"Actually not," said the President. "I have such a lot to do here, and with ambassadors and the trans-Atlantic cable, there's really no need, is there?"

The French Prime Minister said he had been left feeling a little ill by the trip, whereupon the entire delegation sat down in chairs provided by the White House staff.

"We have come to ask," began the delegate from Norway, "under what conditions you would return your troops and your missiles and your economic aid to France."

"Under no conditions at all," said the cordial President Wheeler.

"None at *all*?"

"None at all. You people have been crying go home for a number of years, and so we've decided to do just that. Now, if you will excuse me, gentlemen, I have some papers to sign. Oh, wait, we can save time."

He turned and spoke to one of his secretaries, who ran into the White House and presently emerged with a small packet of papers. President Wheeler took them one by one, bracing the sheets against the back of a handy Secret Service man, and began to sign them. When he was done he leafed through the packet.

"Britain . . . Italy . . . India—no, India isn't here . . ."

He extracted seven sheets and handed them out to the delegates, including one to the Secretary of the United Nations.

"What are these?" the delegates asked, all a-tremble.

"Similar announcements to those we have handed France. The one for you, Sir—you *are* from the United Nations, aren't you?—withdraws American subsidy of that organization and gives you three weeks to clear out of New York."

"*Us?*" said the Secretary-General, stuttering. "Y-you w-want us t-to clear out? B-but why?"

"On the grounds, perfectly reasonable I think, that you spend billions to no purpose at all except as to act as a sounding board for Soviet propaganda and as a base for Soviet espionage in this country."

The delegation gasped. President Wheeler went on.

"Now, if you will excuse me, I must attend to other matters." They did not move, and Willmoore Wheeler suddenly turned back to them.

"If you must know, I am working up an order telling my diplomats I do not want to see any more pictures of them shaking hands with Communist gangsters, or drinking martinis with them over the bodies of the millions they have murdered."

The English Secretary possessed a face which mottled under three persuasions: one was a toast to the Queen, the second the beating of a good horse; and this was the third.

"Good Heavens, man! You don't mean you would interdict the amenities traditional to diplomacy?"

"I do indeed," said the President. "You British have been telling us for fifty years we are children at the conference table. From the results, I do believe you are right. With the hands of our diplomats engaged, the one in guarding our pocketbook, the other close to the holster, I think we will compensate for our naiveté, don't you?"

Flexibility

President Wheeler proceeded with his scandalization of the world. He announced greater military aid to West Germany, Spain, Iran, Korea, Formosa, Turkey and Greece; he issued a policy statement that henceforth economic aid even to the most reliable of anti-Communist nations was to be in the form of business loans by private individuals to foreign concerns. Wielding his pen like an axe, he cut off all aid to Tito, Gomulka and Kadar. He sent demand notes to several of the NATO nations for payment of past debts. Nehru received a thirty-word cable suggesting the immediate return of Kashmir to its proper owners; simultaneously, Pakistan received a message assuring that country that there were some obsolete B-47s available at Orbach Basement prices.

Dozens of other orders followed: one announced that any further bombing of Formosa territory by Red China would be considered an act of war by the United States; another the revocation of truce in Korea, on the grounds that the Chinese had violated every provision of the agreement; and finally a long White Paper announced that the new and flexible

American policy he had promised during the campaign was to be directed toward the extermination of Communism. This paper was accompanied by the severance of American diplomatic relations with Soviet Russia and her satellites.

The confusion of the world knew no bounds. Europe was embarrassed to discover that its fulminations were aped word for word by the Soviets. Everybody, except a muleheaded majority of the American people and President Wheeler, declared that the United States had thrown the world into a terrible mess and exposed it to terrible danger. Ambassador Hagan's reaction was ambiguous. He embarked upon a two-week binge and got himself run over by a Paris taxi. Lying on a hospital bed, with a distressed wife by his side, he opened his eyes once, blinked, and said: "We are saved." Whereupon he expired, obviously bereft of his senses.

Farewell to All That

Europe decided that to survive the war which this madman American President was bent upon precipitating (oddly enough, the Soviets were acting most circumspectly: they had actually withdrawn from North Korea, although this move was attributed not to President Wheeler's ultimatum but to Soviet peace-mindedness), for Europe to survive, it was regretfully decided, it must drop such precious traditions as trade barriers, national cantankerousness, and the do-it-all central state. In such short order that Europeans themselves were amazed, Europe amalgamated into a loose federation of nations, tightened its collective belt and began to produce divisions in the field which before had been populated by promises only. The advice of German Economics Minister Erhard was eagerly sought, and out went controls and subsidies. France—always the extremist—actually abolished labor unions; Britain, the temperate nation, simply converted them into social clubs which, like the monarchy, were allowed to reign but not to rule. Italy, being a little bloody-minded, shot a number of Communists, but the nation was still Italian enough to prefer the horror of a few riots to the worse horror of foreign domination.

5

The Soviet Union did its best to capitalize upon the American threat, but the more *Pravda* harped upon this theme the more Europe reacted in just such a way as was displeasing—by strengthening her economy, and lifting her guard. "Perfectly right," said the British Secretary. "We must not leave a cricket field unplayed in our determination to stand firm against the wicketness of the United States."

The Soviets were caught in a terrible predicament. If America attacked, which she seemed to be getting ready to do, Europe could not really be depended upon, despite its humiliation. And if the Soviets attacked, Europe would either have to fight on America's side or suffer what President Wheeler had announced as America's latest, newest, and most flexible policy, namely: "All who are with us, are with us; or they are against us. In which case, the fate of the nations whose vacillations have allowed evil to befall them becomes their own concern, and one of no concern to this Nation." He had added, "We will not bury you, but we certainly see no reason why we should unearth you."

No Perch for Doves

Meanwhile, American action was becoming increasingly intolerable. America was acting as if she *wanted* to provoke a war. She sent ships and troops to the Middle East and unseated Nasser, telling the Soviet Union that interference on her part by any indirect method would not disguise the fact that the Soviet Union had taken sides against the United States, and such interference would be met appropriately. To hammer home the point, one hundred ICBM's flashed over Soviet cities and exploded with a deafening atomic roar, seventy-five miles high in the stratosphere. The Soviet leaders objected strongly, but nobody listened. The Soviets tried to take the matter to the United Nations, but the United Nations was still searching a new home, and Geneva, the only likely spot by tradition and record of success (Soviet) in such matters, did not seem to be interested in footing the bill. It did the Soviets no good to call for a Summit conference, because there was no summit any more up-

on which to perch peace doves. There were only the United States and Soviet Russia, and it was apparent President Wheeler did not give two figs for World Opinion.

Meanwhile India was demanding more aid than even the Soviets could promise without blushing red. Syria had disappeared from the Middle East, and the Arab nations had suddenly swung about to the American side, prompted by a note declaring that since the rich oil fields were surely to become a prize of war, the United States would be pleased to know where that sector of the world stood. Chiang Kai-shek—supported by the Seventh Fleet, divisions composed of runaway peoples from the satellite nations, and a new combined South Korean-American drive in North Korea—had successfully penetrated Red China. It was not less disturbing to know that great concentrations of armed strength had lined up along the Soviet western flank, and that the new Radio Free Europe was provoking the satellites by assuring them that any move for self-determination would be supported by arms and capital, and by military strength in the event of Soviet aggression.

It was apparent that Russia must either go to war now or never. Unfortunately, in the eleven months of confusion following America's dramatic reversal of form, the people of the United States had been barraged by government propaganda, this time directed toward the conclu-

sion that peace at any price could be bought only by the death of the Nation, and that only by calling the shots now would the United States survive. (President Wheeler was held by some to be unscrupulous in his use of the weapons discovered by his predecessors.) Every Soviet atrocity of the past forty years was reviewed in picture and story. Futuristic movies of life in America under Soviet domination were shown. The people, in a word, had become trigger-happy, and the production of hydrogen bombs, missiles and bomb shelters had grown enormously. To fight such a nation it was necessary to have more than earth-satellites carting dogs about. More was necessary than paper claims of armed might. And if a war should be fought on fairly equal terms, what would happen to the Soviet system—even if the United States, along with Russia, was effectively destroyed as a world power?

Now the Soviets began to call for peace at any price, and over the next two years they paid in the coin of China, Hungary, Poland, Rumania and East Germany. Europe by now was a veritable fortress, and a fortress bastioned by a sound and free economy. Although one or two nations elected to continue with the Soviet Government, it was not long before the sickle and the hammer of the Red Empire glowed palely on the Eastern horizon, and then sank from view altogether.

"You fail to realize three things: First, people don't sit any more—they flop; second, standards must be relaxed in an ever-increasing spiral downward in order not to frustrate morons; and third, all changes are improvements."

6

Mr. Nixon's Bitter Harvest

JAMES BURNHAM

"The wisest princes who adopted the maxims of Augustus," wrote Edward Gibbon, "guarded with strictest care the dignity of the Roman name." Nor did they imagine that such a guard would be sufficiently maintained by sermons on international morality. "The terror of the Roman arms added weight and dignity to the moderation of the emperors. They preserved peace by a constant preparation for war; and while justice regulated their conduct, they announced to the nations in their confines, that they were as little disposed to endure, as to offer an injury."

For centuries under both Republic and Empire, Roman citizenship was a magic cloak protecting its wearer throughout the Mediterranean world. If that cloak were violated anywhere —whether by or without the intention of the local authorities—Rome's retribution was sure and swift. Every great nation has had such a confident, jealous pride in its own good name, and would not otherwise have been great. To be a citizen, a member, of a great community must be a badge whose worth cannot be weighed on a scale of common ounces. To sully that badge, worn even by the humblest individual, must be a crime that the entire community is obligated to punish, at whatever cost.

This was the attitude—more of feeling and tradition, of course, than of analytic reason—of nineteenth-century Britain; and the rest of the world took nineteenth-century Britain at its self-evaluation. Until a generation ago, when the Liberal-egalitarian ideology began to prevail in its governing élite, this was the attitude also of the United States.

Honor and the Fathers

In its past the United States was unusually, often rather arbitrarily jealous of what it asserted to be the rights of its citizens. To enforce their recognition by other nations was a primary problem of the first quarter century's foreign policy. President Washington, in his Second Annual Address, used words similar to Gibbon's: "The aggressors should be made sensible that the Government of the Union is not less capable of punishing their crimes than it is disposed to respect their rights and reward their attachments." Four years later he plainly expressed the attitude of jealous honor: "There is a rank due to the United States among nations which will be withheld, if not absolutely lost, by the reputation of weakness. If we desire to avoid insult, we must be able to repel it."

The immediate motive for founding the United States Navy was (in President John Adams' words) to forestall and avenge "the injuries committed on our commerce, the insults offered to our citizens . . . [which] are to be attributed to the hope of impunity arising from a supposed inability on our part to afford protection." The unwarlike, isolationist Jefferson had nothing but applause for Lieutenant Sterret, Captains Preble and Bainbridge, Consul Eaton and the other officers who—without declaration of war or explicit orders— took repeated quick and ruthless action against North African raiders who injured the persons or property of Americans. When the rights of American citizens had been harmed and the flag dishonored, it was self-evidently proper that Sterret, on his own initiative, should have captured a Tripolitan cruiser "after a heavy slaughter of her men, without the loss of a single one on our part," and that Capt. Bainbridge should decide on his own that a vessel "was of right to be detained for inquiry and consideration." Jefferson scornfully rejected the argument of "those who expect us to calculate whether a compliance with unjust demands will not cost us less than a war."

The War in 1812 was joined because of British "impressment" of our poorest citizens. Throughout the last century the U.S. government took frequent occasion to demand—from Russia, Japan and China, Germany, the Ottoman Empire, Spain, the states of Latin America—a due regard for the rights of U.S. citizens and respect for the U.S. flag, even when these rested on claims that the other nations had never allowed.

Please Kick me Again

It is not probable that Joe McCarthy knew the detailed formal history of this problem, but it was a symptom of both the depth of his traditional American feeling and his insight into the critical issues of the present that he so often stressed it in private conversation as in public debate. McCarthy knew, *felt*, that a nation that abandons its consuls— like Angus Ward—to Asian jails, that stands passive while its soldiers die slowly in Siberian slave camps, its aviators are brainwashed in filthy Chinese cells, its planes shot down by an Adriatic gangster, its diplomatic establishments smashed and burned, its flag cursed, its troops turned over by their own commanders to the mercies of alien courts—McCarthy knew, felt in his guts, that a nation which not only endures passively such infamies but continues placating intercourse with those who perpetrate them is rotting from within.

The rocks, spittle and obscenities hurled at Mr. Nixon and his wife were a part of the harvest of these shameful seeds. Why should anyone —Communists or the local government whose job is to control the conduct of Communists and other criminals toward visitors—have respect any longer for American citizens and the American flag? If we do not respect ourselves, why should others respect us?

And the nation's response to the Nixon rocks? Abjectly confess how badly *we* have behaved. Pour out more money to the nations that have allowed these things to come to pass. And hasten toward a peaceful summit chat with the master-thug who ordered the befouling attacks.

Let us not wonder, then, at the contemptuous wisecrack with which Khrushchev announced Sputnik III.

7

Learning to Read: Child's Play

Teaching a child to read is easy: all you need to do is channel his intelligence and curiosity— and shield him from 'Progressive' teachers

ISABEL PATERSON

Since parents began to protest that their children were not being taught to read, write, spell, or master elementary arithmetic in the public schools, the response from the teaching profession has been overwhelming. The spate of verbiage poured forth, in counter-offensive and justification, by "educators" and "educationalists," is beyond computation without an electronic calculator.

I have not studied this edifying output at length. To be candid, much of it is written in a peculiar and hideous jargon (called "teacher talk" by one of its exponents) from which the human eye rebounds like a tennis ball. Possibly the dialect does double duty; aside from the content, it might be offered in evidence to show why teachers would hardly consider reading and writing desirable accomplishments. One teacher did vouch that the reason "why Johnny can't read" is that he, the teacher, didn't think it necessary. Fussy parents who remain dissatisfied with the veracious simplicity of that statement have a wide and various choice of other answers. That the answers do not agree precisely shouldn't be held against them. Irrelevance is the most effective aid to stupidity in an indefensible position. If the unconvinced complainers aren't wearied into acquiescence, they may be baffled beyond hope of ever getting to the point.

Thus it has been asserted that the public schools are no worse than they always were, which is to say that they never did teach Johnny to read. This appeal to tradition was documented by comparison of marked report cards for pupils past and present, although marks nowadays appear to be subjective flights of fancy. Lately I saw in a note from a child this arresting bit of news: "I got strate A's in spelling." I don't doubt it. But I am bound to admit that she is a highly gifted child. (Modern authorities on educa-tion say that the gifted or notably intelligent child is a grave problem in school.)

Another explanation is that a teacher is obliged to wait indefinitely for "reading readiness" in a child. By what token the readiness becomes manifest is not clear. Other teachers seem to intimate—they don't make an explicit offer—that if their salaries were jacked up they could, or would, really teach their pupils something. Or perhaps they mean that jacked-up salaries would hire better teachers; I cannot be positive which.

Some years ago teachers sternly admonished parents *not* to teach their children at home because that would conflict with the methods used in school. Home-taught children, able to read, would throw a school class into dire confusion. But recently I came upon an article by a teacher urging parents to teach their own children to read, with the provision that the said parents must consult the teacher. Presumably the teacher would impart to the parents the method by which the children failed to learn to read in school. I have before me an article which sets forth the "so-called word recognition method." This method requires "a bombardment of pictures labelled with words." But, the article asks, "what's to prevent Johnny from confusing B-A-L-L with F-A-L-L when the picture is missing?" Do not suggest idiotically that Johnny can tell B from F if he has learned the alphabet. Johnny has not learned the alphabet, and what's more, he isn't going to if his teacher can head him off. An assistant in the library of a famous university informs me that students who do not know the alphabet matriculate there. I doubt if they stay the course; but what of it? Under bombardment, Johnny has been so "stimulated to evaluate" and his "understanding has been deepened" so profoundly by "visualizing chicks and cows" and saying moo, moo and peep, peep, instead of "memorizing the spelling and parroting the pronunciation" of words, that it would be superfluous for him to attend a university.

Shocking Episode

If heedless parents should instruct their children secretly, I know what would happen. An unfortunate child was left in my care while her mother was in hospital. And the child had to stay at home for a week on account of a bad cold. Aged seven, she had spent a full year in school; and by some oversight she had picked up most of the alphabet. During that week I taught her to read. It was sheer indolence on my part; teaching her was the easiest way to keep her occupied. She liked learning. (So do most children; it is their nature to.) The episode is more shocking inasmuch as I had no textbook, and used some of Kipling's verse as reading matter, because it was at hand. Subsequently, at the end of the quarterly term, I happened to see the child's report card. Her teacher had written on it: "You will notice that Susie has now learned to read *by our method*." (My italics.) I'm sorry I don't know the method of that school by which a bright child takes a year to learn most of the alphabet. And I must add that the child's real name is not Susie. I don't want to bring the authentic Susies under suspicion at school.

The deplorable truth is that on chance occasions I have taught quite a few children to read, with no failures. Most culpably, the way I teach scarcely deserves to be called a method. Nobody could spend years acquiring it. And it is too late for me to reform. I began when I was ten years old, teaching three younger children to read. At that age I spent five or six weeks on the job, teaching an hour or so daily; however, writing and spelling lessons were included. My pupils had learned the alphabet previously. Nobody then knew enough to stop them; it was an era of dark ignorance. Nobody had heard of "reading readiness"; and I certainly did not crave to teach. My mother set me the task, and my juniors were ordered to learn. So I did and they did.

It wasn't painful; I was rather interested to discover that they did not all learn exactly alike, though I taught them alike. (That is all right because *they* do the learning, each in his or her own way from the same material.) The difference is in the two types of mind, one type which tends to memorize by graphic form and position, that is, by the eye-memory of an artist; and the other type which seems to incline more to ear-memory, by sounds; each of course reverses to to recall *both* sounds and shapes. But you have to watch for the eye-memory in the beginning, or a young child may spell the word at the top of a spelling list when you have asked for the word at the bottom—because the child learned the spelling in the order from top to bottom, and is mentally recalling it in that order. All you need to do then is to point out the error, and the child will correct it. Eye-memory may be the slower in the beginning; on the other hand, after some correct practice, it may become extraordinarily quick; the artist's eye is indeed a seeing eye.

The sad aspect of this juvenile episode is that I didn't get a "thrill" out of it; whereas "progressive" teachers are "thrilled" if a child recognizes a word (though of course he can't spell it). If Johnny actually learned to read I fear a progressive teacher would be stricken with St. Vitus' dance. Or would he be dismayed? My own insensibility I attribute to a wrong habit of mind. I expect children to learn. They also expect to learn. We are reasonably pleased by the accordant result; but it lacks the novelty, the *frisson*, of surprise.

Having given due notice that trouble will probably ensue if parents teach their children to read, I may as well proceed to tell them how to get into trouble with the least exertion, if they are bent upon it. First, we may

answer the question, "why Johnny can't read," by general propositions.

1. If a child past mere infancy cannot read, there can be only two alternative reasons:

Either it is incapable of learning to read,

Or it has not been taught.

This is a logical proposition.

2. Any child of normal intelligence (including sight and hearing) is capable of learning to read from the time it can speak in apposite, intelligible sentences.

This is demonstrable by experiment. But the assertion that the child is capable of learning to read is a rational induction from the given premise that it has already learned to talk. Because the intellectual process of reading is essentially the same as that of apposite speech, differing only in the specific opportunities of learning naturally open to an infant. In both instances it is a process of abstraction and intermediate notation by arbitrary signs indicating things, actions, relations, everything that language can communicate. In speech the signs are vocal sounds. In reading the signs are visible marks. The baby doesn't need formal lessons in order to learn speech, because in company of adults it hears the sounds and simultaneously sees objects, actions, etc., which they signify.

Babies: Intellectual Beings

Having learned speech, learning to read is literal child's play. The only difficulty is obviated by brief and simple formal instruction; which is necessary because otherwise the external features of the process are not wholly visible and audible. If one reads a book silently in the presence of a baby there is no clue whatever to the process involved. If one reads aloud, still the words are unlikely to signify anything in view to which the baby can refer or attach them; and there is no evidence that the words are derived from the book. At best, the child may get the impression that it is proper to hold a book while talking at random.

A baby is as nearly a pure intellectual being as possible. Its very first mental employment involves abstraction; with its vision not yet focused for detail, what it observes is the relative position of objects in space, an

impersonal concept. When hungry or uncomfortable it cries, but it does not *think* of its own needs, neither in retrospect nor anticipation. It is engaged in contemplation, in learning something of the nature of the universe. And a baby's power of learning is so prodigious that if we did not take it for granted we should be in a constant state of amazement. The advantage of the adult consists largely in what he has gained from experience by means of that native power. That power of conscious knowledge does not belong to a creature which exists by adapting itself to its environment; it connotes a being who lives by adapting its environment to itself. (And that's where Darwin left himself and modern education out on a limb.)

Presumably the reason we do not fully appreciate the marvelous intellectual feats performed by babies is that we have forgotten the actual experience and truly we cannot imagine ourselves back into the condition of an infant. There is not even a fair analogy available. We cannot imagine ourselves as situated in a physical universe of which we have no knowledge whatever, no comparable experience by which to apprehend any part of it, no speech to ask questions, no physical means at first to move about freely—"no nothing," in the vernacular. *That* is starting from scratch. And that's what a baby does. Within a year it has usually got going on its own feet, utilized its mobility to investigate the qualities of things by its five senses, begun to observe conduct, and attained a basic knowledge of speech. A baby understands a good deal of speech before it can talk, because it hears clearly before it can articulate intelligibly. Also it becomes aware of time, of time elapsed rather than future time, at about the age of ten months; I don't know how and neither does anyone else.

Now if reading and writing were used for communication among adults only by means of a blackboard and reading aloud, with the alphabet permanently inscribed above, every child would learn to read as early as it learns to talk. (I trust that nobody who reads this will be over-persuaded to the extent of demanding that adults confine themselves to the blackboard method as described above. It is neither necessary nor convenient. But would that objection give pause to a progressive pedagogue? It never has; rather it seems to spur him on. I shudder at the prospect.)

Anyhow, the longer instruction in reading is deferred after the child can speak, the less "ready" the child will be, because the extreme rapidity with which a young child observes and memorizes tends to slow down and diminish. During the period when a child is memorizing something new every waking hour, twenty-six items, the letters of the alphabet (one of the greatest inventions of mankind) slipped into the young mind one by one, are as easy as pie. Yet those twenty-six signs, mostly denoted in sound by monosyllables, contain all the components of words, the elements of reading. I am not saying that it is imperative that a child should learn to read in its second year; I am saying that it is easily possible. Of course the child can still learn quickly for a good many years; but I should certainly advise that it be taught to read by the age of five, or earlier if you like, because early reading tends to facilitate correct spelling. Also rapid and correct readers usually have learned early.

Begin then by teaching the alphabet. It won't take very long, if you will be so kind as to refrain from distracting the child by blether about cows and chicks or saying this letter looks like something else and see the curly tail of that letter and B stands for blah-blah. With the complete alphabet in its usual order before the child, point to a letter, say "That is A" or B or C, etc.; and have the child repeat it. One letter may be enough for one lesson. (It would save time and effort if the alphabet were shown in four types, that is, printing and cursive each in both capitals and small letters, and in four lines, so that each letter can be identified in its four types at once. If you think the child won't understand their identity, you are mistaken. Odds on it has better brains than you have.) After several repetitions, ask the child to name the letter without your naming it first. Also recite the whole alphabet and have the child repeat it after you. That's all, until the child can name each letter at sight and recite the alphabet by heart.

Then go on to reading, and teach it in just the same way, naming a word, having the child spell it out, and giving the child the sounds of the letters in the word. As soon as a child has caught onto a few short words, tell it that long words are no harder to read than short ones, being made up of short sections. Don't push the child; but insist on correctness; do not allow the child to mumble, jumble, guess and give up. Guessing can be averted by proper timing; if a child can't remember, naturally it will hesitate; then you must name the letter or word before guessing begins.

Never be impatient. A child naturally accepts parental authority, and will do the best it can if it is not terrified or distracted. Don't grudge praise on just occasion.

Finally, the younger the child, the briefer the lesson should be. If you undertake to teach a child between two and three years old, five minutes is long enough to exact close attention, increasing to an hour or so by

the age of seven. If the attention of an infant could be fixed for a considerable time, it would have no chance of survival in a world containing a multiplicity of objects which may impinge on it and which therefore must be observed at a glance. Two or three lessons may be given in a day if you choose. One a day will ensure a steady advance. If you will pay attention yourself you will see when the child is really unable to concentrate any longer; let that end the lesson. In compensation, the child has an astounding faculty of learning in a flash.

Very well, the result will be that Johnny can read, and you and he will both be in for plenty of trouble. At school Johnny will be given insipid rubbish to putter over, until he is bored to stupefaction. You'll have to maintain his interest in reading at home. It is unlikely that he will get any higher marks. The prevailing system of marks was contrived to "equalize" the children, not to record the facts.

What Johnny and his parents are up against is a nation-wide vested interest of professionals who draw six years pay for teaching a child rather less than it could learn in about the equivalent of a year's time in school. There is also a paid lobby to advocate that interest, and a lot of politicians anxious for votes. And there is officialdom in general, the fraternity of bureaucrats, always ready to spring to the aid of their kind. Finally, though of much slighter influence, there are publishers whose "backlog" of textbooks is important to them— and a deep gouge in the taxpayer. Johnny's illiteracy is a valuable property, not precisely for him, but for a great many other people, who have put themselves across as the recognized authorities on education. To meddle with their major asset is to invite unpredictable reprisals.

Here is a curious item which got into the public press. Mr. and Mrs. Charles Dameron of Silver Springs, Md., adopted an eight-months-old baby girl, named Dori. Mr. Dameron is a Washington city fireman. The Damerons own their home. They are both comparatively young, of pleasing appearance; and Dori looks happy, in a family photo. Dori has grown to be two and a half years old and the Damerons thought it would be nice for her to have a brother. They applied to Maryland's Montgomery Social Service League to adopt a boy baby. The Social Service League said no, they would not allow the Damerons to adopt another child. Why not? Well, little Dori had been "tested." *She could read.* The Damerons had taught her! Dori (not the Damerons, of course) was accorded a very high IQ because she could read—an accomplishment which any normal child could be taught by the same age. Miss Elizabeth Montgomery, of the Social Service League, said: "If we had another very bright child, we would place it in a home we considered had superior advantages."

Let that be a lesson to *you*, if you intend to teach your Johnny to read. And don't say I didn't warn you. Some official egghead will surely find or make occasion to insult you publicly, personally, and gratuitously— for bucking the system. Still, if you are determined, here's luck; and in the long run Johnny may thank you.

The Case of Paul H. Hughes
—The Liberal Light that Failed

[handwritten annotation: Article is veiled support of McCarthy through criticism of libsls hypocrisy]

WM. F. BUCKLEY JR.

*"The notorious Hughes case never ceases to deserve retelling,"
the* New Republic *commented in a recent review of* Up From
Liberalism, *"but what does [it] prove about Liberalism?" If the
Hughes case deserves retelling, one wonders why the* New Republic *not only doesn't retell it, but has never yet given its readers
a full account of the case they nonetheless call "notorious." It is
not only the* New Republic, *but the entire world of Liberal journalism which perseveres in its silence about the little confidence
man in Washington who made a dozen prominent Liberals jump
through his hoop in the course of the anti-McCarthy hysteria in
1954.*

*NATIONAL REVIEW alone covered the case exhaustively when it
came up in 1956. Our readership was then under ten thousand.
Even so, we have received repeated requests to review the case.
We proceed to do so—on the fourth anniversary of the Hughes trial.
We tell it not only because the story is fascinating, but because we
do believe, making bold to contradict the* New Republic, *that the
case proves a considerable lot about contemporary Liberalism. As
does the continued suppression of the case. We publish here-
with an account of the case adapted from* Up From Liberalism,
by William F. Buckley Jr.

*Let us do away with confidential in-
formants, dossiers, political spies . . .
No one can guess where this process
of informing will end.*

Joseph L. Rauh Jr. in
The Progressive, May 1950

Certainly Joseph Rauh would never
have guessed that his own use of confidential informants, dossiers, and
political spies would one day result
in a jury of his peers' refusing to take
his word over that of a self-confessed
liar and confidence man.

From time to time in the course of
events a symbolic incident suddenly
plants before our vision the concentrated meaning of a complex historical process. Though humbler in scale
and more banal than the mighty ex-
emplars that we find in history books,
the trial of Paul Hughes was such an
incident. Paul Hughes was a minor
scoundrel. But he dealt with major
figures on the American scene, and in
the nature of his dealing with them,
lies the key to major contemporary
enigmas.

The witnesses who appeared in the
trial of Paul Hughes are the responsible leaders of powerful institutions
that are at the ideological core of contemporary Liberalism. They included
Joseph L. Rauh Jr., Chairman of
Americans for Democratic Action, and
the most conspicuous and active civil
rights lawyer on the American scene.
Telford Taylor, prominent civil rights
lawyer, sometime chairman of the
National Committee for an Effective
Congress—a forceful Liberal lobby of
lustrous membership. Philip Graham,
James Russell Wiggins, and Alfred
Friendly, the three top officials of the
Washington Post and Times Herald, a
leading organ of American Liberalism.
James Wechsler, co-founder of Amer-
icans for Democratic Action, editor of
the *New York Post.* General Corne-
lius Mara, White House aide and in-
timate of President Truman. Clayton
Fritchey, editor of the Democratic
Party's official magazine, *Democratic
Digest,* and deputy chairman of the
Party's National Committee. Also in-
volved in the Hughes case, though not

as witnesses, were Robert Eichholtz,
Washington attorney, Rome representative of the Marshall Plan under
the Truman Administration, and generous financial contributor to the
ADA; Paul Porter, former high official of the Roosevelt and Truman Ad-
ministrations, former publicity director of the Democratic National Committee; Clark Clifford, special counsel
and leading adviser to President Truman (1946-1950).

Here was in no sense a casual selection of unrelated individuals. The
evidence shows that they and their
institutions are actively interrelated—
"interlocked," as one says of business
corporations. These men know each
other intimately, confide in each other,
collaborate actively, give each other
mutual support and assistance. It was
they who were, historically and philosophically speaking, up for judgment at the trial of the 35-year-old
half-literate confidence man, Paul
Hughes.

From FBI to ADA

Consider the story.

In January 1954, Paul Hughes, recently discharged from the Air Force,
was still without a regular job. Immediately after his discharge the previous summer, he had approached the
staff director of Senator McCarthy's
Subcommittee on Investigations—with
a lurid tale of high treason at the
critical American Air Force base at
Dhahran, where he had recently been
stationed. Mr. Francis Carr took notes,
checked the story (as it was his duty
to do), arrived at the conclusion in a
matter of days that it was a fabrica-
tion, and refused further association
with Hughes, whom he never saw
again. Hughes tried the FBI. Again
his story was checked; again he was
shown the door. Paul Hughes crossed
the street.

11

He called on retired General Mara, friend of Harry Truman and big Democrats who, after a few sessions with Hughes, put him on, enthusiastically, to Clayton Fritchey, editor of the *Democratic Digest.* He was a secret member of the staff of Senator McCarthy's committee, Hughes lied to them, and was disgusted by what he saw going on about him. He was prepared, *pro bono publico,* to report secretly to them the secret doings of the Committee. They signed him up zestfully, dutifully accepted the aliases he imposed on them ("Yale" and "Ewing"), and paid him, over a period of a few months, $2,300 for "expenses." In January, evidently seeking to broaden his clientele, Hughes approached the worldly Joseph L. Rauh Jr. Before he was through with him, he had 8,500 of Rauh's dollars.

A Call to Glory

Hughes unfolded to Rauh a phantasmagoria of treacherous doings on the part of McCarthy and his associates—so grotesque and bizarre, so beyond the normal imagination, that they would surely have struck Rauh as incredible had they been imputed to a Communist, rather than to Senator McCarthy. But Rauh was instantly taken in, and asked Hughes for more and more, so hot was his lust for anti-McCarthyana.

Hughes obligingly brought in a 94-page document which is, in its way, a work of genius. One might easily suppose, on reading it, that it was the work of a master psychiatrist seeking, simultaneously, to assuage and to aggravate a patient of unbalanced political outlook. The salve was there—for here was confirmation in abundance of the worst one could imagine about McCarthy; and also the galvanizer—here was a call to glory, a call for extraordinary exertions to destroy the monster McCarthy.

There was something in this remarkable document that fed on, and then quickly nourished, every Liberal political neurosis of early 1954. Here was evidence of a secret and dark alliance between Eisenhower and McCarthy; of tantalizing rivalries between the staffs of the Jenner (Internal Security) and the McCarthy (Government Operations Investigations) committees; of imminent plans to enter into forbidden communica-

tion with Igor Gouzenko, the inaccessible defector who blew the Soviet spy ring in Ottawa and was still being kept under wraps, nine years later, by the Canadian Government; of marital problems developing between Senator and Mrs. McCarthy; of a clandestine White House conference at which a smear campaign against the Democratic Party was programmed; of McCarthy's personal views (revealed through a transcription of miscellaneous animadversions) on such disparate persons and things as Attorney General Herbert Brownell, Air Force bases, Drew Pearson, ethics, Leonard Hall; of McCarthy informers scattered about in the White House, in the Central Intelligence Agency, in the State Department; excruciating teasers about informants whose identity had not been disclosed; and the whole wrapped up in a chaotic package of notes, official memoranda, inter-office communications, secret transcripts, here virtually illiterate, here eloquent, always steaming with drama, and emitting a sex appeal irresistible to professional anti-McCarthyites.

Trial for Perjury

Thus the nine-months-long association had begun. Now, two years after the fateful encounter, Joseph L. Rauh Jr. sat in a federal courtroom in New York, at the trial, for perjury, of Paul H. Hughes. After leaving Rauh, *et al.,* it transpired, Hughes (in a maneuver too complex to go into here) had, while posing as a private investigator, informed a grand jury investigating the redefection of Harvey Matusow to Communism, that Joseph Rauh and his associates had been instrumental in persuading Matusow to disavow the sworn evidence he had given in previous years against his sometime associates in the Communist Party. (Rauh *et al.* denied any foreknowledge of Matusow's

---

From the Document that Sold Rauh

(On the strength of a 94-page document composed by Paul Hughes, Joseph L. Rauh entered into an arrangement with Hughes to report to him [Rauh] regularly on the activities of Senator McCarthy and the Government Operations Investigations Committee. Below are some excerpts from this document.)

. . . as McCarthy is presently violating some very serious military and civil laws, we should obtain photographs and written evidence and witnesses to that effect. The result of evidence of this nature is not only elimination but also prosecution by the Federal Government as well. You must make a decision relative to whether you want McCarthy removed permanently or not. If you do, it is relatively a simple legal matter. . . .

There are many important military and civil officials in the Washington area alone willing to go to any extremes to remove McCarthyism from the political scene. Any coordination desired in this matter is relatively simple to obtain. Surely no obstacle exists in coordinated observation of me during my unauthorized procurement of classified material and my subsequent handling and disposition of same. Under coordinated but secure surveillance, observation will disclose that I surreptitiously procured [according to instructions from McCarthy] various amounts of classified data; photographic evidence, controlled, will pinpoint McCarthy personnel receiving unauthorized classified material from me. Phone taps can be utilized, initially, to tie in all illegal incidents performed by me to specific McCarthy staff personnel. Phone taps can be further utilized for admissions by staff personnel of security violations and compromises of classified military projects. . . .

. . . being nice, too ethical, or squeamish, will accomplish less than nothing where McCarthy is concerned. . . .

about-face.) The grand jury, in exploring Hughes' charge, had unearthed the story of his dealings with Rauh, and indicted him for perjury in the Matusow matter. A second charge against Hughes was that he had perjured himself in telling the grand jury that Rauh had associated with him knowing all along the fraudulence of his representations.

Rauh sat down on the witness chair with the unenviable task of persuading the jury that, though a sophisticated and experienced man of the world, he had worked hand in glove with Hughes without ever suspecting him of being a phony. Hughes' court-appointed defense attorney took on the obligation of attempting to persuade the jury that this was unthinkable; so the legal battle went forward between two competing points of view, 1) that Rauh was a knave (argued by Hughes and his lawyer), and 2) that he was a fool (argued by Rauh and the government).

Rauh told the jury that he had been interested only in developing a legal case against McCarthy, not in having a prurient view of McCarthy's personal affairs. In that case, why did he not instruct Hughes to limit his reports to evidence of legal wrongdoing? Rauh began to hedge.

Q. Wasn't it your testimony, Mr. Rauh. [Hughes' lawyer asked] that the sole thing you were interested in with reference to Senator McCarthy was evidence of the illegal acts; and any other type of information, no matter how derogatory about Senator McCarthy, you were not interested in at all?
Rauh. . . . I said what I was interested in was illegal and unlawful acts. I don't remember whether I ever specifically said [to Hughes], "No matter how derogatory it is, please don't furnish it." That might go a little bit farther than (interrupted).

Alfred Friendly of the *Post* (alias "Dinwiddie") had an equally difficult time explaining why he had jotted down—in longhand—page after page of idle anti-McCarthyana after talking with Hughes,[1] which had nothing to do with allegedly illegal activities. Clayton Fritchey more or less gave up the attempt to persuade the court

1. Court Exhibits 52A through 52D.
2. Mr. Rauh has other views when it comes to the question whether loyalty risks should be allowed to hold down government jobs in nonsensitive positions.

Joseph L. Rauh Jr.

that his interest in McCarthy's affairs was limited. Why was he so interested, he was asked, in the fact that, according to Hughes, McCarthy had a sympathizer on the *Louisville Courier-Journal,* in violation of no known or conceivable law? "What did *that* have to do with illegal activities?" the judge asked. "It happened—a friend of mine happened to be publisher of the *Courier-Journal* . . .," was the answer.

Case of the Cooking Editor

The Court wanted to know why, if Hughes' employers were exclusively interested in McCarthy's alleged illegalities, they had not turned the whole matter over to the Justice Department, rather than keep it within the bosom of the National Committee for an Effective Congress, the ADA, the *Washington Post,* and other factional instruments of a political movement. Several witnesses had a go at answering the question. "Did you explain to Mr. Hughes why you called in Mr. Fritchey and, let's say, not Mr. Brownell?", General Mara was asked. "I don't quite—well," said the General, "the only reason I called in Mr. Fritchey was, I felt he had newspaper background, that he could analyze this thing. . . ."

Attorney for the Defense. [Rauh had just admitted that Hughes informed him that McCarthy's spy on the *New York Post* was the *Post's* cooking editor.] Did you call Mr. Wechsler, editor of the *Post,* and tell him?
Rauh. Yes, sir.
Q. You didn't feel that the cooking editor was going to slant any recipes in McCarthy's favor, did you?
A. That wasn't the purpose. That wouldn't have been the purpose to have somebody there.
Q. What *was* the purpose of McCarthy having a spy as the cooking editor?

A. Because a cooking editor like anybody else has access to all the records, files and clips and other matters on the paper and to all the discussion. It doesn't matter who the person is. I didn't feel he should have *anybody* on the paper.[2]
The Court (interrupting). You don't believe in having spies?
Rauh. No, Sir.
Q. Unless they are **your own?**
A. Unless you are trying to uncover illegal activity which I was trying to do.
Q. You didn't think McCarthy was trying to **uncover illegal activity?**
A. No, I didn't.
Q. You thought you were the only one trying to do that?
A. I thought the *Washington Post* and I were the only ones trying to do that.

—leaving the fate of the country in a very few hands, the jurors must have thought.

—Had Rauh done anything he was ashamed of? He regretted, of course, having been taken in; nothing else.— What about the ethical problem of dealing with such a man as Hughes? Well, neither he nor Fritchey nor anyone else had known he was a confidence man.—But surely they knew from what Hughes himself said, that he was a shady character?—Had not both Rauh and Fritchey received from Hughes a hair-raising program of suggested action against Senator McCarthy in the teeth of which they formed their association?

Q. [Attorney for the Defense]. Do you recall whether Hughes at any time expressed any opinions which caused you seriously to doubt his ethics or morality?
Fritchey. No, not one single thing, no.

The Great Partnership

Excerpts from a memorandum to Clayton Fritchey by Hughes, dated December 1953, and subsequently incorporated in the report prepared for Joe Rauh:

Phone taps can be utilized [against McCarthy] . . . Don't discount the tremendous value in just bargaining power of recorded phone discussions. . . . A program of this type, although not nice, can result in harm to no one except [McCarthy] . . . As mentioned earlier, being nice, too ethical or squeamish, will accomplish less than nothing where McCarthy is concerned. McCarthy has stated many times, "Ethics went out the window with buttoned shoes." So therefore I don't see the necessity for us [sic] to send a boy to do a man's work. If both federal and civil law enforcement agencies use the same unethical procedures to bring to justice criminals, are we not justified in using similar methods to expose [McCarthy] . . . ? It is most easy to prove and document [McCarthy's guilt] . . . by relaxing somewhat on ethics. This perhaps is probably what I'm best suited for. . . .

Joe Rauh and Clayton Fritchey evidently agreed; and the great partnership was founded.

The Dose Increases

In the course of the months to come, things got better and better. Getting reports from Paul Hughes was, for Joe Rauh—and for his friends Fritchey and Friendly—like taking dope. The dose had to be increased every time; and, always obliging, Paul Hughes always increased it. By the time the summer was well along, and their addiction complete, Hughes was driven to rather desperate measures to keep up the flow of information on the rascality of McCarthy. He had already tried, successfully, a melodramatic tale about how he had had to move his wife and child to another state for fear that McCarthy, when he discovered he had been double-crossed, would send around some of his thugs to wipe out Hughes' family. And then, a few weeks later, he had tried to get money from Al Friendly, of the *Washington Post* (who was acting as substitute paymaster while Rauh was in Europe)—to turn over, said Hughes, to an investigator on McCarthy's staff to be used by that investigator to buy off a girl he had gotten into trouble. But what did all this have to do with the *Washington Post*, he was asked. Obvious, said Hughes: by getting the investigator out of a jam, he could further ingratiate himself and get still *more* intimate secrets about the doings of McCarthy and the committee!

By midsummer, dizzied perhaps by an equatorial sun, Paul Hughes took a step which, notwithstanding a six-month run of steady successes, he must have deemed a little chancy. It must have been with a quiver of trepidation that he told his thirsting little group that Senator McCarthy and his staff had amassed an arsenal of pistols, lugers, and submachine guns

in the basement of the Senate Office Building. Why? Well, *presumably* to protect themselves when they went out after evidence. But perhaps, Hughes must have hinted enticingly, for other reasons . . . (He knew from experience that his job was confined to the mere planting of seeds which a legion of neuroses could be counted on to water.)

Things became almost unbearably tense. A little later, Hughes told

Paul H. Hughes

Friendly (Rauh was still out of town) that McCarthy was on the verge of sending someone to New York to pay cash for secret information snitched from the State Department by an employee. Here at last was an illegal act! Friendly got hold of his boss, Philip Graham, publisher of the *Washington Post,* and the two went hand-in-hand to the office of the Attorney General, Herbert Brownell, to tell him breathlessly that they had got hold of something hot. They couldn't tell him, they said, just what it was, but any day now it would happen; and he must hold himself ready, day and night, to put an FBI man at their disposal so that they could catch the lawbreaker *in flagrante.* They insisted on, and got, Brownell's unlisted home telephone number, so that they could reach him at whatever hour Hughes might call in.

Having secured Brownell's promise of help, the publisher and the editor of the *Washington Post* went back to the barricades to wait, anxiously, final word from Hughes that the great illegal act for which they had all been praying and paying was about to take place.

Nothing happened.

After he had squeezed all the juice out of that one, advancing one reason after another why the rendezvous,

week after week, did not come off (concluding reason: Brownell must have told J. Edgar Hoover, Hoover must have guessed it involved McCarthy, Hoover must have tipped off McCarthy; whereupon McCarthy called off the operation), inventive little Paul Hughes simply went on to something else.

It went on, and on, and on. In October, the *Washington Post,* bracing itself for the climax, prepared twelve articles on Senator McCarthy, based on the information Paul Hughes had given it. And then, almost as an afterthought, a reporter, Murray Marder, was assigned to verify some of the information on the basis of which the *Post* was about to break into print. Marder went off to see three or four employees of the Bell Telecommunications Laboratories (which manufacture secret equipment for the Signal Corps), whose "affidavits" testifying to the way in which McCarthy had browbeat them Hughes had furnished: and lo and behold, the workers didn't even exist! The affidavits the *Washington Post* was about to splash over the front pages were fictitious! It was in a state of near panic, one must suppose, that the researcher tore off to Cornell University, next stop on the verification tour, to interview a professor who, Paul Hughes had reported, had been blackmailed by McCarthy. If the professor refused to point an accusing finger at a few Communists on the Cornell faculty (never mind if they *were* Communist), McCarthy had allegedly threatened him, the Committee would publicly reveal that, in his misspent youth, the professor had had an illegitimate son. Unlike the workers at the Bell Telecommunications Laboratories, the professor *did* exist; but he was very much startled by the story of his victimization. The poor old man had *never* been in touch with McCarthy or any members of McCarthy's committee, at any time; and on top of that, far from having misspent his youth, he had, the professor insisted stoutly, led a life of conspicuous rectitude.

The disappointment of the *Washington Post* must have been terrible. The series was killed. The bill was toted up: Hughes had collected over eight thousand dollars from Joseph Rauh, and over twenty-five hundred dollars from Clayton Fritchey; to say nothing of the consumption of hundreds and hundred of valuable hours of some of the highest paid lawyers and publicists in Washington. Indignation flared.

But never out of control. The *Post* did *not* vent its indignation by publishing an exclusive story on the strange life and activities of an anti-McCarthy careerist. Joseph L. Rauh Jr., his perfervid concern over lawbreaking notwithstanding, did *not* report to the Justice Department the illegalities of a man who went about town getting money under false pretenses from credulous Liberals, flashing forged credentials as an alleged member of a Senate Committee. Clayton Fritchey did *not* complain to the police that Hughes had subsequently tried to blackmail him. General Cornelius Mara did *not* complain that Hughes had given him a bum check. No, these forgiving men were prepared to just let Hughes recede from memory.

But the irrepressible Mr. Hughes would not cooperate. He looked around for fresh bait—and decided to con the FBI, much as Raffles decided, finally, to have a go at the Crown jewels. From that point on, his career moved to a rapid end. On the basis of what he told the FBI, he was subpoenaed by a grand jury, and in due course the government decided to prosecute him for lying before that jury. The government was confident it would win a conviction. It saw no reason to doubt that a person who *admitted* to being a *professional* liar could be proved to have lied, in these specific instances, to a grand jury. But the government prosecutors overlooked one thing: in order to prove that Hughes was a liar, it had to prove that Rauh, Friendly, and Fritchey were *not* liars. That proved an insurmountable obstacle. With the result that, today, Hughes is a free man.[3]

When Is Venality Venal?

I do not pretend that the recounting of the essential facts of the Hughes episode does not afford wry amusement. For Rauh and company had for years moralized about the venality of the secret informer—even when used under sanction of custom, law, and relevant administrative rulings, subject, in the end, to all judicial safe-guards. Now it developed that even while they were loudly condemning the use of "political spies" and "secret informers," they were themselves making deliberate, extended, and blanket use of a man whom they believed to be a political spy and secret informer—one who, moreover, had told them explicitly and in writing that he was not merely being personally disloyal to his employer, but was prepared to use illegal methods to get his alleged information.

But I do not recount the Hughes story merely to chronicle a great hypocrisy. There is much to be learned from the Hughes case and its aftermath—particularly if one bears in mind that Joseph L. Rauh Jr. (I name him as a matter of convenience; one must not forget the company of persons involved in the Hughes operation) is a rewarding object of attention by anyone seeking to understand the operations of the Liberal mind. Let us always remember that not one Liberal publicist—not one, I should say, that I know of—expressed disapproval of Rauh by condemning his affiliation with Paul Hughes. Not the editorial writers of the *New York Times*, the *New York Post*, or the *New York Herald Tribune* (the *Washington Post* and *New York Post* were of course compelled to publish brief, self-serving editorials and, duti-

---

3. The indictment of Paul Hughes was on six counts of alleged perjury committed in testimony before a Federal Grand Jury in 1955. The first four counts cited statements made by Hughes to the effect that Joseph L. Rauh Jr., et al., had discussed Harvey Matusow during 1954. The last two counts concerned Hughes' statement to the Grand Jury that Rauh was aware that Hughes' representation of himself as a McCarthy secret investigator was false, and that Hughes' reports on McCarthy's doings were doctored. On February 3, 1956, the jury acquitted Hughes on the first two counts of the indictment and was "hung" (unable to reach a unanimous verdict) on the remaining four counts. A juror subsequently reported that the division on count 3 was 6-6, and 11-1 in favor of acquittal on the other three. In November of 1958, the government recommended that Hughes not be retried and gave its reason: "During the trial the credibility of the major government witnesses was severely attacked by its defense . . . There is no reason to believe that a second jury would be any less receptive to the contentions made by the defense." An official opinion on the credibility, before a jury of their peers, of Joseph L. Rauh Jr., Alfred Friendly, and Clayton Fritchey.

4. When **National Review**, shortly after the conclusion of the trial, chided Liberal publicists for not commenting on the case, Rovere wrote me: "I agree with you that the Hughes case is full of import. . . I know that I shall deal with the Hughes case in [my forthcoming book]." The forthcoming book turned out to be **Senator Joe McCarthy** (Harcourt Brace, 1959). It contains not a single mention of Paul Hughes.

---

fully, did so); not the Alsops, or Marquis Childs, or Roscoe Drummond, or Doris Fleeson, or Drew Pearson, or Thomas Stokes, or Richard Rovere.[4] This must mean either that they saw nothing in that behavior to criticize, or that fraternal loyalty to a fellow ideologue prevailed over the sense of duty. The former hypothesis is especially interesting. It would seem clear that Rauh's enthusiastic use, in pursuit of anti-Communists, of methods whose use in pursuit of pro-Communists he persistently denounces, is a measure of his evaluation of the relative threat (and relative objectionability?) of the two forces. And indeed, spokesmen for Liberalism have often insisted that anti-Communism is more dangerous to America than Communism. But the reason usually advanced for making such a claim is that anti-Communists tend to use despicable, totalitarian methods. Like secret informers. If the same spokesmen are prepared to sanction the use of such methods to persecute politically offensive persons, what grounds have they left on which to oppose the anti-Communists whose *methods*, they say (as distinguished from their aims) render them objectionable?

A week after Paul Hughes was freed I pondered the question, more relevant than ever: What can one do to kindle in the Liberal bosom a spirit of antagonism toward the Communists equal in intensity to that which moved the Liberals to fight against Senator McCarthy? The horror of the philosophical postulates of Communism has not sufficed, nor the horror of Communism's historical record. What then? I wrote: "A few years ago a witty observer indulged in a little wishful thinking: 'If only,' he said, 'Mao Tse-tung, back in 1946 or 1947, had criticized Margaret Truman's singing! China might have been saved!' We cannot, it seems, count on the evil in Communism to instill in us the will to fight back. Something else will have to furnish the impulse. Perhaps some day, in his cups, Nikita Khrushchev, moved to repay a long outstanding diplomatic courtesy, will sputter out, 'You know, I like old Joe—McCarthy, that is.' Then will the Liberals mount their chargers, and join the fray, prepared to shed their blood to devastate the newly discovered enemy."

15

Mayhem at Notting Hill

During the London race riots, "the respectable people of Notting Hill were on the side of the hooligans." A prominent journalist tells why

COLM BROGAN

[handwritten annotations: "theme", "Attacking liberals as Hypocrites on punishment"]

"So a nigger got chivved. What's all the fuss about?"

These were the charming words of a young Londoner who had just been arrested for applying his razor to the face of a Negro he had never seen before.

They set the tone of part, but only part, of the race rioting which has shaken English liberalism to the depths of what it has in place of a soul. In fairness to the Liberals it must be said that they were genuinely shocked and, in fairness again, the newspapers that were loudest in their condemnation of Little Rock were also loudest in their penitential talk of motes and beams. In fact, they overdid the breast beating, for Little Rock and Notting Hill are by no means comparable. In Little Rock the forces of the law were used to bar Negro children from a school, and in Notting Hill the forces of the law were used to protect the colored population. On the other hand, it is hardly likely that a Negro in Little Rock would have a milk bottle filled with petrol flung through his window for no other reason than the fact that he exists.

The English race riots are profoundly interesting for they are the product of two things—the welfare state and racial inequality. The welfare state has produced quite large numbers of dull-witted youngsters who have never had to make an effort or take a risk of any kind in their pampered lives. They have never had any discipline at home and often little enough at school. They have more money and leisure than they know what to do with and they have no resources in their empty heads. Their indifference to religion is total for though they learned nothing at school they heard of some things. They have heard of Science and so they can say, "I don't dig all that Adam and Eve stuff." End of

argument. *Darwin locuta est.* The burden of their lives is boredom and they seek to escape from it by indulging their sexual lusts with the most squalid and ungracious promiscuity. The more vicious of them indulge in the even more thrilling lust of violence when the pretext and occasion offer. These were the storm troopers of Notting Hill. They don't care in the least about the color of a man's face. All they want is a face to kick.

The Liberal Reversal

Needless to say, the Liberals would not dream of admitting that the welfare state had anything to do with the formation of such character. A distinguished psychologist who made an acute analysis in the *Times* actually mentioned the demoralizing influence of the welfare state, though he stepped back hastily in the next sentence; but the representative progressive, while he might admit that all is not perfect in the welfare state, would certainly say that what is needed is more welfare. The Liberals have eagerly seized on the element of pure hooliganism and tried to spread it over the whole picture. They have even done a somersault in their views on punishment. Liberals are strongly opposed to stiff, retributive sentences, for they maintain that the first and almost the only purpose of court sentences is reform. Retribution is barbaric and deterrence does not deter. If a young savage bashes an old woman for profit or for pure pleasure, someone is quite certain to say that he never had a chance. "It is Society that should be in the dock and Society is all of us," is the unvarying rubric.

But racial equality is just as sacred a tenet as enlightened penology. More so, in fact, for the Liberals are now loud in their demand for stiff sen-

tences on the race rioters. Their sacred oracle, the *New Statesman*, piously declared that this was one of the few cases where punishment really did deter. From which it appears to follow that if a thug hits an old woman, Society must be severely reprimanded, but if he hits a young Negro who is hitting back he must be slapped down.

This might be funny enough if the sudden Liberal eagerness for sharp punishment did not blind most of them to the grimmest fact of the situation. The fact is this. The great majority of the respectable people of Notting Hill were on the side of the hooligans. Notting Hill is a curious district, a between-tides district. It is a district where the desperately respectable upper working class rubs shoulders with the desperately genteel lower middle class, and both live on the verge of the *Lumpenproletariat*. Even though most of them live in old and shabby terrace houses, they would dearly like to live elsewhere. This they indicate by spotless lace curtains, polished brass and scrubbed doorsteps. But it is not enough for the housewife that her own house is neat and clean. She is affronted if all the houses in the terrace are not the same.

Now it happens that a fair number of the colored immigrants are not neat and a number are not even clean. In an old and grimy working-class district there is a very real sense in which cleanliness is next to godliness, for cleanliness implies an endless struggle against adverse circumstances; it is a test of character. By that standard the Jamaican who is dirty or careless is condemned as a moral failure.

But the English who attach such importance to cleanliness and good order attach at least equal importance to peace and quiet and privacy. It is not possible in any intelligent view

[handwritten annotations at bottom: "How welfare State ruins children", "No Morals"]

to blame the immigrants because they have not much liking for privacy but a lot of liking for exuberant noise. But it is unintelligent to expect an intelligent view in Notting Hill, especially among the women. Mothers had been driven to the verge of breakdown by the strain of trying to pacify screaming children who could not sleep because of the infernal noise coming from an all-night calypso party next door or in the flat above, night after night. The inquirers who rushed to the field of battle heard the same response from woman after woman, often in the same words. "I don't approve of the Teddy Boys but they did more for us in four days than the police did in four years. We can sleep now." The men gruffly agreed. These were the men who lifted no finger to help the police, even when sadistic thugs were attacking perfectly innocent immigrants. Some of these were the men who joined in the attacks, perfectly mature and responsible men. But their targets were not indiscriminate. They were out to "get" certain immigrants whose manners and morals had outraged them for years.

Background for Race Hatred

I understand that Americans who know England well are astonished and dismayed to find that an outbreak of pure race hatred could occur among people of such amiable and quiet-going ways. I share their dismay but not their astonishment. For a number of years I have taken time off to nose around the racially mixed quarters of various English cities and I have long taken it for granted that if there was any country where race fever would flare up provided the number of antibodies was sufficient, that country was England. After all, the American working class have such a fantastically mixed racial background that some degree of acceptance of differences of moods and morals has been drawn in unconsciously with their mothers' mixed milk. Also, Americans are inclined to favor an open kind of life, while the English are an enclosed order. The English objection to an open kind of life is literal as well as metaphorical. A Jamaican, a Barbadian or a Nigerian, bred in a hot climate, will instinctively throw wide

open his doors and windows on a warm day, but to his English neighbors this comes near to indecent exposure. To an American this may be as hard to understand as to a Jamaican, but you may accept (or reject) my assurance that it is true. It is the fundamental reason why Joe McCarthy never had a chance of a fair hearing in England where it is thought objectionable to wash even clean linen in public.

But race hatred did not emerge merely because of different customs which are morally neutral in themselves. The discovery that the Negroes did not have a single friend in Notting Hill was one that the Liberals found very hard to take, and they have tried quite desperately to explain it away as the product of ignorance, inherited prejudice and economic circumstances. These factors certainly played their part. The Negroes are sorely pressed to find any sort of accommodation largely because there is a silent but very effective color bar which denies them accommodation in nearly all the pleasant districts. As a result they crowd in wherever they can.

However, economic and social difficulties are not the whole story, as the Liberals would like to believe. Not even the most progressive of progressives can deny that there is a West Indian tradition of quite casual promiscuity. When that tradition is transplanted to an area where there is a somewhat puritanical tradition, there is bound to be trouble. The behavior of a number of white girls with the immigrants is sufficient evidence that there is plenty of native promiscuity, but the West Indian pursuing his lighthearted amours is cheerfully open about it. He is totally unaware of the need for some salutary hypocrisy, and his lack of discretion often looks like an insolent flaunting of his conquest of a white woman.

This in itself is enough to stir anger, but the really savage rage is provoked by the Negroes who live luxuriously on the immoral earnings of their paramours. A very intelligent West Indian who is doing well in a car hire business said "I can't blame the English for getting mad." He pointed across the street. "Three houses over there were broken up last night. Why? There's a Negro in

every one of them who puts his wife on the streets every night."

At the height of the troubles a white woman burst out into the street. She told the story of her daughter who had married a Negro, been corrupted by him into prostitution, and convicted of soliciting. "I never look at her," said the mother, "but just think of your own flesh and blood becoming nothing but a dirty paragraph in the Sunday papers." An Englishwoman's anguish must be deep before she will utter such a cry in public.

The Liberals maintain that there are proportionately no more Negro pimps than white. This is not true, but even if it were it would hardly affect the issue. For it is the inexplicit feeling of the average Englishman that a white pimp degrades one white woman; a black one degrades white womanhood.

Yet the Liberals remain stubbornly blind to the facts, as one striking example goes to show. The reporter who covered Notting Hill for the *Manchester Guardian* left no doubt that the Negro share in the local vice was quite disproportionate. He told of one girl who tried to deny that she worked as a prostitute for her Negro master, but whose head was cut and arms badly bruised. The reporter followed the Negro who drove the girl in his car to Bayswater Road and left her to get on with her work. A woman correspondent complained to the *Guardian* that the article (which was purely factual) was bound to stir up racial trouble. How did the reporter know that the girl was not selling herself voluntarily? (Presumably she had cut her own head and bashed her own body.)

There can be no doubt that the amount of sexual vice practiced by Negroes is grossly exaggerated in inflamed minds, but it would be surprising indeed if it were not more than normal, remembering their background and tradition. The chaplain of a large prison once told me that the Negro prisoners often could not comprehend why they were in prison at all; the crimes for which they were convicted carried no moral disgrace in their own eyes. The drug traffic is also grossly exaggerated, and all this is extremely unfair to the amiable and respectable immigrants who ask for nothing more than to get a job and a room and to be left alone.

But there it is. The police may or may not succeed in damping down violence, but the British have had a taste of the color problem and a good many of them are ready to retch. Certainly the police will get no help from the white working-class natives of mixed areas. During the last Nottingham outburst a Guardsman in full uniform was among the attackers throwing milk bottles. No man could be more conspicuous and no man more certain of heavy punishment if caught, but he was throwing all the same.

There is an informal Anglo-American lunch club in London which meets every week. I once sat beside a high-ranking American general while a discussion on race was going on. Some of the English members were much less than tactful in their remarks on American customs and prejudices. The general listened quietly and then said to me, "I wouldn't disagree with a single word these men said. But wait till you've got fourteen million of them."

The general was an optimist. I certainly won't wait. If the number ever comes near one million and the tensions mount proportionately, I shall hie myself to parts West, where color is not a really serious problem. Little Rock, for example.

Cartoon by John D. Kreuttner

From a Traveler's Notebook

The author of *National Review's* popular feature, From the Academy, offers some random impressions of Europe in the fall

RUSSELL KIRK

[handwritten: Nostalgia for Medvl tradition]

Castleford

The grim colliery town of Castleford, in Yorkshire, was an important Roman station; but it no longer has either a castle r a ford: nothing but miles of dreary streets of dismal houses, with here and there a gloomy pub. It is a big place, densely populated, portions of it condemned and derelict. Civilization's only outpost, aside from the neo-Gothic Anglican church, is the Theatre Royal, where a little band of young actors struggles valiantly against cinema and television. Thus far, their only popular success has been *Dracula*.

The Socialists dominate Castleford, of course, and I think the Communists are not negligible. Ugliness nurtures ugly politics. In such hell-holes as Castleford—a place so hideous that it has acquired a kind of perfection, being the apotheosis of its kind—the wonder is that a sizable minority of working-people still vote Tory.

The scraps of Merry England, old rural England, still lie hard by Castleford. The town is nineteenth century; the countryside, in part, still eighteenth and seventeenth and even sixteenth. From the ridge where Castleford stands, on a clear day—not that there are many clear days in damp and smoky Castleford—you can see the towers of medieval churches. One ancient village, Methly, is an easy walk away. It retains one of the finest little parish churches in England, and Americans come to see the feathered angels, in glass and in stone, in its choir. Up a slope above the village is Methly Hall, a house of the Earls of Mexboro—until the Coal Board took it. The Board has dug an immense open-cast pit right up to the terraces of the Hall, and the vast derelict house—much of it is very old—stares with its dead eyes into the devastation. Methly Hall was all beauty; Castleford is all ugliness;

and the end in England is not yet.

It is not poverty that creates radicalism, nor yet prosperity that nurtures the conservative. But poverty in ugliness and boredom—there, indeed, is good soil for the Communist. Poverty in a society which is intoxicated with getting and spending; poverty among folk who have lost the hope, and even the knowledge, of any world but this—there the fanatic ideologue finds his disciples. The people of Castleford have a sour and envious look; and those who might have been their leaders have left this dismal spot if

they could. Ugliness drives out the able and hardens the hearts of those who must stare at it all their days.

A good deal of sentimental pity is wasted on the miners in the illusion that they hate their work. The miner's work is not disagreeable to him; but the places where he lives, in England at least, must be abhorrent to anyone, even a native. Nowadays the English miner has good wages, easy hours, a new house furnished by the county council, plenty of beer and cigarettes, and political power. But he is no better contented than before; if anything, he is more of a radical.

The Welfare State in England has made sure that the miner is well fed and lodged; but it has not given him heart. The new blocks of council-houses it builds for him are uglier far than his old cottage, though more comfortable perhaps. By ruthless town-planning demolitions and rent acts, the Welfare State abandons to the housebreaker all the old landmarks and bits of charm which may have survived the industrial era; in

the countryside, through punitive taxation, it destroys the great estates and great houses—the countryside, which "he loved . . . just the indiscriminating feel of it." And in exchange for his dog, his prowling for a rabbit, his search for mushrooms—why, it gives him cheap television. And it leaves him an ugly customer.

Nuremberg

The noble walls are one of the most beautiful survivals of the medieval world anywhere in Europe; and until the last war, everything within their great circuit was old and fine. Nuremberg's misfortune was that Hitler chose it as a center for Nazi rallies. The population, in fact, was not particularly Nazi: many of them went to the concentration camps. Yet because Hitler had a liking for the place, the British and the Americans bombed old Nuremberg whenever they could; and in the last days of the horror, when the war was over in all but name, they burnt it to a cinder.

It is said that a diehard SS regiment was within the walls then; if so, a simple encirclement would have forced their surrender in a day or two. But we were in no mood for mercy, and after two or three hours not a house in the old town was habitable. The art of Dürer, the romance of Hoffmann, flamed up from the gel bombs and were gone forever. The jail outside the walls—and all legitimate military objectives were outside the walls—we spared, so that we could hang people.

Yet Nuremberg has come back from its fiery grave. Everything within the walls that still stood has been patched and painted; the gutted churches are roofed again, and their wonderful pictures and carvings and ironwork hang once more. The astonishing energy of revived Germany, undeterred by the Russians beyond the Elbe and the possibility of a holocaust ten times worse than the Allies' assault, has put life into Nuremberg again, in part rebuilding things where and as they were, in part raising new structures in some conformity to the old character of the town—and in part modernizing garishly, so that the main shopping str   dazzles even an American visitor by the eager competition of its neon signs.

In outward things certainly, and in a good many inward things, the Germans—especially the Bavarians—remain the most conservative people in Europe. Much more than the French or the Italians or the Spaniards, they love their old towns. Nuremberg will be a good place to live; Trier has healed its wounds; Cologne, risen from its ashes, is a beautiful city. All this is in striking contrast with England, where whole blocks in big cities like Sheffield still lie under heaps of rubble, and where the rebuilding at fine old places like Exeter is in execrable taste.

But I am told that the invisible scars at Nuremberg are deep and festered: the postwar generation has no enthusiasm for ideology, but neither has it found anything else to love. Once the physical rebuilding is accomplished, where will the Germans turn for occupation? Once the leaders of antique mold, like Chancellor Adenauer, cease to be, who will replace them? In Nuremberg, a friend tells me, most people in their twenties and thirties have been divorced once

or twice; they stagnate. Those younger still cast eager glances at America —a land which, they think, never is bored.

Medieval Nuremberg was a little world: it sent its beautiful handicrafts to all Europe, and within those Gothic walls a civilization stood complete. But now the vigor drains out of it, as out of nearly all provincial

capitals, to the great centers: to Munich and Bonn and Berlin. The immense castle looming over the town ceases to invoke, for most Nuremberg folk, even memories of Hoffmann; for they have seen Hollywood movies, and therein the Promised Land.

During the Second World War, the deliberate devastation of famous ancient towns was evidence of the decadence of our time. The RAF seems to have begun the business, with raids into Bavaria against places with hundreds of Gothic houses and not one factory. Very promptly the Luftwaffe joined the game, with the "Baedeker" bombings of Coventry and Exeter and Norwich and whatever other beautiful cities it could reach through the fog. In the fullness of time, a New Zealand general smashed Monte Cassino for the exhilaration of it, and a South African air marshal wiped out Dresden when the fighting had stopped. The Germans thoughtfully burned the Roman ship at Nemi, and finished the bridges at Florence; in Russia they effaced every trace, where they could, of medieval beauty. We Americans came late to the game, and did not really have our hearts in it; our vandalism, for the most part, was accidental. Yet we planned to drop our first atomic bomb on Kyoto, the Rome and Florence of Japan, a target wholly unmilitary; only the weather prevented us. When the Russian observers came to southern Italy, they were annoyed to see the Greek temples at Paestum still standing; they wanted to know why the Americans hadn't blown them up. No point in it? Nonsense: "They're Italian, aren't they?"

Cunninghame Graham has a story about an Italian officer who let half his platoon be picked off by revolutionary snipers, rather than shell a Renaissance tower. No one had any such notions when Nuremberg was gutted.

Vienna

St. Stephen's Cathedral was burnt out in the last days of fighting, before the Russians took Vienna; but it has been so handsomely restored that the stranger to Vienna never would guess it had been harmed. (Most of the new building in the city, however, is not handsome.) The Opera is restored, too, and I sat in the old imperial box and listened to Mozart. (I had some little difficulty in getting that far; for I hadn't extinguished my cigar when I entered the sacred precincts of the Opera, and swarms of functionaries advanced fiercely upon me, shouting "No smoking!" They took me for a peasant from the hinterland, because I was wearing a Salzburg cloak; but once they discovered I was an American, whose person was inviolable, they bowed me into my imperial splendors.)

A few days earlier I had been in the presence of the gentleman rightfully entitled to that box: Archduke Otto von Hapsburg, who for some years has been living at Pöcking, in Bavaria. A week later, the newspapers were full of rumors that the Archduke had opened negotiations for returning to Austria.

Even more than St. Stephen's, the dominating feature of old Vienna is the great imperial palace of the Hofburg—which, almost untouched by the republican years, seems to be waiting for the Hapsburgs' return. Vienna is not a republican city. In this aristocratic, nostalgic place, the waitresses in the famous cafés confer the titles of Count and Baron upon the more dignified customers—if they leave tips. Every political faction contains ardent monarchists, always excepting the Communist Party.

If Otto von Hapsburg returns to Vienna, he will regain possession of his family's great estates, long since seized by the Austrian Republic in a kind of blackmail; but to return, he must—according to the present constitution—abjure his claim to the imperial crown. Presumably he would not have to abjure the claim of a brother or a son, or promise not to be elected President—or Regent. The Socialists say they have no objection to his return: they think his coming would split the Christian Democrats into monarchical and republican factions; and besides, there always have been monarchical Socialists in Austria, and the Socialist Party took no active part in dethroning Otto's father, the Emperor Karl.

Not many months ago, a large party of leather-jacketed Viennese youth, on their motorcycles Marlon Brando style, roared all the way to Pöcking to call on the Archduke. He and they got along famously, and they swooped back to Vienna singing his praises. En route, they happened to pass the President of Austria, in a limousine escorted by a strong force of guards. "Look at that!" said one of the boys. "That fellow needs a gang to protect him, and the Archduke doesn't even have one policeman at his door!" Toryism, according to Newman, is loyalty to persons. Perhaps the ancient longing of youth for heroes, and the need of a people for some symbol of their national identity, will incline the restless crowd of young people toward the great name of Hapsburg.

Among the Archduke's partisans in Vienna one finds old-fashioned conservatives, liberals, socialists, even some former Nazis; a great many Catholics, of course, in this Catholic stronghold, and—increasingly—Jews. Before the Second World War, there were two hundred thousand Jews in Vienna. The Nazis murdered or swept away all but two thousand; now there are twenty thousand. What the intelligent and energetic Jews of Vienna perceive is that never were they so secure as when under the Empire.

Bernard Shaw's play *The Applecart* had a successful American revival two years ago. In *The Applecart*, the witty and generous and wise king baffles all the bullying politicians by whom he is encompassed. There are strong similarities between Shaw's King Magnus and Otto of Austria-Hungary. Possibly the applecart at the Hofburg may be upset one of these days.

Avila

Cold, dry, austere, and in part derelict, the ancient and noble city of Avila stands upon a high spur of the sierra, looking in winter upon snow-covered mountains. Though its population has grown to twenty thousand in this century, there were half again as many people in medieval times. Nothing thrives in Avila nowadays: a neat new automobile-body

factory, beyond the station, has a manager and a few workmen but no contracts; and some sort of new veterinary school, a square, ugly building erected by the present government, never opens its doors.

Whatever is old in Avila is beautiful; whatever new, ugly. The splendid eleventh-century walls enclose the wonderful Gothic cathedral, many crumbling palaces and convents, red-tiled houses big and little, and innumerable bars. Avila is stern, chaste, and hard-drinking: to take one's brandy in the bars, indeed, is the only amusement, except for the American movies.

George Santayana spent his childhood here, within the walls. His dignified father was of the number of those Spaniards "filled with envy and respect" for the modern utilitarian world of England and America. Many people in Avila nowadays feel this admiration and longing for things American: they go to the films, and come away with a confused impression of a society in which everything glistens and everyone has plenty of money, a flashy new car, a smart house in the suburbs, and a pretty girl; and they ask themselves why Avila cannot be like that. For a year or two, they have been making some endeavor to convert Avila to efficiency and modernity and the Hollywood image of America.

But these efforts are clumsy and dismal in execution. Out toward the railway station, towering apartment houses have been built. The architect, I take it, never saw Avila, or else did not know his business; for these grim, shabby structures are less comfortable—not to mention beauty —than the old houses that were demolished; their windows all face the cold north, and the fierce winter wind torments the inhabitants, huddled over their braziers. The church architects do no better, despite the wealth of good ancient church-architecture right under their eyes. A fine, vast eighteenth-century convent, which easily could have been adapted to modern uses, is being demolished to make way for an American-style diocesan college, all glass and flimsy color; while the Bishop is "restoring" the outside of his palace to look like Walt-Disney crazy paving, and is doing the same sort of thing to the stone interior of the cathedral.

What one sees even in Avila, holy and impoverished Avila, goes on at a faster pace elsewhere in Spain, as in nearly all of Western Europe: a confused neoterism in outward things. It is true that the Spaniard still clings with some tenacity to spiritual and cultural tradition; but in this, as in most matters, the Spaniard is abstract. What P. E. More called "the demon of the absolute" is the curse of Spain; in politics it leads to fanatic ideology, in religion to bigotry, in private life often to a perpetual haggling over petty points.

Old Spain is dotted with American troops and tourists now. If the Spaniards do not understand America, neither do the Americans understand Spain. At Palma, not long ago, the American Navy marched a band —uninvited—to the bull-ring, and burst into rock-'n-roll as the wearied bull awaited the matador. The Spanish crowd, for whom the corrida is a serious drama of valor and death, rose up furiously, shouting and cursing in protest; but the American Navy apparently took this wrath for applause, for they marched back the next week and repeated their rock-'n-roll performance.

Once I heard a president of the Chamber of Commerce of the United States declare, in a public address, that we Americans are not conservatives, but revolutionaries; and that we are going to turn the world upside down, change all other people's tastes and beliefs, and teach them to buy our products and make them like it. I do hope that we will not be so foolish as to essay this role.

We might spend $50 million in foreign aid in Avila, and demolish everything old. But our new creation would not be American; it would be only a sham. And the Spaniards, at once or after a little lapse of time, would hate us for what we had done.

The Strange Case of Dr. Dooley

I. Facts

According to available records, James Milton Parker Dooley was born in Bloomington, Illinois, on December 10, 1902. He was educated in local schools and graduated from Illinois Wesleyan College in 1923. From there he went to the medical school of Johns Hopkins University, where he won his Phi Beta Kappa key. After three years he was sent to Labrador for a year's special work in surgery. The next year, 1927, Parker Dooley received his medical degree and was granted an outstanding two-year resident appointment to the surgical staff at Johns Hopkins Hospital.

In 1929, just as the young Dr. Dooley was completing the second year of this appointment, a request came to Johns Hopkins from Father Frederick H. Sill, an Episcopalian minister who for many years was headmaster of Kent School, the well-known preparatory school located on the bank of the Housatonic River across from the village of Kent in northwestern Connecticut. Father Sill asked Johns Hopkins to name a panel to investigate a number of unexplained deaths among the students. This was done, and one recommendation of the panel was the appointment of a school physician. The assignment was proposed to Dr. Dooley, who accepted "because it offered an opportunity for some original research and would also provide some money to pay off some of his accumulated debts."

Dr. Dooley stayed at Kent School for five years, from 1929 to 1934, where, along with his duties as resident physician, he conducted biological research into streptococci and undulant fever that received national notice in medical circles. This brought him, in 1934, a full-time teaching appointment at Cornell Medical School in New York. He also was made chief of the outpatient clinic of New York Hospital, which is affiliated with the Cornell Medical School. Dr. Dooley has stated that, during this period, in order to continue active work with patients he turned down an offer from Mayor La Guardia to become administrative head of all New York City hospitals.

A remark a few weeks ago by a nine-year-old boy to his mother touched off the strange case of Dr. Dooley. Admonished to stay away from a disreputable neighbor, the boy asked his mother, "Why don't you like him? Is he a pig like Dr. Dooley?"

Such a remark about one of the leading pediatricians and citizens of northwest Connecticut was surprising to say the least. Particularly so coming from a child, as Dr. James Parker Dooley was widely known as a friend and benefactor of children.

The ensuing investigation and the reaction to it in the region bared a microcosm of philosophical and moral ferment which, incredibly, went unnoticed in the national press. Believing that the episode has an urgent meaning for our society, the editors have chosen to treat extensively of the strange case of Dr. Dooley.

In 1939 Dr. Dooley transferred to the faculty of the Pediatrics Department at the University of Chicago. He became one of the leading figures there and at the famous Bob Roberts Hospital for children. After the war, for a while, he moved his laboratory down to his old college (Illinois Wesleyan), where he found time to teach a course in Latin American history.

He had long wanted to study tropical agriculture. In 1946 the government of Haiti invited him to go into one of its primitive villages to try out public health methods. Dr. Dooley accepted this offer. In the mid-summer of 1946 he arrived in New York on his way to Haiti, but found no ships immediately available. To escape the city's heat while waiting for a ship, he went back to Kent.

About four miles from Kent village, a descendant of an old New England family, Miss Myra Hobson, a spinster in her seventies, lives by herself on a now inactive family farm comprising 1,200 acres of pasture and woods that stretch across the foothills of the Berkshires. In the middle of her property, deep in the trees and half a mile from the road, there is a small lake, or pond. On the shore of the pond there is a rough wood cabin, such as fishermen or hunters are wont to use. This cabin, by modern standards, is unadorned: there is no running water, no electricity, no furnace, no telephone.

Parker Dooley settled in this cabin, in the cool woods, while waiting for his ship. But he broke his leg, and had to give up his journey and his assignment. While his leg mended, it became known that he was there. Cases were brought to him. His months in the cabin multiplied, and soon he joined a small medical clinic that functioned in the village. His work expanded throughout the neighboring communities: Sharon, Salisbury, Lakeville, Washington, Warren, Cornwall, Falls Village and even farther afield.

Dr. Dooley maintained an office, along with three other doctors, at the Kent village clinic, although his name did not appear on the door. His practice grew to comprise, it is said, 2,500 children. He became school physician at the local public school. When a Health Center, devoted to children's problems and supported by contributions from the leading families of the region, was started at Salisbury, Dr. Dooley became the leading professional figure. He often spoke at meetings of Parent-Teacher associations and before other community organizations.

Dr. Dooley continued to live in the woodland cabin, and the cabin continued as it was. Without a telephone, messages had to be brought to him. He had no car, and through sun or rain or snow he walked the four miles to the village, unless his landlady, her sister or one of his other friends happened to drive him in. His life was spare and frugal. Though his practice was large enough to have brought him a considerable income, his fees were small—indeed, bills were often overlooked altogether.

Dr. Dooley stayed for nine years in his cabin.

Not long after he settled there, Dr. Dooley initiated a long-term special project. He became acquainted with the plight of certain children, ranging from nine to sixteen or seventeen years in age, who from one cause or another had come to be regarded as gravely delinquent, unmanageable or intractable. These cases often came to light through courts, hospitals or other public institutions (not all in Connecticut), sometimes through physicians, clergymen or relatives. Dr. Dooley determined to handle some of these cases by having the children take up lengthy residence under his direct supervision in the cabin. In all, under what came to be known as "the cabin project," twenty-two children stayed there, for from two to four years. Some of them stayed in the neighborhood a year or two longer, still under Dr. Dooley's care, but living in the foster-homes of parents who admired and believed in Dr. Dooley's work. This cabin project became well known, not only in the region but widely through New York and New England. The boys shared the rough life of the woods. They chopped kindling, hauled the water from the hand pump, slept in sleeping bags on the floor. They walked more than a mile through the trees and down the road to board the morning bus for the local elementary school or the regional high school at Falls Village. The disorders of many of the twenty-two were lessened under Dr. Dooley's care; and it is generally believed that in some cases the improvement was outstanding.

In March of this year, the cabin received through the Salisbury Health Center a strange and moving case. The subject was a ten-year-old boy, who will be called "George." George, though good looking and seemingly intelligent, suffered from a derangement that impelled him to emit periodically—without any volition and almost without awareness of it—a piercing, anguished bark, or howl. The medical term for this affliction is "lycanthropy." It was well known, though differently explained, in ancient and medieval times, when it led to the tales of werewolves howling in the night.

The trouble had not been lessened by any previous treatments. It was so severe, and so agonizing to others

who heard it, that George was unable to attend school, go to movies or join in any social activities. When Dr. Dooley accepted the boy as a cabin patient, he told his mother it would be best if the family stayed away. The mother, distressed and baffled by the child's strange malady, readily assented.

George had a number of brothers. Dr. Dooley suggested that two of them —Peter, aged 13 and Mark, 9—should visit at the cabin, since, he said, their histories were relevant to his study of George's illness. Peter came for some days, and Mark was there during the week from August 1 to August 7.

When Mark first came home he said little about his visit, but a few days later, when his mother had occasion to scold him and to tell him to stay away from a neighbor of whom she disapproved, the child asked:

"Why don't you like him? Is he a pig like Dr. Dooley?"

This totally unexpected question led the mother to make immediate inquiries, the results of which she quickly turned over to the State Police. On August 14 the police, on the basis of direct evidence of active homosexual encounters between Dr. Dooley and the cabin patient, George, as well as the two brothers during their visits, drove up the dirt road to the cabin and arrested Dr. Dooley for "indecent assault and risk of injury to a child."

Dr. Dooley, pending trial, was placed in the jail at Litchfield, the county seat. He made no attempt to raise the $7,500 bail, though he could easily have done so. He did not deny the acts which formed the basis of the arraignment, but entered a plea of *nolo contendere* —that is, waiving jury trial, he placed himself at the disposal of the Court.

On October 4, Judge Elmer W. Ryan, sitting in the Superior Court at Litchfield, heard the case, with Thomas F. Wall appearing for the State and Charles R. Ebersol representing the defendant. Judge Ryan also accepted a lengthy statement prepared by the defendant, together with a large number of affidavits, letters and other documents.

On the next day, October 5, Judge Ryan gave his verdict. He rejected what Mr. Ebersol had held to be explanatory and mitigating circumstances, on the basis of which he had asked for the defendant's acquittal. On

the evidence and admissions, Judge Ryan was convinced that Dr. Dooley "is a sex pervert . . . the aggressor in these acts." He found him guilty on two counts of the indictment. Under the laws of Connecticut, Judge Ryan sentenced Dr. Dooley to from one to six years in the State Prison. James Parker Dooley is now serving his sentence, at Wethersfield Penitentiary.

II. Opinions

Here, it would seem, the case of Dr. Dooley is at an end. The story, though odd—even fantastic, in some of its details—is sadly routine in pattern. A man transgresses the law. The transgression is discovered and confirmed. He is punished, in accordance with the law. When Judge Ryan spoke his verdict, the case was closed. Such is, usually and normally, society's view; and such was in fact the view of the greater number of the ordinary citizens of that Connecticut region—the farmers, artisans, merchants, laborers and some part of the teachers, lawyers, writers, artists and the wealthy who are scattered here and there through the hills.

But this was not the end, nor has the case yet ended.

On the day of the trial, the bare room in which the Court sat, open to the public, as demanded by Anglo-Saxon legal tradition even for such a case as this, was filled with spectators. These were not the farmers, artisans, merchants and laborers; nor, except for a marginal few, were they mere idlers. More than fifty of them, well dressed and assured in manner, were a selection of the region's intellectual elite. Most of them were women, the women recognized as community leaders, who head charity drives, belong to clubs, run the Parent-Teacher Association, the Association for the United Nations, the League of Women Voters. Almost without exception they were Liberals, by their own classification—though of course many who think of themselves as Liberals were not there, and would not have agreed with those who were.

These spectators, or nearly all of them, came to the courtroom to signify in a kind of public demonstration their sympathy with, their support of Doctor Dooley, their rejection of the judgment the Court inexorably must hand down. They were in agreement, and many of them continue to be in agreement, with Dr. Dooley's explanation and views as these were expressed by his attorney, Mr. Ebersol.

What, then, was the explanation offered for these admitted actions which, *prima facie*, were subject to a triple condemnation: intrinsically, in and of themselves; as an adult's violation of children; as a physician's violation of his sacred Hippocratic oath?

Mr. Ebersol did not deny the homosexual encounters, nor did he contend that they had been limited to the three boys or the specific occasion specified in the legal charges. He made it clear that there had been other patients and other occasions. And in that open courtroom, within the hearing of those spectators, Mr. Ebersol, corrected occasionally by the defendant and plainly following the defendant's information and instruction, reviewed certain of the encounters with a specificity of detail not often found outside of medical textbooks. Against this factual background, Mr. Ebersol offered as defense his analysis of Dr. Dooley's purpose, end, and motives. In sum, Mr. Ebersol, for Dr. Dooley, contended that these encounters were an integral part of a new, pioneer and revolutionary technique of psychiatric therapy.

On October 6, the day after the sentencing, the *Lakeville Journal*, the most influential newspaper of the region, published a letter from Dr. Dooley:

"To the Editor:

"I have not been a reader of the *Lakeville Journal* nor do I know your name. Some one sent me a clipping from the August 18 (?) issue of your paper, telling of my arrest and imprisonment. This account was so sympathetic that I thought you might be willing to publish a statement from me about my work at Kent.

"The work in question was a project for the study of disturbed and sick children in residence in a woods cabin on a lake, part of an old farm four miles from the village. During nine years, twenty-two children stayed there for long periods; and many more, for a short time. This project was separate from my clinical pediatric practice in the village.

"The people in this locality grew accustomed to seeing derelict children become respectable junior citizens of the community. The methods used to

accomplish these results were always experimental and unorthodox, and occasionally illegal.

"The first two children in this study were from the middle west, and were placed in my care because their parents were familiar with my work in Chicago. With no exception, each subsequent child came because the parents or some agency had first hand knowledge of the results in the case of some child who had been at the cabin.

"In the management of disturbed children many general approaches have been used, among them: force, admonition, kindness, and traditional psychiatric medicine. None of these has been so successful that a further search for methods is not indicated.

"In this project, the approach was to induce the child to go back in his life to the age when his trouble started, and then to guide him anew up to his present age along lines which would be more comforting to him and more acceptable to others. Some observers thought that the children progressed because I was so nice and the woods so pretty. Actually, accompanying a child in a deep regression may be a raw and bloody business, not a trip for the squeamish.

"Naturally I don't enjoy losing my freedom, but the fact remains that I knew the law, and knowingly violated it. That the methods used on occasion may have been technically illegal does not invalidate the soundness of the results.

[Signed] PARKER DOOLEY
9/23/55

"Ed. Note: This letter was received prior to the arraignment reported elsewhere in this paper. At the doctor's request it was withheld until after the trial."

The core of the defense was contained in Mr. Ebersol's review of the case of Robert,[1] another of the cabin patients, now sixteen, whose experience at the hands of Dr. Dooley he related as illustrative.

"BY MR. EBERSOL: Mr. Wall [State's attorney] has referred to the case of another child, a sixteen-year-old boy; and I shall refer to him as Robert. A homeless ward of the State, no usable family, he came to the cabin on Thanksgiving Eve, 1952. He was still there when the Doctor was arrested. He came on the request of the juvenile court. From that day on, except for a rare day when he visited elsewhere, and for three or four weeks in this summer, the Doctor spent some part of every one of approximately one thousand days with him; and for many weeks of those days, early in his stay, he was never out of the Doctor's hearing. Upon his arrival, about all the Doctor knew of his history was his unusual record of eight runaways from foster homes and institutions. Only several months later, after repeated requests, did the Doctor obtain from the Division of Child Welfare of the State Department of Welfare a social summary of the information on the boy.

"The Doctor then learned, for the first time, that he was an illegitimate child, and that in addition to his chronic runaways, there was chronic thievery, chronic lying and deception, chronic truancy from school and chronic school failures, and chronic sex offenses.

"Quoting from the State report which the Doctor got several months later, 1951: 'A report from the director of the county home revealed that he displayed homosexual behavior at the County Home to the extent that he became ostracized from his own age group. In April, 1952, he was in trouble

[1]All the names of patients are, of course, disguised.

again; and the juvenile court authorities advised his [social case] worker that he was taking a short cut through some fields in his neighborhood on his way home from school and, upon encountering two younger boys, he took ten cents and a jacknife away from them. He then made homosexual advances to the other children, but the juvenile court took no action on this." End of quote.

"Here, then, was a radically, desperately sick boy with whom the agencies, the State and the court, did not know what to do.

"THE COURT: How old was that boy?

"BY THE ACCUSED DOOLEY: Thirteen years and five months.

"BY MR. EBERSOL: Thirteen years and five months, Your Honor. This was the situation when, three runaways later, he was brought from the juvenile detention home in Hartford to Dr. Dooley at the request of the juvenile court. A radical case requiring radical, unorthodox and experimental treatment when all else had failed. As a psychologist wrote of Robert, 'Robert needed someone to love him' and that the Doctor did, being father, mother, brother, or whatever and whenever the boy needed him.

"Here, again, I wish the Court might be able to read the Doctor's detailed report on Robert's regression and progression. Particularly upon his arrival and in his early stage, he needed and benefited by the permissive environment in developing a sense of assurance, trust, and belonging to someone. One by one, although in no planned order or at any one time, each of his chronic symptoms had to be dealt with down through his regression and up through his rebuilding. The sexual deviations were only one of these but, since we seem most concerned with them here, they will receive more attention now. Here let me emphasize, however, that by no means did all the cabin boys have sexual problems nor were sexual solutions the solutions to other problems that were there.

"It was clear, then, that Robert was schooled in homosexual intercourse of every kind before he came to the cabin. In permitting himself to become involved in Robert's sexual acts, the Doctor did not seduce him but only changed his attitude towards a pre-existing situation. As the Doctor prefers to say, he took the badness out of

the act and left the act hanging there, neither bad nor good.

"Doing this might be very unwholesome for the child if the Doctor's purpose was, as we claim, to satisfy—was, as the State claims, to satisfy his own lust. If, however, his purpose was, as we claim, to guide the child out of sex perversion to a more socially acceptable sexuality, then the successful spiritualization of his homosexual acts may be a wisely chosen first step; and in judging the Doctor's work, it would be well to remember that some very well-intentioned and energetic people had failed him when he was younger, when he was easier to work with. This morning, I received from the Doctor the last few pages of his case report on this boy.

"And I would like to read, just briefly, from them. 'That this boy was moving toward a homosexual way of life with me is simply not true. He was being freed of infantile needs, folding up and packing away his late-discovered and now tenderly completed infancy. He was not learning homosexuality. He was most certainly unlearning homosexuality.'

"As for results, it has been reliably reported to us that a psychiatrist, examining Robert after the Doctor's arrest, found him to be a well-integrated boy, and could not, after reading the report on him, written before his going to the cabin, believe that he was, in fact, the very same boy he was examining.

"This, then, very briefly, is the background of the cabin project, the laboratory for the study of children by an experienced, serious student.

"THE COURT: May I interrupt to inquire—?

"BY MR. EBERSOL: Yes.

"THE COURT: Is there a claim that this form of therapy has taken Robert out of the class of homosexuals?

"BY MR. EBERSOL: I don't believe it has been completed, yet, Your Honor. Doctor had not had an opportunity—I believe that he felt he had at least another year's work on Robert.

"THE COURT: Very well.

"BY THE ACCUSED DOOLEY: Less than a year.

"BY MR. EBERSOL: Less than a year, the Doctor says. I have been attempting,

here, to give the Court the whole picture in outline form into which must be integrated the acts which formed the basis for the information against him.

"These acts are condemned and prohibited by law as indecent, unchaste, impure, obscene. This, the Doctor knew and understood when he engaged in them; but it appears to me, the motive and intent of the actor may and does change the whole character of the act and its consequences. Killing on the battlefield is sanctioned in wartime; and, often, the killer is rewarded with medals while killing in peacetime is murder, punishable by death."

The homosexual encounters with George's brothers, Peter and Mark, were also explained by therapeutic theory. It was necessary "to invite the relatives in and to associate them with the child in varying combinations and

situations which were calculated to show the structure of the relationship. . . . Although Peter, thirteen, did not appear to upset George, he threw some light on George's case. . . . He began coming to the cabin whenever possible. . . . All this time, the Doctor was carefully studying him and his relationship to George. . . . He was, then, convinced that Peter could not have heard of George's [homosexual] experience with the Doctor before Peter had almost exactly a similar one with the Doctor. That is, it was not the Doctor being the aggressor, but the permissive environment; and the boy taking the initiative. After that, further acts of this nature with Peter had only—were only in continuance and furtherance of this study."

As for the younger brother: "It was of importance for the Doctor to learn whether or not Mark had had any of this experience because he felt that George's yelp had a sex-guilt expression—or had been a sex-guilt expression, and that this sex-guilt was pretty well now gone as far as George was concerned. So that this perfect younger brother, Mark, was just the one who would make George feel most guilty if he were in the habit of sex play with him, and then the symptoms might return. As Mark was such a snuggling child with the Doctor and so demonstrative physically, it was easy for the Doctor to learn whether he had the same desire for genital play as his two older brothers had shown. It . . . [became] quite clear to the Doctor that he had not."

Mr. Ebersol added: "Here, I do not wish to imply that all the sexual acts of the Doctor with the boys, on his part, were merely permissive; but I do assert that they were all engaged in by him with the same purpose in mind."

Mr. Ebersol read into the record a series of letters and affidavits that had been written in support of Doctor Dooley and of his unorthodox therapeutic methods. Excerpts from some of them follow.

A former patient wrote from Cambridge, Massachusetts: "I consider it a great fortune to know and to have been served by a doctor who would risk so much for his patient. Few men would go so far."

A master in a private school wrote: "We . . . are desperately sorry that your wonderful work has had to be interrupted. . . . Our belief in your personal integrity has not been changed. We realize that your medical skill and knowledge caused you to take steps not readily understood by a layman."

The President of a Massachusetts Parent-Teacher Association wrote: "It appears to us that you are suffering the penalty that often lands on forerunners, both in science or art. The threat of popular disapproval or of law infringement is set up to warn off the fainthearted or the criminal . . . So, in the doghouse or the jailhouse we find the best and the most mixed-up together or, rather, to use a less harsh term, the most creative and the most destructive. . . . In a sense both are threats to stable status quo society; and yet the first group are the seeds of tomorrow's best harvests.

". . . The size and character of your practice is evidence enough that your ways are sound and practical. No doubt it would be easy to find points where your methods carried you across the frontiers of the legal or the moral codes and made you vulnerable to accusations like the present ones; but we do not see that such pin-point out-of-context challenges have any validity. They may be true, but, lacking the whole truth, they are a kind of lie about you and your purposes."

Mr. Ebersol's culminating affidavit was written by one whom he describes as "an outstanding authority in the field of child guidance and family life who, with her husband, both psychologists, have conducted a school for disturbed children for more than twenty years. These people are in Court, here, today, Your Honor." Before they transferred their educational work to a rural environment, this couple, whose name is, as Mr. Ebersol notes, well known, for some years conducted a prominent school for normal younger children in New York City. The following are excerpts from the letter:

"It would seem to me that he had every professional and human urgency to do exactly as he did and I could wish that he would fight for that right. Perhaps I can make myself clearer with a simple example. Two men may cut open a woman's stomach. The one, Jack, the Ripper, commits a criminal act of assault. The other, Dr. John Doe, Surgeon, performs a life-saving miracle. Both men have performed, essentially, the same act. The intent of one is sadistic. The intent of the other is life-saving and knowledge-seeking for the purpose of further life-saving. The result of one is death; the result of the other is a chance for life. Are both these men to be regarded in the same light?

"Must the surgeon when attacked by ignorant, if well-meaning persons, plead guilty to assault along with Jack the Ripper[1]; and, if he does, does this not help to identify his act, in the public mind, with that of Jack?

"The Law necessarily follows, rather than precedes human experience. But if scientific exploration ceases until legal processes catch up, where would human progress be? History has presented us, again and again with the dilemma of brave men of insight and vision who have elected to proceed at

---

[1]In quotations from the Court record, the exact style of the Court stenographer is followed.

whatever personal cost with the task of blazing new trails. . . .

"One could hardly imagine that the seriously disturbed children brought to Dr. Dooley, the so-called hopeless cases, could respond to anything or any person external to him. To use psycho-lingo, their transference was to him. It seems obvious that these youngsters had to work through their anxiety in the acquiescence and acceptance of his own person.

"Knowing what small amount I do about children, it seems to me that Dr. Dooley did an enlightened act of professional and personal giving of himself that could be conjectured to have made cure possible for these children. . .

"Scientifically he has given us clues to understanding children and the deep roots of their disturbances that few other scientists have even dared to look at, let alone expose.

"I feel that my own knowledge of children and effectiveness to them in time of trouble has been vastly increased by these observations."

One of Dr. Dooley's physician-colleagues at the clinic had given Mr. Ebersol his "Credo on the doctor." The colleague was in Court, and with his permission, Mr. Ebersol read from this Credo:

". . . He has always been known as a fearless pioneer in new fields. He has never sought favor, wealth or self-aggrandizement. He is primarily interested in fundamental biological processes . . .

"His actions, as described by himself, represent the exploration of little known problems with equally little known techniques. The problems were unorthodox; the approach equally so. To assume that he allowed himself to indulge in self-gratification ignores a completely selfless past and loses sight of the incredible amount of time and energy devoted to maintaining, feeding and teaching the boys under his care. This was a twenty-four-hour, seven-day job without interruption. This was the work of an exceptionally devoted man, for a man with very unusual singleness of purpose.

"There is no doubt in my mind, speaking as a physician, but that Dr. Dooley's actions represent an extension of scientific research into the sexual problems of adolescents. I am not competent to judge as to the value of what he accomplished with them or discovered. I have no doubt as to his motive."

Judge Ryan's verdict did not close the issue in the minds of Dr. Dooley's firmer adherents. In a public letter, Dr. Dooley's nine-year landlady declared her full confidence in him and his work: "The cabin provided a place for his work and I have been close enough to be acquainted with many of the problems of the children, and to observe the day to day progress of these patients. . . . You may rest assured that the innate integrity that is Dr. Dooley's has in no way been impaired; rather has it been all the more demonstrated. . . . The treatments used surely in time shall be considered justified by the results achieved. . . . It is my fervent hope that in time he may return to the cabin on the mountain."

The *Lakeville Journal*, which had on the sixth published the report of the trial and the text of Dr. Dooley's letter, followed up on the thirteenth by giving over a large part of its editorial page to letters on the case. One of these, the shortest, is a plain, flat condemnation expressing surprise "that a publication as respectable as the *Lakeville Journal* condones a practice as vile as sex perversion especially by a pediatric physician." All the others are pro-Dooley, with the exception of one letter from a physician which suggests that Dr. Dooley could himself be helped by psychiatric treatment.

Dr. Paul W. Stoddard, Principal of the large Housatonic Regional High School, wrote: "Some time ago I offered to testify on Dr. Dooley's behalf at the trial, but the offer was refused by his lawyer, who, however, included a statement on our behalf in his plea to the Court.

"This case is without question one of the most confusing that I have ever known. . . . As one grows older, the more he is convinced that seldom is black all black or white all white, but that the pervading color in this world is some shade of gray! . . . I cannot defend Dr. Dooley for the particular acts that brought about his arrest and imprisonment because I do not know all the facts. . . . The Regional High School has been the richer that Dr. Dooley lived among us."

Another letter, signed by both man and wife, ended: "If he becomes free to practice again, we and our children will continue to be his patients. . . . The prosecutor demanded that he be made to pay heavily his 'debt to society.' In truth, a far heavier debt is society's to those very few of its servants who, living entirely in the present, spend *themselves* with no heed to the cost, burning their bridges *before* them."

One man wrote to accuse the prosecutor of "sensationalism." "As to Dr. Dooley's 'illegal method' in the case of the ten-year-old boy," he commented, "only the very cold fact by itself was the matter of the accusation leaving completely out the spirit in which it was done."

Another writer made an almost inevitable comparison: "Personally, I not only do not agree with [Judge Ryan's] decision, but feel that it is a very unfortunate one. It subjects a truly great, pioneering physician to a grave ordeal. . . . It makes one feel that society has not gone too many steps forward since the trials of Giordano Bruno, if a physician, using unorthodox methods in his studies to help mankind, can be incarcerated for doing so."

III. *Judgment*

There *are* innumerable shades of gray, yet black is black, not gray, and white is white, and the assertion that because gray exists black does not is philosophically ignorant and morally irresponsible. To say that because Bruno should not have been burned at the stake Parker Dooley should not have been imprisoned and disgraced is to fail to make distinctions as basic as those upon which it is necessary to rely to assert the difference between the unfolding world of scientific inquiry

Kreuttner

"Gentlemen, I have absolutely nothing to conceal."

and the unchanging world of moral absolutes.

The case of Dr. James Parker Dooley is not confusing; it is Dr. Dooley's well-wishers who are confused. And their confusion is so great, and so serious, and so endemic, that we must look after our moral skins.

The form of argument used in defense of Dr. Dooley is identical to other arguments that have become famous in our day. It is the argument that rests on the instrumental conception of man as a mechanical bundle of conditioned reflexes, and on the metaphysical doctrine that the end justifies any means. Modern ideologues have explicitly relied on these doctrines, most glaringly when Lenin contended that "better two thirds of mankind perish than socialism fail." Stalin put this more colloquially, in justifying his reign of terror, when he reminded us that "you can't make an omelet without breaking eggs."

Indeed, as one of the doctor's sympathizers observes, the law follows, rather than precedes human experience. The law is the formalization of convention, and there is a convention-in-the-making, at least among substantial numbers of men and women of substantial education and means in the Housatonic Valley and, one must suppose under the circumstances, throughout the country. These men and women are, however, rather the passive victims than the makers of ideas. From their schooldays on they have been fed the rich diet of modern "scientism" under the fashionable brands of Dewey, Freud and Marx as sold on the market by the Max Lerners and the Albert Lynds. They have been taught that "scientific progress" is the purpose of human existence, and that all measures contributing to Science and Progress are justified. In accepting Dr. Dooley's scientific therapy, they are only applying, in all innocence, the principles of their masters.

In this they show themselves more honest if more indiscreet than the nation's public spokesmen for the views which they have absorbed. These spokesmen will continue to greet the Dooley case as they so far have, with a deeply embarrassed silence, or will shy away from it with protests of horror. But we cannot grant them the moral luxury of either silence or protest. Those who believe that scientific progress is not subject to the restraints of traditional morality cannot at their convenience, for reasons of sentimentality, taste or tactical usefulness, draw back from the consequences of such a position. Dr. Dooley's ingenious and powerful defense is an unavoidable deduction from their own principles.

These principles accept a total experimental attitude toward the human personality provided only a) the experiment works, and b) the person conducting the experiment is motivated by a concern for the "welfare" of the object upon which the experiment is made. That is what the arguments in behalf of Dr. Dooley reduce to, plain and simple.

To be sure, the judge ruled that in point of fact, Dr. Dooley was gratifying his unnatural desires. He arrived at this decision after ruling implausible the explanation advanced as to why in order to cure George, who was sick, it had been necessary to violate Peter and Mark, who were whole. Dr. Dooley's defenders dismissed the judge's ruling on the matter as a further reflection of the incompetence of the layman to adjudicate matters involving "brave men of insight and vision who have been elected to proceed at whatever personal cost with the task of blazing new trails," and thus satisfied themselves as to Dr. Dooley's motives.

What if Dr. Dooley had been demonstrably out to satisfy his own sexual instincts to the point of being insensible to the welfare of his patients? His friends would have turned their backs on him.

The other stipulation—the therapy must be successful—is similarly provided for, for there are abundant testimonials from doctors and parents familiar with Dr. Dooley's work.

What if, as the result of Dr. Dooley's experiments, George and Robert and others had turned into unrestrained and aggressive homosexual marauders? Why then, too, Dr. Dooley would have been deserted.

Dr. Dooley then met the two standards his defenders implicitly exacted of him. That is why they supported him.

To deal with the second criterion first: Is rape not wrong if the result of it can be shown to benefit the "patient" —or the society in which she lives? And would the Nazi doctors who ex-perimented with human victims in order to benefit society — and, in a sense, the wretched victims who were thereby put out of their misery—have been heroes rather than brutes, "the most creative" rather than "the most destructive," had they come up with a cure for cancer? Is this what Dr. Dooley's lawyer meant to say when he reminded us that we are living in a raw and bloody world, where life is not for the squeamish?

Dr. Dooley's defenders argue, in effect, that only man's subjective motivations (which modern psychologists themselves tell us may be only a bundle of self-serving rationalizations) determine whether an act is socially objectionable. Whereas a lie is a lie, they would say, it is reprehensible only if the person who commits it means to deceive, or to do harm. A theft is a theft, but not punishable if the thief steals for exalted motives. Espionage is espionage, but not censorable when the spy (as with Klaus Fuchs) claims he acted in the higher interests of mankind. The sexual violation of children is the sexual violation of children, but is not evil if one intends good for the children. By this standard, the only relevant line of inquiry into the demonstrably deranged Jack the Ripper lay in asking whether he intended to do good or evil to his victims—or patients, if that inquiry yields a particu-lar verdict. At a certain point, in such an inquiry, one quite naturally loses sight of just what it is that is "good" or "bad."

Which leads to a final explanation, on which a number of Dr. Dooley's defenders must subconsciously have based their defense, and that is that homosexuality—as therapy—is itself not wrong. That conclusion is hotly urged by the man who compares Parker Dooley to Giordano Bruno. What Dooley did, he is in effect saying, is not substantively different from what Bruno did; hence the tormentors of Dooley are related, through time and space, to the executioners of Bruno.

Bruno rejected a theory of the universe, and was burned at the stake in an age when offenses of that kind were deemed to be outrageous affronts upon society. Experience shows that the treatment of Bruno—and of Galileo and Socrates before him—was unwise and inhuman not because these philosophers have proved to be "correct," for their conclusions continue to be the subject of discussion, but because tolerance toward intellectual dissent is in most circumstances pragmatically useful and humanly desirable. But is the metamorphosis in our attitude toward diverse opinions to guide also our attitude on moral practice? Is it then an anachronism to punish Parker Dooley for his "unorthodox methods"?

"After the seventh adverse FBI report on this man I immediately began to consider the advisability of making a note to remind me to look into the possibility of asking him to think about the idea of requesting a transfer to a less strategic job."

Kreuttner

That is the tacit assumption of Dr. Dooley's sympathizers, and those who reason as they do, in and out of the Housatonic Valley. To be sure, the force of Dr. Dooley's personality helped to unbalance what would have been the normal judgment of some of his supporters. But among them, there are intellectually nubile men and women, apt students of dedicated relativists and nihilists who spend out their lives in a metaphysical desert, helpless at the hands of seductive practitioners of experimental nostrums who demand no less than human beings for guinea pigs, recognizing no restraint imposed by a natural philosophy or the human personality, promising only that It Works. Homosexuality: Unlearning by Doing, preached James Parker Dooley, and doctors and lawyers and teachers and housewives came running, baring their terrible vulnerability: the length to which the promises of progressivism would carry them.

The Self-Importance of Picasso

Modern Art of Picasso like Communism — No meaning, abstract, Nihilist

The New York exhibition of a genius prompts the question: What will the artist-nihilist burn for inspiration? Himself? Even Picasso is not enough

WILLIAM S. SCHLAMM

Modern Art is selfish

And what is one to do when the cliché happens to be the *mot juste?* Yes, on seeing Piscasso's overwhelming Seventy-fifth Anniversary Exhibition, which the Museum of Modern Art will keep open in New York till September 8 (and the Art Institute of Chicago will show there from October 28 to December 8), the most pertinent thing I can say is really, "And how this man can paint if he wants to!" For the banality of this statement, I apologize. And, having apologized, I'd like to invite my reader on a journey into second thought.

Three floors and the basement of the Museum of Modern Art break down under the weight of this life work. It lifts the roof. It is very likely the last time that the West will have an occasion to encounter, in this age of atrophied creativeness, an artist who stays in a perpetual state of fecundity. The sheer magnitude of the work done in fifty-eight years (the oldest canvas exhibited is a watercolor of 1898, when Picasso was seventeen, the newest is an oil painted in June 1956) evokes reverence for the divine spark in man. And then, as one wanders from one eruption of this Protean talent to the next, a painful sadness overcomes the delight. This man can paint; perhaps no man, ever, could paint better. But this man has lost his soul to his self. The normal megalomania of the genius has, in him, reached beyond the confines and the proportions of human nature. God's world began to bore him. And so the genius, in his Promethean *ennui,* went out to create his own world. And he failed.

What we call Modern Art was of course born before Picasso (1881). But the Modern Artist—this unprecedented mixture of guts and spleen, spirit and dope, manna and rot—is entirely his design. It is, in fact, his replica. The Modern Artist *is* Picasso.

Picasso has, in almost sixty years of overpowering productivity, set the artist's arrogant self against the created universe. With this, he has lifted, so to speak (and appropriately in Freudian terms), the subconscious of Modern Art into the conscious mind of the Modern Artist.

This was the fissure that separated Modern Art from the continuity of art that had flowed through history for two thousand uninterrupted years. In the nineteenth century the artist discovered that the painting existed, and had merits entirely in its own terms, without any reference to the painted. From there it was just a short jump to the final and essential tenet of Modern Art: that not even the painting mattered, but only the painter—that the painter's achievement was his "signature," his personality restlessly expressed throughout the length of his total opus, rather than the finished and finite individual canvas.

The Matrix of Decay

The artist, in other words, had flown off on the tangent of his self. For thousands of years, till the middle of the nineteenth century, the artist had lived in the obsession of "service": there was something objective outside him—God, or Beauty, or Nature, or Form—that he had to grasp, to arrest, to project in his painting. The artist's life, even if he personally was proud and haughty, was a debauch of dedication. He was (and considered himself) but a tool, an executor, a servant—select, yes, even privileged, but also driven and under orders. And then, as Nietzsche first noticed in a shattering moment of fright, "God was dead." Could dedication stay alive? Dedication to what?

In this matrix of general decay, Modern Art moved faster towards the explosion of traditional form than any other kind of human creativeness. The word and the sound—the media of all other arts—are incomparably more tied to accumulated experience ("tradition") than vision. This is perhaps due to the immense fact that, when we open our eyes, we see the unfathomable wonders of Creation, the sunset and the glaciers and the ocean and the stars; but we hear—with the rare exception of the thunder and the bird—only man's language and rather fatuous noises; so that our eye is *prepared* for the unexpected, but our ear and our mind only prepared for what we already know.

Yet whatever the reason is, the fact remains unquestionable: that the painter's power of seduction surpasses that of the poet and the musician. And the greatest seducer of them all, for more than fifty years, has been Pablo Picasso. In art, this century is his. It could not escape him even on perverse detours: each of them was designed by Picasso.

This Seventy-fifth Anniversary Exhibit, organized by an exemplary intelligence and with an almost smothering generosity, makes it definitively clear that Pablo Picasso has stood at the beginning of *every* "ism" of the last fifty years. Each time this Titan switched around, a new "art movement" started. Was it only his vitality, the immense prowess of this passionate painter? I wonder. In fact, I know that it was far more. His every whim was formative because his every whim was significant for the position of the artist in this disjointed age.

In the first place, Picasso became the general pattern precisely because he is arrogantly self-concerned. For the contemporary artist, who no longer "serves," it came with the force of liberation that an artist *can*

29

be so arrogantly self-concerned. Every other focus had dissolved. So the self must be the focus. And here was an artist, a Titan, who had the courage to worship his self. And thus Titan became the formative god.

The truly offensive element in all the perversities which, in succession, have become the "isms" of our century is the impudent cocksureness of their "message." Each time Picasso started another fad, and up to the moment when he staggered into the next, the very *last* "ism" strutted with the claim that it had better be taken as the *definitive* school of painting in our time. Now the painter would be maimed, and art would choke, if he were not internally free to experiment with his every means of expression. But an artist proves his maturity and his worthiness by knowing *when* his work has reached the definite character that entitles it to our attention. Up to that moment, the artist will experiment and suffer and destroy—above all, *destroy*—in the exhilarated inferno of his solitude. When he finally shows, he *knows*.

Not so Picasso. During the sixty years he has painted so far, he has never had a moment of doubt that his every stroke was final, valid, incomparable. His insatiable and yet so easily jaded appetites were the source of pompous revelation—simply because revelation, in this nihilistic world, could come from nowhere else. And, being revelation, though only for the moment, it had to be released to the world, each time, with the solemnity of definitive truth.

This, come to think of it, throws another light on Picasso's celebrated fecundity: perhaps he has not painted more than many other painters—perhaps he has only *shown* more. In some cases (Van Gogh, for example) we happen to know of major canvases literally torn to shreds by the painter before anybody could see them. In other cases we are entitled to *assume* such self-criticism. Without any doubt Picasso is the first major painter who loved himself *all* the time.

And this is intended to be taken literally: he loved himself or, rather, his self all the time. He loved, in fact, nothing else. He *knew* nothing else. Fortunately it was a fascinating self; or else the "art appreciation" classes of the world would have been even

drearier than they were. But one's self cannot grace art with the final dimension that makes an artifact a lasting and essential statement on the human condition. Some of Picasso's paintings will be exactly this—but merely because, in spite of his adulated self, in particular cases Picasso was moved by a greater (if only private) love. This, I am happy to report, seems to be true for his work of the very last few years: a force of great joy, of almost humble delight with form and color, again breaks through those stilted artificialities which he had acquired over the decades. But, viewed as a life's work, the opus of Pablo Picasso will remain one protracted statement on his self.

"But He Sees It That Way!"

When the Philistine complains about the horrors of Picasso's distortions, the partisan of Modern Art replies desperately: "But he *sees* it that way!" Very well. Then my quarrel with the Modern Artist is that he *sees* it that way. And why does he? Because, I contend, he is jaded. It may be a Titan's jadedness, a Promethean jadedness—it still is jadedness, the worst possible sin I can imagine. The Modern Artist looks at the created world—and he finds it wanting. Worse, he finds it boring. Worse still, he finds it ugly.

That the ultimate reason for Picasso's studied distortion is simply *ennui*, the exhibit in the Modern Museum proves to me beyond a doubt. Here, in the staggering succession of year after year after year, one feels almost physically how his senses have become surfeited—and how his boredom with the *human* form grew irresistible to him. And yet, he can't leave that form alone; for his appetites are human. So he must distract himself, amuse himself, by creating ever new perspectives, distortions, squints. In this exhibit one learns to understand Picasso as the sensuous painter who grows desperately tired of his senses and yet can't help being sensuous.

What clinches the case for me are the absolutely delightful animal sculptures Picasso has produced during the last few years—the painted terracotta owl of 1953, for instance. If there exists a more delectable animal sculpture, since the miracles of

Egyptian mastery, I've forgotten it. But consider what this means! The aged Picasso, after several lifetimes of distorting the human form, joyfully *"imitates"* the gracefulness of animal nature! Why? Because, it seems to me, the "naturalistic" beauty of the animal has never yet bored him. The *ennui* was confined to the human form which had fascinated his senses to the point of distressed satiation.

It should by now be pretty obvious that I admire and do not love Pablo Picasso, that I consider him a towering genius and fundamentally reprehensible. Now like those of my readers who might resent that I call a Communist a genius, I know that Picasso is a Communist. Yet I also know that he is a genius—and what are we going to do about it? I for one propose to devote some attention to the fact that geniuses can be Communists, rather than conclude from their being Communists that they can't be geniuses.

In Picasso's particular case, it does not even surprise me that he became a Communist. It seems to me, in fact, that the Modern Artist, in general, is under very serious pressure to become one. For the Modern Artist is dedicated to nothing, he "serves" no objective mandate, and does not accept any discipline but that of his own self. The sinister trouble is that no man can live in such utter isolation. Thus, to keep body and soul together, the Modern Artist will be terribly tempted to *simulate* a broad and general kind of dedication. And Communism is very much what he might find convenient—a terribly general, terribly abstract, terribly "profound" dedication which, actually, does not mean a darned thing to him as an *artist*. Embracing the wholly abstract dedication, he can safely remain the uncommitted, isolated, contemptuous painter-nihilist.

That the Modern Painter is in this kind of trouble is, of course, also an indictment of his time. He did not choose to avoid dedication; his *age* has banned it from our experience. It is an undedicated, lukewarm age. In this under-chilled society of ours, to find the warmth that alone can make him create, the artist must burn himself. And so his self, his only fuel, becomes his only god. This is the story of Pablo Picasso.

Chappaqua Builds its Dream School

Are we building a high school or the Taj Mahal, asked the bewildered taxpayers of Chappaqua when confronted with a seventh bond issue

PRISCILLA L. BUCKLEY

Secretary of Health, Education and Welfare Folsom says the United States must build 14,000 to 20,000 additional classrooms a year to take care of the growing school population. The U.S. Chamber of Commerce says those figures are inflated. But there's no disagreement over the fact that more classrooms—more schools—are needed. The debate centers on whether the local communities and the separate states should go it alone, or whether the federal government should step in. But in the discussion, one important consideration tends to be overlooked, and that is: How luxurious are these new schools to be? Should they be equipped with lavish cafeterias, fully outfitted gymnasiums, instruments sufficient for an 80-piece orchestra? Many communities are finding that the cost of the bare additional classrooms is, like the cost of a boat hull, just the beginning . . . .

The story of Chappaqua, New York, is (let us pray!) unique; certainly it is for the ages. Even so, Chappaqua's problem is, pretty much, every town's problem.

Chappaqua is an unincorporated village which sprawls over twenty square miles of Westchester County, some thirty miles north of New York, and encompasses the towns of New Castle and Mt. Pleasant. Together they have a population of approximately 40,000 and the per capita income is, relatively, very high. Like all suburban areas within easy reach of New York, Chappaqua has experienced a population boom since the war. Moreover, since Chappaqua has always provided first-rate public education, prolific young couples predominate among the new residents, aggravating the classroom shortage.

In 1954, the elders of Chappaqua determined to build a new high school, to be ready for the fall term in 1957, equipped to handle the projected 47.15 per cent increase in school enrollments between the years 1952 and 1957. The voters of Central District No. 4 proceeded to authorize a bond issue of $2,100,000, the sum of money deemed necessary to build and equip a 28-classroom school. The $2,100,000 figure was generous, given the fact that a 28-classroom high school, at today's prices, averages about $1,370,000, a recent survey indicates.

With a promissory note for over two million in pocket, the School Board set out to build itself a high school *par excellence;* a high school that would, it was whispered about, bring cries of envy from parents and educators in the rival school districts of Mt. Kisco and White Plains.

The Board purchased a 25-acre lot on a rolling hillside overlooking the Saw Mill River Parkway, within sight of the *Reader's Digest* building. The firm of Perkins and Wills which had attained national prominence some years before, following a *Life* spread on modernistic schools, was designated as architects. Perkins and Wills proceeded to design a campus-type school—bands of low-lying structures that hugged closely the contour of the land. Each consists of five classroom "units" (everything about the school is spoken of in "units"), a gymnasium, an auditorium, a library-cafeteria, and an art-music shop (nine buildings—or, rather, units—in all). As a concession to the northern winter, these units are joined by long, covered but unenclosed, walkways.

One thing, however, was clearly wrong with the initial plans: the fly-space was insufficient. Fly-space (for the uninstructed) is that space over a stage from which scenery is lowered and raised by pulley and rope during a play. To add fly-space to comply with professional (Broadway) standards would cost an additional $9,000,

the architects said; so after some discussion, the town voted a second bond issue. (June 6, 1955. Bond Issue No. 2; new total cost, $2,109,000.)

On With the Building

The plans were now complete. The architects congratulated the School Board (presumably on its taste in choosing them) and the School Board congratulated the architects on their plans, and contractors were invited to bid on the job. It was somewhat of a shock when the lowest bid turned out to be 36 per cent, or some six hundred thousand dollars, higher than estimated. But the School Board, undaunted by adversity, devised a marvellous solution—another bond issue. At a stormy public meeting, an economy-minded group of citizens, among them a number of local architects and contractors, demanded that the plans of the school be modified to reflect the income of the people who were building it. They suggested certain changes, such as the substitution of two-storey buildings for the proposed one-storey units, thereby effecting economy in foundation, roofing, plumbing and, later on, heating. But the Board argued that any major alterations in the blueprints would mean a ten month delay in completing the school, and therefore doubling up the already overcrowded classes. The argument won the day. Three weeks later, the voters approved a supplementary $530,000 school bond issue. (Oct. 15, 1955. Bond Issue No. 3; new total cost $2,639,000).

By the following spring it had become apparent that the school population was growing faster than anticipated, so the Board asked for authorization to go ahead with the construction of an additional eight-classroom unit which originally had been scheduled for 1965. In the interest of economy, this one would be a two-storey building, situated under the brow of the hill where it would not clash esthetically with the main school. A $245,000 authorization was duly voted. (June 21, 1956. Bond issue No. 4; new total cost $2,884,000.)

Peace reigned on the school front as construction got under way, until the eruption of the Great Rock Scandal. Building has always been expensive in Westchester County, and especially expensive in and around Chappaqua. Any resident familiar with the swampy ground of the low-lying areas and the rockiness of the high ground knows why. Notwithstanding, it was originally estimated that only 300 cubic yards of rock would have to be removed (at a cost of $3,600, or $12 per cubic yard). But when the contractors started laying the foundations and running pipes between the buildings, they found rock everywhere they turned—so much that by the end of January 1957, 11,-000 cubic yards had been removed—at a cost of $141,054.45! (This time the estimate was not 36 per cent, but 36 times off.) And the end is not yet in sight. To remove the rock and level the football field, an additional $55,000 will be needed.

Funds for the rock removal came out of the $161,678 "contingency fund" which had been established to cover the cost of the school's equipment and any unforeseen expenses that might arise. Having spent the entire contingency fund before the first inkwell had been bought, the School Board had no recourse but to turn, once again, to the voter. And this time, it asked for three authorizations at once (proposed Bond Issues No. 5, No. 6, No. 7; new total cost $3,277,000); 1) $40,000 to buy 15 acres of land adjoining the new high school; and 2) $53,000 to buy 16 acres in another section of town to be used at some future date for a new grade school; and 3) $240,-000 to complete and equip the high school. It arrived at the $240,000 figure this way: Costs were running $303,-678 over estimates and had eaten up the entire contingency fund of $161,678, leaving a deficit of $142,000. The difference between $142,000 and $240,000 is $98,000. Why did the School Board think it needed this additional $98,000? Because, it seems, the original estimate on equipment

for the school had in two years time been revised, i.e., raised, from $157,-000 to $255,000—63 per cent—during a period when the cost of living in the metropolitan area had increased about three per cent.

The Board refused to break down the $255,000 figure because, it said, it is customary to set aside a certain percentage of the total cost of any school as a handy yardstick to compute the cost of equipping it, and this was what it was doing. In Chappaqua that percentage was approximately eight. And by taking the rock blooper alone as an example, it is only too easy to see how the equipment costs could have soared 63 per cent in 24 months.

The rock cost $141,000 more than estimated. To that $141,000 we proceed to tack the architect's commission of six per cent, $8,460 (and let's have no quibbling over whether the architect is entitled to a commission on a $141,000 miscalculation). We add $8,600 to the $141,000 and find that the rock removal cost is now $149,460. We then take eight per cent of that figure (the ratio of equipment to total cost) which comes to $11,956 and add it to $149,460 for a grand total of $161,416—which is the amount the taxpayers actually were being asked to pay because somebody failed to make adequate test bores of the rock formation. (A firm of engineers consulted by the School Board in the spring of 1957 found that pre-construction tests to determine sub-surface conditions on the site of the new high school were "inadequate.")

No!

So the matter stood on March 2, 1957, when the voters of Chappaqua trooped to the Town Hall to cast their ballots on the three new bond issues proposed by the School Board. To the consternation of the school authorities they voted 1) no, 2) no, 3) no—no! to the 15 acres adjoining the high school; no! to the 16 acres for a new grade school; no!—by a resounding two to one—to the proposed $240,000 deficiency appropriation. Which left the School Board high and fundless with its showplace high school nearly completed, but totally unequipped.

And there it rests at the moment.

Once school authorities have been properly chastised (the School Board's single act of public contrition has been the announcement that it will hire only eleven of the fifteen new teachers authorized for next fall), Chappaqua undoubtedly will approve whatever expenditures are necessary to complete and furnish the school. But the taxpayers, alerted by the vigorous *Newcastle Tribune* and economy-conscious citizen groups, will do so knowing that their brave new high school is, and will continue to be, an unnecessarily heavy burden. Already they are asking what the cost of maintenance will be for a campus-type school. How many men must be added to the payroll to shovel off the walkways between "units" in winter time? To keep the snow off the acres of walkway roofing? To wash the thousands of yards of plate glass which separate the class rooms from the corridors? How much heat will be dissipated as children, running from building to building, open the doors? What about the cleaning and maintenance of the extra lavatories and washrooms necessary in a multi-unit construction? What will the taxpayer ultimately shell out because the rock formation forced the builders to place heating pipes under the roof instead of under the floor? (Or does hot air go down in progressive schools?) Will the town find (as one contractor claims) that the open walkways will eventually have to be enclosed for reasons of health? And at what price?

They are asking, too, why was it necessary to have separate football, lacrosse and baseball fields? Why an auditorium with slanting floor so that it can never double as a roller skating rink or be used for a school dance? Why professional fly-space? Was there any real necessity, they ask, for the costly glassed-in study alcoves off each and every classroom? Why the luxury of single-loaded corridors—that is, corridors serving only one set of classrooms—when double-loaded corridors would have meant substantial savings in wall and foundation costs? Finally, they are asking, why is Chappaqua spending between $4,120 and $4,463 (depending on whether the extra $240,000 is or is not authorized) per pupil to build a high school when schools in comparable suburban areas around New York and Philadelphia are costing between $2,000 and $2,200 per pupil?

The recklessness of the venture is, of course, reflected in the soaring tax rate. Between 1952 and 1957, the tax rate in Chappaqua rose from $42.67 (per thousand dollars of assessed value) to $72.23! And all but $6.00 of that increase was earmarked for the schools. By 1960, the rate is expected to reach $100 per thousand, a

level which may satisfactorily solve the school problem since it will assuredly drive out of town many of the young couples who moved in to take advantage of the schools. As it is, taxes already have driven from Chappaqua retired citizens by the dozen who find that inflation plus rising taxes is taking too large a part of their fixed incomes. What it adds up to is this: Chappaqua had every right—it was in fact a clear duty—

to build a new high school. But the frills and furbelows, which have no bearing whatever on the quality of the education, there was no need for; and in return for them, Chappaqua has mortgaged its financial position for a long time to come. Chappaqua's story is, and will be, repeated across the nation so long as the mechanistic notion persists that the best possible education can be found only in the best possible physical plant.

Before You Say No...

A Correspondence, Non-Fictional, between
A Young Boy
    A Housewife
        A Headmaster
            and Young Boy's Brother

March 7, 1958
Dear Mrs. Heath:

I wish to ask you a great favor. My brother David goes to Cranwell and he says they go easier on brothers, so I might have a chance to get in even though my grades aren't so terribly good. But I need three letters of recommendation and I have one from a priest and one from a nun and my father says he thinks the third one better be from someone who is not a priest or a nun. You are not a priest or a nun but yet you know me intamitely from me having delivered your paper even that bad day right after Christmas when their was no school and the Times boy didn't deliver his customers, and from those Catholic Christmas cards you always buy,  and from the jack lantern pumpkins I helped you carve three years in a row, and the Easter Eggs, and a lot of other things. (Like the time I picked up John when he broke his arm and taught Priscilla how to ride a two-wheeler.)

Before you say no, I did break the trampoline but I didn't honestly know how heavy I was, because I grew very suddenly and the only reason I was always on the roof was because of my gliders which you said I could get if they were on the roof, and the time you wouldn't let me come in your back yard for three weeks that time, Catholic Word of Honor, John started it and it was not my fault because Scout's Honor, I only gave John the most compleatly gentle kind of tap so he would go home so Georgie Cunningham wouldn't beat him up, because you know how Georgie is when he get's mad. Because John threw a mud ball at him on his bycicle. Not that you were wrong, but that I'm explaning now, because you were so mad then you wouldn't give me a chance to explane, because John got their first and he fed you a lot of garbage. But I still like John, he is a fine young boy, he has been well brought up by his Mother.

But even if sometimes you don't get along with me too well, I always think of you as my "Oldest Friend" so I hope you will do me this great favor of writing me a letter of recommendation.

Thanking you for your trouble,
    Respectfully yours,
    PETER BAILEY-GATES
P.S. Thank you for the pennies of which I already had the 1926 San

Francisco mint but I did not have the 1921 Denver. Do you have a 1905 Indian Head, I will pay one nickel, clear profit of four (4) ¢?
    Respectfully yours,
    PETER BAILEY-GATES

March 7, 1958
Dear Peter:

I would be glad to write you a letter of recommendation to Cranwell, and I am very flattered that you asked me. Of course, I will have to tell the Truth, the Whole Truth and Nothing But the Truth, so I hope nobody will be careless enough to allow my letter to fall into the hands of the police. I can't tell you how much I would miss you if you had to spend the next ten years in a reformatory.

    Respectably yours,
    MRS. H.
P.S. No, I haven't got a 1905 Indian Head, which saddens me very much, but what saddens me more is the fact that even after three years' acquaintanceship you don't know me well enough to realize that I also know that this particular penny is worth $6.00! You and your 4¢ profit—hah! I've told you and *told* you about my high I.Q. Don't you believe me? However, just to show you I bear no grudge, I will give you my duplicate of the 1911 no mint mark—for free yet!
    Respectably yours,
    MRS. H.

P.P.S. Don't worry about my letter. I will bet you one dollar (from me) to one doughnut (from you) that you will get into Cranwell—not because you're such a hot-shot, you understand, but because if I'm crazy enough to like you, your priest and your nun are probably suffering from the same form of insanity. On the other hand, they may know you even better than I do, God help them!

Respectably yours,
Mrs. H.

March 9, 1958

To Whom It May Concern:

Peter Bailey-Gates has been in and out of my house almost daily for the past three years—by "almost," I mean those short sentences of exile which I have been unkind enough to impose upon Peter—and in that time I have come to know him very well indeed: as friend, paper boy, fellow penny-collector, and as combined decorator, waiter and entertainer at my younger children's birthday parties.

I have found Peter to be unfailingly good-humored, well-mannered and considerate—all of which qualities stand him in good stead in his relations with the public, which are many and varied. I am sure that no boy in New England, much less West Hartford, has been engaged in so many intricate business enterprises as Peter Bailey-Gates. I have bought, hired, subscribed to, invested in, paid and been paid interest on fully a dozen of his ventures in the last three years—not even counting his snow-shoveling, leaf-raking, apple-picking and garbage-can-toting, for which my own young sons are recruited. Peter's financial sense is, however, no deterrent to his feeling for what is fitting and proper: when he washed the car of the 70-year-old spinster who lives nearby, for instance, he was careful to explain (lest I should find out, I suppose!) that he had refused payment only because she had "no man to make money for her"; again, when he asked me to take an ad in his projected *Colony Road News* and I was so irreverent as to reserve two inches of space for the slogan "HOORAY FOR MRS. HEATH," Peter offered to refund my dollar because he had caused my ad to appear as "COMPLIMENTS OF A FRIEND." I must, however, state categorically that Peter has faithfully and conscientiously fulfilled his share of every and any contract between us,

whatever it may have been. (And the fact that one or two of these contracts have been rather clearer to Peter than to me, has been indignantly attributed by my own children to my habit of doing jigsaw puzzles, reading, watching television programs and saying "Uh-hunh" simultaneously, when I should have been *listening*. My husband affirms this judgment.)

Lest my young friend sound barely lower than the angels, I must add that his fertile imagination combined with his 13-year-old sense of humor have led, on occasion, to my addressing him with "harsh words and unkind"—("You know perfectly well that when I told you last Tuesday you could climb upon the roof to get your glider, I didn't mean you could buy ten *more* gliders and *aim* them at the—and by the way, I hope you didn't buy them with the lottery money for the bicycle horn—when are you going to *have* that lottery, anyway? I bought those tickets six weeks ago!" And much more.) These irrational, if predictable crises of the adult world leave Peter possibly repentant, probably remorseful, but certainly unruffled. He is more sophisticated today than three years ago, when, at the age of ten, he frequently urged me not to get my liver in a quiver. Today, when Peter and I have what he refers to as "a difference of opinion," he retires with complete equanimity to his own back yard until such time as my ill-humor subsides. My change of mood is apparently picked up by Peter's extra-sensory perception within the hour, for whenever I decide that the time has come for forgiving and forgetting, he appears at my front door within fifteen minutes, to assure me he *has* forgiven and forgotten. By way of proof (or penance?) he then resumes without rancor his status as our daily visitor.

Needless to say, our friendship is steadfast.

ALOISE BUCKLEY HEATH
(Mrs. Benjamin Heath)

March 15, 1958

CRANWELL PREPARATORY SCHOOL
Office of the Principal

Mrs. Benjamin Wild Heath
29 Colony Road
West Hartford, Connecticut

Dear Mrs. Heath:

I am very grateful to you for your

detailed and colorful description of Peter Bailey-Gates.

Many of Peter's accomplishments can be put to good use at School. Leaf-raking and snow-shoveling are part of the punitive curriculum. Endowed with all the energy which you describe, I am sure that Peter will be an early candidate for demerits.

We will try to keep pace with Peter. What substitute we will have when the occasion arises for Peter to "retire to his own back yard" we will try to figure out during the year.

Sincerely yours,
CHARLES E. BURKE, S.J.
(Rev.) Charles E. Burke, S.J.
Principal

March 15, 1958

Dear Mimi and Dad:

Please excuse the paper, for I'm in study hall, and since something happened tonight, which made me feel pretty proud of my little (little? Ha Ha) brother Peter, I thought I'd tell you about it, unless you already know, This has also changed practically my entire attitude toward Father Burke who has practically never been known to crack a smile in the memory of the oldest graduate.

Not more than five minutes ago, during the break between study hall hours, Father Burke called me and showed me a letter which Mrs. Heath had written to him about Peter. It described Peter to a tee. All of the letter was praiseworthy about him, and had been written just about Peter and nothing else. Father Burke was astonished and asked me if it was all true, and I told him it was, and he said in that case PETER GETS IN! ! . . .

Say hello to the little kids for me please, and tell them "Big Dave" will be home soon.

Love and prayers,
YOUR SON DAVID

Dear Pete—Boy, does Mrs. Heath sure have your number. Father Burke said he can hardly wait to get you up here to knock it out of you. Love and kisses.

DAVE

Hoffa: Tragedy of a Tough Guy

The "tough guy" who helped build the Teamsters into a labor empire is on his way out, says the author, but the empire will remain and its power will be used for ends he cannot even imagine

GARRY WILLS

[handwritten annotation: Anti-Union — Teamsters Union Reflects Hoffa's Crimes]

The American public, brought up on gangster movies, is always anxious to meet the real thing. The Kefauver and McClellan shows were popular in the same way that a Humphrey Bogart show is. The crowd came to see gangsters, and in Jimmy Hoffa they were not disappointed. He has spent his life imitating the Bogarts who imitated the Capones and Costellos. Carrying his cocky little body like James Cagney or Edward G. Robinson, speaking the same "me and my pals" language, hunching his shoulders at a question like a man responds only with his fists, he was a caster's dream come true.

It was pathetic to see this man who has all his life tried to convince others that he is a tough guy despite his five feet four inches, trying at a stroke to destroy the role he had so carefully built up. He appeared on his last morning before the Committee, scared but smiling, ostentatiously carrying his brief case; to a bored press table he moaned about the executive meetings he had been at all night, the work he had done on the Teamster constitution, the further meetings he must attend that evening. To the Committee he kept bringing up the "Constitooshun" he was reworking; re-emphasized his title of vice president; tried with disastrous results to use dignified language. (A beautiful example: Senator Ives, noting the vast power Hoffa would have for good or for evil as Teamster president, asked him what he meant to do about it. "I will live up to both responsibilities," he solemnly assured the Committee.)

Even so blundering an attempt to be legislator, vice president, and business executive is a far cry from the early Jimmy Hoffa, who used his fists, indeed, though never so much as he liked to imply. Jimmy grew up in Detroit and in the Teamsters, two tough societies in the early thirties. He organized his first strike when he was seventeen, was elected head of a local at nineteen, and of the Detroit Teamsters at twenty-one. Something of the boy wonder even now, he was then determined not to be five-four and cherub-faced.

Points of Power

Detroit was, in the thirties, the feared center of the coming revolution, where the Reuthers came and went preaching, picketing, and organizing against the impossible odds of autodom. But Jimmy's heroes of that era were the boys of the Purple Gang, tough guys who could win a truck driver's respect. He did not work with the Reuther brothers, but rather after the pattern of the Dunne brothers in Minneapolis, who formed a Teamsters' tactic that demanded a Jimmy Hoffa for its execution. The Teamsters' Union deals with a scattered and diffused membership; where the Reuthers could organize a stable group of workers in a plant, the Teamsters had to tie all the small owners and operators who roam the highways into a powerful unit (for power is the prime fact and drive of labor's efforts). The Dunnes in Minneapolis met this difficulty by grouping their fluid elements around stable points of power; the qualification of these power-points was stability, not literal status as "teamsters." For instance, they used the teamsters to help railroad workers strike, then reversed the process and bound the truck drivers' protest into a pressure that could tell. This set the pattern for Teamster growth, so that even in the recent hearing, when Hoffa was asked about his union's toilet-seat manufacturers and rosary peddlers, he said "We organize anyone we can."

Another method of binding the fugitive drivers into a net across the highways was to gain control of terminals, then of all trucks working out of them, then of any that came to pick up goods or services in that terminal or that whole city. This method, called "leapfrogging," made it necessary to have all warehousemen, servicers, and salesmen "organized," so that we find the union's constitution claiming rights of jurisdiction over "*all* dairy employees . . . *all* cannery workers."

Dan Tobin, the czar of the Teamsters' Union, fought this new kind of expansion, but without success. He opposed the Minneapolis union's bloody strikes, and wanted the union restricted most literally to truckdrivers. But the Dunne brothers' approach won the new blood, and Tobin found his meager 100,000 of 1933 become a kingdom more vast and pivotal than he had ever imagined. Power once attained in this despotism is rarely overthrown, and Tobin ruled the organization built on a vision not his own.

Even with this program outlined, the Teamsters had to deal with the thousands of individual truckers, cluster them around these power nuclei—a job made difficult not only by the unrooted state of drivers, but by their character. A tough group at any time, in the early thirties the truckers still had many of the prohibition drivers in their ranks, men who, like longshoremen, had a background in hijacking, weighting their loads, sabotaging their rivals. They were a hard group to deal with. To expand Tobin's reign with the Dunnes' tactic, two men were needed, one who understood the mathematics of power and could organize from the center, and one who could scout the bushes and run men into the net.

The two men appeared; Dave Beck, who has gone the way of Tito's and Mussolini's vanity and become a puffed-up living caricature of himself, but who was the brains behind the organizing of teamsterdom's four conferences, and little Jimmy Hoffa, who could talk the trucker's language with a boy's self-importance and use a man's "persuaders." Together, and needing each other, the two men built an empire. Despite rivalry and the recent demise of Beck as an open power, the organization binds them together even now; each is too committed to the thousand "deals" they have managed together to strike at the other without hurting himself. When Jimmy, ducking and running on his dazed last appearance before the Committee, shifted blame for some acts where no one but Beck must bear it, no recriminations followed. The next day they smiled from the news photographs in their old pose, flabby cheek by firm beaver-jowl.

Unseen Empire

"Jimmy" to all, a man who deals personally with other men, not with charts and graphs, Hoffa has built and wielded his power as the big city boss did. Power and patronage go together; "deals" are sewed up through an intricate network of friendships, favors, and the honor that does exist among thieves. A man in this position must be able to burn a candle at both ends and all along its sides—dealing with the employers, with the members, with the middlemen—the carpetbaggers of labor—who spring up everywhere, with the side-groups who can throw their power to Jimmy whenever he needs it, with all those who come to him for "something special." Time has revealed the tireless Jimmy spinning this wearisome web, owning trucks himself, throwing union welfare funds to shady friends' insurance companies, acting as trustee of rebellious groups in the union, the man who breaks their spirit and leads them back under bridle. He has leap-frogged from one organizational problem to another, cajoling reluctant locals into area agreements that give him power in large units. Piece by

piece he gave Beck the parts to be fitted into the jigsaw that now covers the nation. It is unfortunate, even esthetically, that all the labor and maneuvering that went into this huge empire can never be recovered from the darkness where such kingdoms are born; it would be a fascinating story of achievement, a kind of inverted epic, an odd heroism of brains and blackjacks. The untold history whose records never were or are destroyed—Iliad after Iliad played out for the enjoyment of the prince of this world—is only hinted at in the few sordid crimes men have uncovered.

The Teamsters, built on power and still afire to augment it, have not

been frustrated. No other union can safely defy them; the men who deliver goods can support or break at will another group's picket line or strike. It is the Minneapolis story all over. Small truckers, that terribly numerous group whose livelihood depends on three or four employees, are at the mercy of the union's agents. Some activities hinge, as the rum-running business did, on the truckers, and the same methods are applied here (often by the same people) as in prohibition days. These are the slot-machine and pinball concerns made famous in the recent hearings, and the men who are milking this business are not parasites of the union but central to it, good friends of the ever-friendly Jimmy. For Hoffa is still available to his constituency, still one who deals person-to-person, who likes to be liked, especially by the tough guys he has always admired. Even under the greatest pressure before the Senate Committee,

he would not name a single name when he spoke of cleaning out the union.

The rise of Hoffa is covered by these impregnable friendships, by the mutual engagements assured from all parties to shady doings, and by the cloak of virtue thrown around a labor leader's use of direct violence. But a sample of these methods—as much as can ever be pinned on the big gangsters, the ones caught only, as Hoffa still may be, for evading the income tax—was uncovered by the House Committee's 1953 Detroit investigation. There the public first saw what kind of deal Hoffa is driven to by his compulsion to "organize." Before this he had been arrested seventeen times, six for brawling; had pleaded *nolo contendere* to an indictment for conspiracy to give one paper company a monopoly and to "organize" grocery stores to do his will. He was put on probation and given a fine, which the union paid. But all these had been limited charges which he admitted and sloughed off.

Tangled World

Before the Committee, however, *connections* were exposed, more important than individual deeds, suggestively extending into the highest echelons of labor and the lowest tiers of the underworld. Hoffa was seen moving through a whole world of extortion, violence, union business, and personal profiteering. His amazing policy of destroying the books at the end of the year was aired; the policy had, naturally enough, been applied only to that local in charge of slot machines, the Teamsters' satellite-business run by William Bufalino, who went to the hospital as soon as the Committee arrived in Detroit. Two women entered the picture, too, on the payrolls of various locals, who turned out to be Hoffa's wife and the wife of his partner Bert Brennan (who shares his office and about five businesses with him), both women hidden under their maiden names. Their payroll status Hoffa tried to explain as a whimsical method one local had of repaying a personal loan; when the amount paid them turned out triple what was supposedly advanced, the loan became, by the natural law of all such explanations, a gift. A truck-rental company was set up in the wives' names, too, put in ideal circumstances through Hoffa's union power, then sold to Carney Matheson, who had originated the scheme.

The kind of tangled world in which a tough guy makes his way became obvious as Hoffa sat there in Detroit with his lawyer George Fitzgerald defending this phony trucking business set up for Carney Matheson. For Fitzgerald and Matheson had bought into a brewery with Jimmy; Matheson, also a lawyer, was supposedly representing the claims of employers *against* the union! Others close to Hoffa were drawing funds from the union for all kinds of private concerns: Paul Dorfman, once a member of the Capone gang, and his son Allen, shared with Hoffa ownership in an oil company and a girls' camp begun on a "loan" from the union. The shuttling of "loans" back and forth in these circles, all cash, all unrepaid, is impressive even to one who expects such things.

The 1953 hearings should have convinced anyone that Hoffa was not, as he pretended, the tough guy who worked only for the good of the gang. Reinhold Niebuhr's recent statement that Hoffa steals only for the union and not from it is simply absurd. Hoffa, it is true, will not live, and eventually vegetate, in a palace like Beck's; he has probably allowed more pilfering by his lieutenants than he has himself executed. Nevertheless, once one deals in the shade for profit, some amount must seem well earned by the "organizer."

Just a Good Show

The recent hearings extended the scenario of Hoffa's dramatic growth to power, but kept essentially the same cast: Brennan, Matheson, the Dorfmans and Fitzgerald again at his side. A few unfortunately newsworthy names, like that of Johnny Dio, entered with an impact which underlined Jimmy's desire to be "one of the gang." Dio and Hoffa took it on the chin, with gangster loyalty to each other, for their phony New York locals and their tapping of grand jury testimony. But all that was here accomplished was a slightly better-focused picture of Jimmy as a criminal. Tough guys are colorful, and the hearings were a lot of fun;

but tough guys have a way of getting things done, and he will probably be elected Teamster president this month. It was a good show, but nothing more. For the Jimmy Hoffa it opposed is nothing more. The important thing about Hoffa is the system which made him, and which will break him, since he has nearly outlived his usefulness.

The Hoffa-turned-respectable who sat and checked off the forty-eight charges, as McClellan read them, like an executive checking over his accounts, knows that he is on the way out. All his heroes are pathetically old, members of the Capone gang or their contemporaries. Even Hoffa's fellow imitators, Cagney and Edward G. Robinson, are through. He has been aping dead men. It is too late for him to learn the new roles of power. Typically, he has begun to imitate other businessmen, not the ideologues—cast in the mold of Reuther—to whom the morrow belongs. The ascetic working schedule and personal habits of Hoffa, a devoted family man who never drinks or smokes, are precisely those of the teetotaler millionaires with their own passion for "organizing." This "labor crusader," like the "captain of industry," makes up for his lack of a real crusade by such devices of pseudo-dedication. Hoffa would now like for some of Hal Gibbons' social-worker aureole to rub off on him, as Gibbons wants the *de facto* power of Hoffa. But Jimmy is a man of one role; having worked at it, he cannot unmake ·the image, ever. There were those who thought Hoffa too smart to have attempted his bribery of Cheasty; but this is the way of all men who organize too long and too successfully, who begin to think they can organize grand juries and congressional hearings and buy and sell anyone. He is reaching the destined end of the tough guy.

Temporary Monarch

He will probably be elected president, a little while to monarchize and kill with looks. But Meany will be after the Teamsters; and he will finally get them. Hoffa will go as Beck has gone. And no one of his never-deserted friends will miss the tough guy. There was some idealism in the labor movement which did not

fear to use this strong-arm man; there is none left in the group which will cynically disown him for their own good name. His fall will not even be dignified by pointing a moral. He will be counted a single gangster, not a product and producer of the power-mentality driving the labor movement no less in its present triumph than in its difficult birth. The organizing will move onto a higher and subtler echelon; the cruder work of this little organizer will be scorned and publicly condemned. Men will take the instrument he forged and use it for ends more vast than he could imagine. Power will mean Hal Gibbons making a government of the union, running hospitals and labor centers (and federal elections), instead of Jimmy Hoffa making it a business, running oil fields and trucking firms and jury trials.

Even such friends of the union as Niebuhr admit that it is a despotism, controlling all the organs for speaking and instruments for acting, disposing of dues and contracts at the leaders' will. He advocates constitutional changes to get rid of the Hoffa element in the union. They never can. The rejected fashioner of power will have his revenge. Americans above all others should know that the complex organism of a society forever bears the mark of its birth. Only a single strange conjunction of interests and desires and ideas could have caused the brilliant compromise which is our governmental system. And the Teamsters' Union, too, is oriented by its birth from power and violence toward further power. The tough guy's power will pass into hands more skillful, and so more dangerous. (Dio recounting on the telephone his fear of an airplane crash points up the fearlessness of Reuther when he was shot. Tough guys are always weak; the man to fear does not boast of his fights, as Jimmy did.) But it does not matter how many respectable pairs of gloves are put on the bare hands that fashioned this vast power-pyramid; the Teamsters' Union will continue to bear the mark of the two men who built it.

The Meaning of Hungary

More perhaps than any other event in recent history, the rape of Hungary has shaken the academic world—maybe enough, who knows, to set it to re-examining some of the premises out of which was constructed the policy of coexistence. In college after college, students and faculty issued statements some of which had a ring to them that lift them up out of the class of formal, stylized protest. In the religious world, the moral insufficiency of America's position caused a number of ministers to probe deeply, and assert the necessity of ceding before transcendent moral compulsions.

NATIONAL REVIEW had intended to take brief notice of a half dozen statements that issued from the academic and the religious world. Instead, we decided, upon setting eyes on them, to devote all our space to reprinting extracts from an address by Professor Frederick Wilhelmsen to the student body of Santa Clara College, and a sermon by the Reverend Stanley Parry of Notre Dame University.

They are statements that reflect the best that the American mind and the American heart have to offer in the present crisis.

—THE EDITORS

We are gathered here this morning to protest Soviet aggression in Hungary. We meet, I trust, not in the spirit of hate. The enormity of the crime committed by the Russian Army in Hungary cannot be measured in human terms. This crime staggers the reason and leaves it limp with incomprehension. It is as though men had surrendered their humanity, had created a vacuum in their souls—a vacuum which was filled by forces from another world and from an order of things so monstrous that it simply is not commensurate to the hate of man . . .

Not ten days ago the Hungarian people had done what no one had conceived possible. . . . Our political scientists, almost to a man, declared rebellion against the industrialized might of a modern state impossible. There is hardly a political analyst in America who has not been saying for years that revolution behind the Iron Curtain not only could not succeed, but that it could not even get under way. What they forgot was the heroism of a Christian people. What they forgot was that the Faith is not of this world. There are no graves for those of us who are of the Christian West; or—better yet—graves exist solely that we might climb out of them. And Hungary, alone and un-

aided, rolled back the tombstone of history.

It was perhaps this taunt thrown in the face of dialectical materialism, or was it panic in the Kremlin which saw suddenly that its soft policy of the past year failed to melt like butter the will of decent men but produced only iron and the determination for freedom—was it this that brought back the Russian troops; that caused them to arrest the Hungarian armistice commission; was it the British-French action in the Suez? Probably it was all of these, but it was something more. . . .

This act of Russian Soviet treason was brilliant, magnificent: it was inspired—by hell itself. Today there is a band of corpses, a Soviet rosary, spanning the bridge between Buda and Pest. The frantic calls for help from clandestine radios have ceased. The voice of Hungary is silenced . . . Yet they still fight on, the Hungarians.

They have been fighting since before they were Christians, since the days when they came riding into the Danubian valley through the Carpathian mountains from Central Asia in the dusk of the ninth century. And as with all the great migrations, the First Hungarians—members of the Old Turkish race—followed the sink-

ing sun toward the West, sensing in some dumb manner that their future lay in the Lands of the Evening. That they were hurried on by the Finger of Providence can be doubted by no one who sees history in the light of the Incarnation. Their first King, Stephen, received the Crown from Pope Sylvester II. . . . A light of Faith in the center of paganism, Hungary poured out its blood through the long Middle Ages and even beyond. That land of Hungary—or, more accurately, the Lands of the Holy Crown of St. Stephen—stood as a shield against the threat from the East . . .

No one understands, really understands, the role of this 1,000 year kingdom, this nation who vested its rulers as late as 1916 in a garment woven by the wife of St. Stephen 900 years before, no one really knows this people who does not understand the meaning of the Sacred Crown of St. Stephen. When the American businessman Mr. Robert Voegeler was released by the Communists, the Russians tried to exchange him for the Crown. They failed. It rests somewhere in safekeeping, perhaps in Fort Knox. The Hungarians believe that no government can last long that does not possess the Crown, not simply symbolically but physically . . . Here is no ordinary crown. Given the land by Pope Sylvester in the year 1,000, it was later built up by a headband encrusted with sapphires and enamel plaques on which are carved the saints. On its top is a globe capped by a cross and beneath is the figure of the Savior reposing: He is surrounded by the sun, the moon, and two trees. Below are the apostles. Until 1945 all Hungarian Courts issued their verdicts "In the name of the Sacred Hungarian Crown." . . .

Not ten days ago the image of that ancient Crown, symbol of Hungarian liberty, promise of Hungarian independence, appeared everywhere in the streets of Budapest. Children carried tommy guns and crosses in their hands, the Crown of St. Stephen in their hearts. Let us think long on this Crown, we who protest this morning and who appeal to the President for action in the United Nations. This Crown is capped by a Cross—what else would one expect from such a civilized people, a people which has always considered its national existence one with the mission of Christ? But this Cross is bent over at a crazy angle: it appears about to fall . . . the bent Cross symbolizes Hungary today, its back bent under the Soviet boot. But although bent, not broken. We must, as the apostle John writes, "harden ourselves in hope." Remember that the Cross always bends: as Chesterton wrote of the early Church, "the heavenly chariot flies thundering through the ages . . . the wild truth reeling but erect."

The Cross reels today in Hungary. But reeling it stands. And like all crosses it stands arms outstretched—crying for your help and mine. Holy God, grant us the courage to embrace that Cross.

PROF. FREDERICK WILHELMSEN

In remote places, in hopeless isolation and with irredeemable commitment, the last noble remnants of Hungarian students are dying violently tonight. I wish to inquire whether they are dying wisely. In the largest sense we cannot affect the innate wisdom of that death. For to die nobly is always wise. But in an America fat with too much living, it may be difficult for many to see the wisdom of Hungarian defiance—so hopeless, so doomed to failure. For us, however, who still remember that by death life is not taken away but only changed, there remains the power to appreciate deeply the nobility of spirit these men displayed. With awareness in their hearts, they preferred death in a hopeless bid for freedom to a prudent life of enslavement.

The only mistake they made was to expect aid from us. In this Hungary thought too highly of us. We have wrung our hands, and passed resolutions. And now that the last Hungarian radio has been silenced by Soviet might and the tranquillity of the dungeon returns upon the land, the danger is that we will try to forget. This evening I pray that the last voice from Hungary will echo in disturbing and corroding tones through the

conscience of the West and stimulate us to a manliness we have of late forgotten. We cannot change the innate wisdom of what they did, but we can, by our response, decide whether their deed will bear its ultimate fruit.

The policies our government should follow in this matter is not my theme tonight. I speak of a sphere of life and decision beyond the reach of the coarse hand of government—that in which the human soul confronts the truth. Here it is that Hungary makes her first and irresistible demand upon us. If our decisions in this sphere are not noble, they cannot even be right anywhere else. And the burden of my theme tonight is this: if you cannot find the nobility of soul to meet those demands, you are indeed a waste people. The students who died in Hungary did not have their lives taken away. They gave them—and gave them most magnanimously. It remains for us to make that gift worth while. In our own souls we must also raise this gift to the level of significance it has already achieved in the souls of those who have died.

In the Providence of God, Hungary has the historic role of defending Christendom against the barbarism that periodically threatens it from the East. Her narrow plains constitute one of the crossroads of history where single battles have decided the course of events for centuries to come. There, in the past, the life of Christendom has been staked on the prowess of Hungarian fighting men and the zeal of the Christian faith. In our day such an issue has once more been met. On the eastern borders of our civilization Bolshevism has organized the negation of God on earth. This negation now confronts Christendom, and Christendom gives a confused response. . . . The light of faith has indeed flickered low in the West. We see too dimly by it.

It has fallen to Hungary, at this moment, to illuminate again the truths by which we live. And so desperate is our confusion that it has required an act of truly heroic proportions to attract our attention. Though it be occupied, enslaved, and abandoned, its spirit has shone forth with an intensity that has lighted up the darkest corners of our society. And the utter abandonment of this act of enlightenment carries with it the urgent intimation that God perhaps

is offering Christendom a last chance to be worthy of its redemption.

In the presence of this noble commitment we cannot remain mere spectators. We are tied to the men of Hungary by too many bonds. They are parts of Christendom—so are we. But beyond all these human integrations there rises the truly relevant one. They are members of the Body of Christ—and so are we. Here we find the truth of the matter. It is not Hungarians who are dying in Hungary. It is Christ who is dying in His members. And so we too are dying. The very circumstances of the Hungarian uprising against Bolshevism focus attention on the spiritual character of the issues that are at stake. A student uprising sparked the rebellion, and the issues are issues concerning truth itself, not some narrow national interest. The attempt was hopeless from the beginning; there was no temporal purpose behind it, but rather a purpose whose farther reaches escape the bounds of history, and whose full significance can be grasped only in the perspective of the struggle between Michael and Lucifer, between Christ and Satan. . . .

The sacrifices made in Hungary will not have been in vain if they teach the confused minds of Christendom this truth. But those sacrifices will have produced their full fruit only when the spirit behind them takes root in each of us. For us, therefore, it remains to resolve that the struggle so nobly begun shall never cease.

Christ is ever dying that we may live. And at crucial periods in human history men are frequently ennobled with the mission of dramatizing this truth on the stage of the world. We must make sure, through our actions, that the fire lighted in Hungary shall not die out, but rather shall spring up anew in our own souls, whose commitment to Christ will keep alive the wisdom the West so sorely needs. With St. Paul, therefore, I urge you:

take up the armor of God, that you may be able to resist in the evil day, and stand in all things perfect . . . having girded your loins with truth, and having put on the breastplate of justice . . . in all things taking up the shield of faith with which you may be able to quench all the fiery darts of the most wicked one. And take unto you the helmet of salvation and the sword of the spirit. . . .

REV. STANLEY PARRY

The Bankruptcy of American Optimism

Europe, says the author, created the myth of America as the land of honor—a myth which America also believed. But the ordeal of Hungary has tried us, and proved us empty

FREDERICK D. WILHELMSEN

The picture of Europe burnt into the folklore of the American consciousness is so well known it is almost embarrassing to detail it. We were the people of the future, they of the past; we stood for progress, they for decay; we for the clean and the civic and the responsible, they for the piracy of individualism and the chaos of selfish reaction. The very existence of our expatriates of the twenties and the literature of protest against Babbitry heightened the dominant self-assurance of the American consciousness.

The picture of America entertained by the poor and the dispossessed of the Mediterranean basin and the European heartland paralleled comically and exactly the picture of Europe drawn by Americans of all classes and regions. This European picture of America has nothing to do with the Puritan legend taught our own children. As D. H. Lawrence pointed out, the Puritans did not seek freedom and the full life. They were men terrified of joy and grace and beauty, men who brooded under the glowering shadow of their avenging God—that God who came back to Christendom riding west on the negations of the desert and the passion of pure religion. The Puritans fled the largeness and liberty of Baroque Europe. (It was only with difficulty that the broad common sense of the English motherland and the humanity of the Stuart Kings prevented the early settlers from turning the first colonies into totalitarian theocracies.)

The vision of America as the land of hope and freedom was the dream of the *Continent* and its toughness is attested by the fact that it has lasted for almost 150 years. Europeans — especially Mediterranean Latins and Slavs——living close to death and poverty and greed, often bruised and hardened by a century and a half of bad governments and corrupt economies, cynical and proud of their matchless inheritance, tired of its burden—looked across the Atlantic to this nation as a symbol of hope and a promise of escape. The American legend—the legend summed up by the Statue of Liberty and the teeming streets of New York, Chicago, and Detroit—was born and nurtured in Europe. Peopled by immigrants, America exists as a vision seen in a dream by men for whom reality had become too intolerable to bear. We are what Europe made us be.

There were Sicilians who greeted our troops in World War II with the request that Sicily be made the forty-ninth state. Each July 5 the jails of Prague are full of young men and women who dared to break out the Stars and Stripes under the guns of their Communist masters. Even the Germans, truculent and resentful after two defeats suffered at our hands, honor this nation by imitating it in all things industrial and commercial. The French, most reluctant of all peoples to alter their way of life, have studied American civilization with an intensity and vigor foreign to our own universities.

The intellectual issue is grasped when we understand that Americans asked the questions and Europeans answered them; that Americans posed as the promise and hope of the future and Europeans agreed, some with enthusiasm and others with reluctance. The existence of Neutralism has obscured the facts marshalled above; it has not altered them: Thus far Neutralists have failed to seize power in even one government in all Western Europe. The Old World might laugh at us; mock us; insult us behind our backs; rob us blind when we travelled abroad as tourists; sneer at our naive optimism and scorn our preoccupation with progress as petty and barbarian. All these were but compliments, the admissions of men who sensed in their hearts that ours was the future.

America Stands Dishonored

That hour of history has passed. Everything can now be dated Before Hungary and After. The air has cleared. It is an air clean like that in a cemetery before dawn. And if we meditate before the tomb of Hungary a terrible truth will come home to each one of us: it is no longer Europe that stands a mendicant before the bar of history; it is America that has been judged and found empty by civilization itself.

In November we Americans stood dishonored before the West. I take this as the central fact of the mid-century. Our resolute refusal to act in Hungary, a refusal subsequently given formally by the Secretary of State *in the name of principle*, has branded us a nation of cowards from Oslo to Madrid. Now the charge of cowardice can be borne by a nation provided its timorous policy masks a fundamental realism. But we Americans are being condemned abroad not only as cowards, but as fools; not only as cowards and fools, but as fools and cowards without vigor, without life, without that substance and being we and all Europe had credited to the American spirit.

That the United States should have failed Hungary because they were paralyzed with fear was at first incomprehensible to a continent bred on the conviction that Americans always risked the future and therefore gained it. That the United States should find themselves maneuvered into the preposterous position of supporting the Soviet Union against their natural and traditional allies, of preaching homilies to the British and French after the abysmal failure to halt the murder of Hungary—these actions were less tragic in the eyes of Europe than stupefying. Tragedy has meaning, but American diplomacy during the past six months has seemed both irrational and craven. It is only now that Europeans, recovering their customary cynicism after the shock of Hungary, are beginning to see the joke. If I read the foreign press aright, it is not America that stands before the civilized world as the Great Fool of the Century: it is Europe for having been taken in for so long by the legend of American daring and idealism.

That these judgments may be severe and even unfair will be argued by some political philosophers here and abroad. That the judgments have been passed by the European man in the street can be doubted by no one sensitive to the temper of European opinion. The fact that we are being condemned on the Continent and in the British Isles should move us to examine the presuppositions not only of American foreign policy but of the mind of which that policy is but an instrument.

The Spell of Words

It is time we Americans faced the realities of the world in which we live. These realities are twofold: the facts of politics and the mind upon which those facts repose. That mind is as much a part of the reality of our time as are the facts themselves.

Among the facts the following are crucial. We can no longer surrender our foreign policy to the United Nations in the name of international morality because the United Nations today cannot stand above power blocs but must work through them. Our policy of "massive retaliation" has proved both a boomerang and an illusion: we have built an atomic and hydrogen stockpile so terrifying in its power for destruction that we are petrified at the thought of using it; it follows therefore that the very "massive" character of our military strength has permitted Russia to act

with impunity in every local situation in which she feels it necessary to bolster her tottering empire. Our much-heralded dedication to moral principle is but the platitude of a Madison Avenue broadsheet. Our conscience, had we the courage to face it, is etched with the burnt-out face of Hungary.

If we faced the world as it really is we would cease the disgusting travesty of thinking that justice has been done the heroic Hungarian people simply because we have given a Hollywood reception to a few thousand Freedom Fighters who are then dumped on the economy to become short-order cooks and street cleaners. Finally, if we took a long look at the magic of the written and spoken word we would discover that we, the most inarticulate people of the West, have been living under the spell of words and only words for better than a decade.

I refuse to argue the above. They are simply facts and, as Newman once wrote, with facts one does not argue but accepts them as they are. The intellectual Left as well as the intellectual Right, both here and abroad, seemed for one sweet moment to close ranks in their joint horror over our total failure in Hungary, our almost comic confidence in declarations of disapproval, and our unmanly surrender to the United Nations of a burden it had no power to shoulder.

Moral indignation will not heal our sins. But it might prod us as the thorn of remorse to probe the Mind from whence comes this seeming insanity.

I use the word "seeming" advisedly. To the political philosopher all action has meaning. Our political paralysis before the world of today, a paralysis clearly observable since the elections of 1952, is a moral and intellectual disease entered into by this nation as a matter of principle. Four years before the events of last November, Eric Voegelin wrote in his *The New Science of Politics*:

Dangers . . . will rather be met by magic operations in the dream world, such as disapproval, moral condemnation, declarations of intention, resolutions, appeals to the opinion of mankind, branding of enemies as aggressors, outlawing of war, propaganda for world peace and world government, etc. The intellectual and moral

corruption which expresses itself in the aggregate of such magic operations may pervade a society with the weird ghostly atmosphere of a lunatic asylum, as we experience it in our time in the Western crisis.

The Gnostic (to use a term made popular by Voegelin) entertains dream assumptions about the perfectibility of man, and the ultimate benevolence of history. Gnosticism, that disease we of the West inherit from I know not where—perhaps from the medieval Catharists and beyond from that Near East which produced the Arabian Nights and the Lamp of Aladdin, that dream drugged with the illusion of a divine power for a glorified man who would right all things and himself make straight the crooked paths of the human heart—Gnosticism, that disease, has worked its poison into the blood of our body politic. But it has now run its course. Gnosticism decayed is the moral and intellectual rot which prevents us from acting today with that vigor which has ever marked the American character. The America of 1957 is a land of Optimists without a goal.

Recently a scholar defined the American mind as a "project." We have been a nation of projects from the Plymouth Rock Foundation to TVA. Our nervous practicality is by no means unique in Western history: the Romans were as practical as Americans. What is unique with us, however, is the American insistence that this nation is dedicated in a special manner to pioneering, to experimentation, to action; and this not for the sake of itself but for the sake of what is often called "the fuller life" for our children and for the generations yet to come. Possessed of a boundless confidence in action; buttressed by the Calvinist conviction that the Good News applied in a particular manner to ourselves; convinced that history is essentially benevolent; trusting, after an initial hesitation, the wisdom of the people; seizing upon mechanization as the anointed instrument of the American Dream—the mind of this people, at first hesitant and unsure because it still remembered Europe, finally gathering strength, then annealed in the blood of Gettysburg and The Wilderness, presented itself to the world as a Thing completely one with its own essence.

The forests have been cleared. The cities have been built. The children have been put to school. The slums are largely cleared. Poverty has been reduced from the mystery spoken of in the Gospel to a problem in social engineering. The fire has gone out of our old Radicalism: it takes real genius today to find a typical American who is oppressed or impoverished. The oppressed lie on the periphery of American society. Mexican migratory workers, Puerto Ricans in New York, marginal farmers, Negroes in the big cities—these are but remnants, the detritus of a people bent on enjoying the fruits of their own productivity. The battle for the Good Life has been won for the broad millions. Our much vaunted American Optimism has reached its goal. We have nowhere left to go.

Perhaps this is why our children dream of conquering the moon. In the meantime, however, they are educated in our great universities to accept things as they are; they learn their lesson well: the scramble each June to lose personal identity and merge the self in the great corporations constituting "The Permanent Revolution" has become a tradition on the American campus. "They no longer sell out at forty; they sign up at twenty-two," according to Mr. Louis Kronenberger, commenting on the comfortable and conformist youth of the day. We were once a nation taking pride in adventure and in the hope of things fresh and new. Today we wish only to become Men in Gray Flannel Suits. The Liberal Dream of the Full Life has conquered the continent and thus destroyed its old reforming zeal. At the risk of violating proper English usage, permit me to suggest that we have become the most "conservative" people in the Western world.

The disappearance of the "inner-directed man" and of the gospel of work and self-reliance have laid to rest the old Protestant Ethic. While still committed to the legend of risk and work and thrift; while still dominated, at least publicly, by the myths of the forests and the great plains beyond; while still preaching the doctrine of American righteousness inhabiting a future whose horizon will be bounded only by the Kingdom of God; while still telling our children and our constituents

that these are the spurs making America the land of restless movement—the life has gone out of them and has left us empty and without a faith with which to face the world. We have come out of two great wars and a depression. We have shifted from a productive to a consuming economy. The simple truth is that Americans today, taken in the large and by the handful, want nothing better than to be left alone so that they may eat the fruit planted and pruned by their fathers.

Optimism without a goal is forced to adopt the strategy of inventing a fiction which passes among people as a reality. We have not invented this fiction consciously; it has been elaborated deep within our corporate psyche as a defense against our unwillingness to face the realities of the world in which we live. We have made words and bare abstractions do duty for a genuine commitment to the real. This was perhaps easier for us than for any other Western nation; we are largely a non-verbal, non-literary people: therefore we are more susceptible to being duped by the power of language. Thus we spoke in November of "responsible action through the United Nations," knowing deep in our hearts, but never saying it aloud to ourselves, that this was a safe tack because it was bound to produce what we *really* wanted: no action at all. Thus we reached the paradoxical situation of proclaiming that responsible action was one with inaction.

Today

Eisenhower as Symbol

Perhaps our President, the most ungrammatical statesman in modern history, is the most apt symbol for the Gnostic mist with which we wrap our determination to do nothing that would risk our fortune or commit our word. He announced to the world that it was American policy to keep alive the hope for freedom within the satellite countries *and* that it was American policy not to encourage rebellion in those countries. Either half of the proposition can be understood and defended in isolation from the other; the two together make sense only in terms of Gnostic illusions about the future, illusions masking a profound determination to stand still and remain as we are.

Speaking recently in San Francisco, Mr. Adlai Stevenson declared that "we can't go on tottering from brink to brink . . . while our leaders assure us that all is well and tell us to relax and buy another car or swallow another tranquillizer." We need not agree with Mr. Stevenson's politics to see that he has captured in a phrase the mood of America today. Tranquillized and relaxed; fat with comfort, chrome, and complacency; soothed by legends that came out of a forest we never saw and out of a faith we hold no longer, we are a nation that has lost the respect of the world.

For years our intellectuals have been telling us that Christendom is dead, that the Old Order has run its course. Today we know it was all a lie. It was not the dream of the future and the Full Life that brought those children into the streets of Budapest: it was the call of Honor and the Decency of Death. It was not the promise of tomorrow but the presence of yesterday that moved the heart of Europe when Hungary freely mounted its cross. What is the West, what is Christendom? "It is a patriotism which is chivalric," wrote Hilaire Belloc. "In our earliest stories, we honor men fighting odds. Our epics are of small numbers against great; humility and charity are in them, lending a kind of magic strength to the sword." Christendom is honor and the fatherland and man with his back to the wall. It is the glory of lost causes and the splendor of certain defeat. It is the risk and the doom, the dice clacking at the feet of the Savior.

Christendom went down into the tomb with Christ in Hungary. It was Christendom when the women of Budapest marched through that broken city, mourning their dead and shouting defiance at the Soviet tanks lining the ruined streets. But Christ was not born in those final days of 1956. It is Good Friday in the West today. Hungary, that Hilt of Christendom, will rise again. If we mourn in America, let it not be for the Hungarian dead; let it be for our own dead honor.

*Connects Mrksm & Conservatism
the liberals switched
today*

Why Did They Fire Bang-Jensen?

His story proves that honor lives on. Does it also prove that honor has no place in the UN? And that UN officials had better not displease the USSR?

PRISCILLA L. BUCKLEY

So far as the public is concerned Povl Bang-Jensen is the United Nations official who refused a year ago to turn over to the UN Secretariat the names of Hungarians who, having been promised anonymity, gave testimony on Soviet brutalities to the special committee that produced the UN Hungarian Report. Bang-Jensen claimed he had been authorized to make that promise; Secretary-General Hammarskjold denied this and accused the Dane of insubordination. Eventually, and to the relief of all concerned, it was resolved that the lists be burned, and so it was that on a blustery January night in 1958, Bang-Jensen and UN Security Officers climbed up to the snow-swept roof of the UN building and consigned four sealed envelopes to the flames.

A good solution, all agreed, and editorial writers who had swung to Bang-Jensen's defense when it was a matter of life and death—the possible life and death of the witnesses and their families in Hungary—turned to other matters. A subsequent report by the so-called "Gross Committee" charging that Bang-Jensen had been guilty of "grave misconduct" was briefly noted and, later, the announcement that the Dane had been dismissed from the United Nations caused a mere ripple.

Those who did think about it must have wondered why it was necessary to take so drastic a step against the man who, after all, had been Denmark's ranking member in the UN Secretariat. If he had exceeded his authority in making a promise of anonymity to the witnesses, would not a formal reprimand, a temporary suspension or some other readily available bureaucratic disciplinary measure have sufficed? The fact is the "affair of the list" was only part of the story. The entire UN Secretariat had been rocked by grave charges Bang-Jensen had brought against UN personnel who, he insisted, had done their best to scuttle the Special Committee on Hungary. It had now become necessary to discredit and get him out of the way—or to investigate his charges.

His Background

Who is Bang-Jensen? He was born in Denmark 48 years ago, and studied economics and law. At the age of 25, he brought out a book, *Retail Price Maintenance and Price Cutting,* which won him the Scandinavian equivalent of the Pulitzer Prize. While researching it in Berlin, he worked closely with the anti-Nazi underground. At the outbreak of World War Two, finding himself in the United States, Bang-Jensen hurried to Washington to offer his services to the Danish Mission, and was instrumental, as chief assistant to Minister Henrik Kauffmann, in negotiating the strategically important "Greenland Agreement" of 1941 which placed Danish air and naval bases on that island at the disposal of the United States. He was credited later with playing an important part in swinging Denmark into the North Atlantic Treaty Organization and away from a neutralist Scandinavian confederation which Sweden favored—an action which did not endear him to the Communists.

In 1947 he took a job as Senior Political Officer in the United Nations' Department of Political and Security Council Affairs, partly because, as a student of international law, he was interested in the development of the organization; partly because he was, and is, a convinced internationalist; partly, to be sure, because the job would enable him and his American wife and two (now five) children to live in the United States. For eight years, so far as is ascertainable, he discharged his duties to the satisfaction of all concerned.

As a person he is attractive, with a slim athletic build, thick, slightly graying hair, an impetuous way of speaking and a quizzical smile.

On January 7, 1957, just two months after Soviet tanks had rolled back into Budapest and smashed the revolution, the General Assembly voted into being a "Special Committee on the Problem of Hungary." Bang-Jensen was appointed Deputy-Secretary of the Group, which consisted of five member nations: Australia, Ceylon, Tunisia, Denmark, and Uruguay. Keith C. O. Shann (Australia) was appointed Rapporteur of the Committee and William Jordan (Great Britain) Secretary and liaison officer between the UN Secretariat, into which flowed many of the reports on Hungary, and the Committee itself.

The following is Bang-Jensen's version of what happened inside the Hungarian Committee.

First, on the matter of the witnesses. His job was to handle and interrogate Hungarian refugees and process the data received from them. Since Soviet and Satellite citizens held jobs in the UN Secretariat, many of the recent victims of Soviet aggression were understandably reluctant to allow their names to be filed with the Secretariat. There was some discussion of the problem. Then early in February 1957 (according to Bang-Jensen) he was told verbally by Dr. Protitch, a Yugoslav Under-Secretary for Political and Security Affairs, that Dag Hammarskjold had agreed Bang-Jensen would be the only person in the Secretariat to know the names. This was followed by a memorandum implicitly to the same effect from Andrew Cordier (U.S.), Hammarskjold's Executive Assistant.

Armed with this authority and another memorandum from Cordier to the Controller authorizing him to allow Bang-Jensen to pay out expense money to the refugees to defray travel

Whistleblower on UN

United Nations and I, legally as well as morally, are bound by this promise [which] cannot be modified without the consent of the witnesses themselves."

Public Humiliation

On December 4, 1957, began the private and personal ordeal of Povl Bang-Jensen, of his wife, and to an extent, his children. On that day he was ordered to report to the Office of Personnel and there, in the presence of Dr. Protitch, he was informed that he had been suspended. Further, he was forbidden to tell anyone of his suspension, a difficult assignment in any event, but especially so since the entire Danish delegation was due to dine the following night at his home. He was then put through the public humiliation of being escorted by two UN guards to his office, whence, under their supervision, he was allowed to phone his wife. They then led him to the front door of the UN building—one can imagine the whispering that must have accompanied the procession through the UN corridors—and ordered him not to return. Exit Bang-Jensen. Or so, anyway, was it intended.

As the bureaucrats prepared their final offensive, Bang-Jensen found himself under attack from another side, the victim of a skillfully executed smear campaign to picture him as dissolute and a psychotic. Where it was started, and by whom, no one can tell. But whereas yesterday Bang-Jensen had been known as a trusted and dependable servant of the United Nations, today it was suddenly common knowledge that he was mentally unbalanced, subject to hallucinations, suffering from a persecution complex. The whispers went the rounds! *He's been a borderline case for years. . . . high strung. . . . had to throw him out physically. . . . Remember that UN guy who tried to break into the Waldorf last year and see Ike? It was Bang-Jensen. Wanted to tell Ike some one had planted a bomb in the UN building; and other fabrications. He's a drunkard* (about a man who drinks so little he barely qualifies as a social drinker). *He's incompetent* (about a man who had just been nominated by Denmark for a new and more important job in the Secretariat). And, of course, *he's a*

homosexual, the charge which figures so often in the character assassination operations of the Communist Party. Was it a Communist operation? It certainly has the earmarks of one; and if Bang-Jensen was on to something which, if investigated, would lead to disclosures of Communist influence high in the UN, then certainly the Communists are most likely to profit from the impeachment of Bang-Jensen. If Communist agents were involved in the attempted sabotage of the Hungary Report, they are surely contributing gladly to the destruction of Bang-Jensen. And if he goes down, will the Report he played so critical a role in producing go down with him? That, precisely, is the line *Pravda* and *Svzda Nep,* the Hungarian paper, have taken in recent weeks. And for the future, a salutary example to check anti-Communist ardor in international civil servants?

Investigating Group

The machinery to dispose of Bang-Jensen was now in motion. On December 4, the day he was suspended, Dag Hammarskjold appointed Ernest A. Gross, an independent lawyer and former U.S. Assistant Secretary of State under Acheson, head of a three-man group to investigate the case. The Gross Committee ordered Bang-Jensen to appear before it on December 13 and bring with him such "documentation as you consider relevant to help you in answering questions." But Bang-Jensen a) had not been informed of the charges against him, and b) was still physically barred from his office and his files, so that even if he had guessed what documents might be relevant, still he could not put his hands on them. The Gross group talked to Bang-Jensen on December 13 and again on the 16th. On neither occasion was he permitted to be accompanied by his lawyer. Those were the only times he was questioned in the course of a six weeks investigation. Never was he confronted with the men he had accused, never asked to comment on their statements, never given a transcript of their testimony, never allowed any of the documents he, and his lawyer, Adolf A. Berle Jr., considered relevant and necessary to the proving of his charges.

In January 15, 1958, the Gross

Group (which had been commissioned as the "Gross Group to Investigate the Bang-Jensen Case," but which now reported as the "Committee to Investigate Mr. Bang-Jensen's Conduct") recommended that the secret list of witnesses be burned. To honor the promises of Bang-Jensen? No; because "they [the names] could be of no present or future use. . . .

> The same irresponsibility which marked his [Bang-Jensen's] method of handling the papers [his refusal to turn them over to the Secretariat?] may have brought about their alteration or defacement in respects impossible now to ascertain. Accordingly, such information as may now be embodied in them is no longer entitled to credence.

Then, three weeks later, the Gross Committee issued a mammoth report (35 pages and 70 annexes) charging Bang-Jensen with insubordination and recommending that the UN Joint Disciplinary Committee take action. It found that Bang-Jensen was not open to "rational persuasion" and accused him of "false and slanderous accusations against his colleagues."

The very weight of the Gross Report seemed impressive evidence of Bang-Jensen's guilt. But it does not appear to stand close scrutiny. For example:

1. It stated that the Chairman of the Special Committee on Hungary, Alsing Andersen of Denmark, had "thoroughly investigated" the charges Bang-Jensen had brought against his colleagues, and found them groundless. Andersen has since admitted that the sum total of his investigation consisted in a one-hour-and-fifteen-minute conversation with the very men Bang-Jensen had accused, during which they simply denied the charges against them and he took their word. In other words, in 75 minutes he had disposed, to his evident satisfaction, of 30 to 40 points Bang-Jensen had raised on one chapter of the Hungary Report alone.

2. The Gross Committee stated that it had carefully investigated allegations Bang-Jensen had made with regard to irregularities during the hearings of the Hungary Committee in Vienna. A puzzling statement in view of Bang-Jensen's insistence that he never told any one what the irregularities he had mentioned in Vienna were. He has challenged the

Gross Committee to produce the document listing the "irregularities" it investigated and found to be "utterly groundless," but to no avail.

The report of the Gross Committee was duly turned over to the UN Joint Disciplinary Committee and Bang-Jensen, at the same time, assured in a memorandum (of March 7) that "all documents required in order to prepare his answers to the charges against him would be made available to him by Mr. Andrew Cordier (Hammarskjold's Executive Assistant) upon specific request."

Still hopeful of beating the system through the system, Bang-Jensen then listed 87 documents he believed necessary to his defense, a remarkable feat of memory since he was still barred from his desk and files and was working with what secretarial assistance he could personally afford. But he never got the papers. Some he says he didn't really expect to get since he doesn't believe they exist, although they were referred to in the Annexes to the Gross Report. Bang-Jensen refused two summonses to appear before the Disciplinary Committee, arguing that he could not defend his position without the documents he had requested; and on the same grounds he refused to submit a written answer to the charges against him. On June 5, the Committee recommended that he be dismissed and on July 3, Dag Hammarskjold informed the Danish Political Officer that he had been fired.

Dag Hammarskjold's statement of dismissal summed up the charges against Bang-Jensen. The lengthy rebuttal Bang-Jensen issued several days later went unnoticed by most of the press. Why?

A reporter for the *New York Post* told Bang-Jensen that his paper had dropped the story because they had heard that Bang-Jensen was insane and also because undue publicity would give the reactionary Right another weapon with which to belabor the United Nations.

So Bang-Jensen now found that when he turned to the press for help it was no longer in his corner. Still refusing to accept his dismissal (he sent back his termination pay check of $17,000 and is reported to have mortgaged his life insurance in order to pay his daily bills) Bang-Jensen appealed to the Administrative Tribunal of the UN—the organization's highest judicial body—not for a reversal of Dag Hammarskjold's decision, but for access to the documents withheld from him. That request has now been turned down.

Reopening of Case Urged

In his appeal, he is supported by the Danish Government, which voted him $5,000 a few weeks ago to help defray his legal expenses in the fight, (and that despite the fact that Alsing Andersen, Chairman of the Hungarian Committee, who sides with Hammarskjold, is head of the Danish Social Democratic Party, one of the coalition parties in the Danish Government). Bang-Jensen has also received the support of the influential "Council Against Communist Aggression," which numbers among its supporters lawyers, professors, legislators, ministers and labor leaders, such men as Representatives Hays (Ark.) and Bentley of the House Foreign Affairs Committee, Dean Roscoe Pound, the Rev. Dan Poling, C. Dickerman Williams and others. They are urging the United States to press for a reopening of the Bang-Jensen case.

And that is where the matter stands. It is a year since Bang-Jensen was suspended. He has been without salary for six months, and at 48 faces the prospect of looking for another job with his character blackened and even his sanity in question. What has he proved?

Well, in the matter of the lists, he proved that honor lives on, even if it does get into trouble with the United Nations Disciplinary Committee. Eighty-one Hungarian refugees sleep better at night because it was a Bang-Jensen in whom they placed their trust. But what of future refugees? Will they trust UN officials?

On the other questions: Bang-Jensen's side of the story, which we have reported here, has not been proved. We have only his word for it about the tendentious irregularities in the work of the Special Committee on the Problem of Hungary. He has not proved his case; he could not without the documents. On the other hand, the UN *has* the documents and *its* case. The Gross Report does not stand up. It is not enough to say—as the Gross Report did—that Bang-Jensen's charges were "utterly groundless"; that, for instance, his charges relating to the suppression of witnesses were so "demonstrably groundless" as to raise serious questions about the "rationality of his behavior." This will not suffice.

Many will continue to believe that Bang-Jensen was unjustly fired—that, as a Danish paper recently said, he was fired not for misconduct but for "too much good conduct." When will there be an impartial review of his case? A review which will center on the conduct of Messrs. Jordan, Shann, Andersen and others, rather than on the conduct of Bang-Jensen?

Postscript: R.I.P.

(Within a year after the article above, Bang-Jensen was dead, NATIONAL REVIEW printed the following editorial.)

The exact circumstances of Povl Bang-Jensen's death do not bear on the question of his heroism. He was a hero because at a fateful crossroads in his life he chose the bitter path of honor over the easy road of expediency. To 81 Hungarian Freedom Fighters, who told him the true story of the Hungarian revolt and its suppression, with their own and their families' lives in balance, Bang-Jensen had pledged his word that their identities would be revealed to no one. He held to his word as the wrath of the UN bureaucracy mounted against him, as his friends began to turn aside and the press to ignore his travail. He held firm as Dag Hammarskjold and Ernest Gross and their sycophants broke and dishonored the man who, more than any other, was responsible for the ineradicable Hungary Report.

The police say it was suicide, and have closed their files. "A perfect suicide," one police official explained—"the revolver in his hand, the bullet in his skull, the spent shell on the ground nearby, the suicide note in his pocket." Perhaps.

On confirmed evidence, Bang-Jensen was last seen at 8:30 A.M. Monday morning, November 23, leaving his Queens residence for his post-UN job at CARE's Manhattan office. His body was found Thursday morning the 26th, lying across a path in a Queens park. But the medical testimony establishes that he had been dead twenty-four hours at most.

Murder?

Where was he, then, from Monday morning until the moment of death on Wednesday?

Many persons normally walk or play near where his body was, including many who walk their dogs thereabouts. How strange that his corpse lay undiscovered for twenty-four hours.

Why have the police made no public report of the exact results of the autopsy? Was there a one or two or three days' beard on his face? What had he eaten, how long before death?

What was written in the suicide note which no one but the authorities —not even his wife, to whom it was addressed—has seen? Were the words, style, syntax, spelling recognizably his? (It was misspellings that first showed the falsity of the Mindszenty confession.) Would the police know it, if they were not? What sort of paper was it written on? With what pen? Was the pen found in his pocket?

A taxi-driver voluntarily notified the police—after the news of Bang-Jensen's disappearance had been printed, but before his death was discovered—that he had driven Bang-Jensen to the UN entrance, which happens to be across the street from the CARE office where he worked. His this testimony been followed up?

High Communist escapees, on the agreement that he communicate it in person to Director of CIA Allen Dulles, gave Bang-Jensen specific information about Soviet agents planted in the UN Secretariat and in CIA. On eight occasions over a period of months, Bang-Jensen tried to see Mr. Dulles—always in vain. But he did repeatedly see, in the effort, a subordinate CIA official, who transcribed a report "for the record" about his dealings with Bang-Jensen. What is the real story of this runaround and this report? Is it true that the report leaked through to the UN Secretariat?

On Friday night, November 20, Bang-Jensen attended a PTA meeting at his children's school and took an active part in the proceedings. His pastor declares that Bang-Jensen's religious beliefs, strongly held, precluded suicide. A psychiatrist whom he had recently and successfully consulted, insists that he had no suicidal tendency. His wife is convinced that he could not have committed suicide, and did not. What is to be made of such data? The pastor reports also that his religion forbids cremation. Yet, on an alleged instruction of the unseen suicide note, his body was hastily cremated and returned for burial in Denmark. Why this unseemly haste, which has as one result the destruction of crucial evidence?

It is easy enough to understand why the police prefer to close a file with a routine notation of suicide. No use stirring up unnecessary trouble. . . . And it is easy to see, in this case, why the MVD and CIA are happy enough to let matters slide. But there are too many unanswered questions. There is no way to cremate *them*, and some of them are going to haunt us—and should—until they are answered.

FREEDOM

SLAVERY

Don't let anyone kid you: the game is worth while.

46

Rippling Creek Club v. U.S.A.

Some playful (and anonymous!) young attorneys in the office of the Solicitor General of the U.S. have let their imaginations go on the trend in Supreme Court decisions . . . and take us forward to 1973

SUPREME COURT OF THE UNITED STATES
No. 367—OCTOBER TERM, 1973

Rippling Creek Club, Inc., *et al.*,
Petitioners,

v.

United States of America

On Writ of Certiorari
to the United States
Court of Appeals for
the Fifth Circuit

(May 20, 1974)

Mr. Justice Smith delivered the opinion of the Court.

This case involves the construction and constitutionality of certain provisions of the Federal Discrimination Commission Act, 42 U.S.C. §9001 *et seq.*, empowering the Federal Discrimination Commission to issue cease and desist orders against "any individual, firm, corporation, unincorporated association or other entity whatsoever," whenever in the Commission's opinion such entity "is engaging, or is about to engage, in any discriminatory action, practice, or course of conduct." 42 U.S.C. § 9004 (b).

The corporate petitioner is a nonprofit corporation organized under the laws of the State of Alabama. Its organization and functions are those usual in country clubs. It maintains a clubhouse in which bar and dining facilities are provided, and it operates a golf course, tennis courts, swimming pool, and other customary amenities. It has, and at all times relevant to this litigation had, a membership of less than the full complement of 500 authorized by its constitution. New members are admitted upon the nomination of five regular members and the approval of the individual petitioners, an election committee of seven members appointed by the board of governors. An initiation fee and annual dues are charged. No so-called "Negro" is or has ever been a member.

On this state of facts the Commission instituted an investigation into petitioners' discriminatory practices, and, finding such to exist, issued on March 27, 1970, an order requiring petitioner to cease discriminating in its selection of membership. 13 F.D.C. 398. This order was duly affirmed, and an injunction issued, by the Court of Appeals for the Fifth Circuit. 58 F.3d 119. We denied certiorari. 391 U.S. 917. More than a year having passed, and there still being no "Negroes" among petitioner's membership, the Commission initiated contempt proceedings. Petitioners were adjudged in contempt, and the statutory punishment of fine and imprisonment was imposed. We granted certiorari to reaffirm basic principles in the administration of the Act. 402 U.S. 933.

Petitioners' primary contention is that the Act can have no application

The Chief Justice, 1958

to, and the Commission no jurisdiction over, purely social organizations. Stripped of irrelevancies, in one aspect this argument is in essence that the Fourteenth Amendment, under which the Act was passed, applies only to State action, and that the actions neither of the corporate petitioner nor of the individuals composing its election committee come within the scope of that Amendment's prohibitions. It is true that only State action is inhibited by the Amendment; but to contend that action of the kind here involved is not State action is to revive the exploded fallacy of the Civil Rights Cases, 109 U.S. 3. As we said in *Saffold* v. *Holder*, 364 U.S. 221, 224, where the ghost of those cases was laid to rest forever:

> To say that action of a corporation is not "State action" in the instant context is to fly in the face of juristic reality. No corporation has or can have existence of any legally significant kind without the active consent of the State. . . . While its activities may in no sense be governmental, the life which enables it to carry on those activities was breathed into its nostrils by the State. What the State's creatures do, the State does.

The similar argument of the individual petitioners can fare no better. In the first case under the Act to reach this Court, *Harrison* v. *United States*, 380 U.S. 11, 19, we said:

> Petitioner contends that even if the repeated pronunciation in public of this word as "Nigra" amounts to discrimination within the meaning of the statute, the statute cannot be applied to him, since this conduct is not "State action". . . . The true bounds of the concept of "State action" have only recently emerged. It is plain that, under the

47

unitary conditions of modern life, to limit the notion of "State action" to those activities carried on by the legislature's express command or implied permission is to empty it of all significant content. The true teaching of *Marsh* v. *Alabama,* 336, U.S. 501, *Terry* v. *Adams,* 345 U.S. 461, and *Edgerton* v. *Shockley,* 361 U.S. 366, should by now be plain. It is that "the State" cannot be dissociated from the community; that action which meets the approval of the community and expresses its mood is as surely "State action" as is the most explicit statute.

We have frequently reaffirmed, and indeed broadened, this holding. *Firemen's Benevolent Society* v. *United States,* 397 U.S. 225; *McCracken* v. *United States,* 388 U.S. 409. Compare *United States* v. *One Book Called "Tales of Uncle Remus,"* 31 F. 3d 922.

But the corporate petitioner's constitutional argument goes further than this; it raises the question left open in the *Firemen's Benevolent* case, *supra,* whether the right of assembly guaranteed by the First Amendment ousts the application of the Act to purely social organizations, whose sole *raison d'être* is the gathering together of congenial persons.

We did not reach this question in *Firemen's Benevolent.* There we held that the Commission had undoubted power to prevent the production of the "ministrel show" complained of, since the Society functioned as an insurer as well as a social organization; but we intimated that this question would be ruled by our decision in *States Rights Democratic Party* v. *United States.* 393 U.S. 1. In the latter case we held that political associations could not hide from the Act behind the shield of the First Amendment, since such associations are by their nature concerned with government, and discriminatory action "is not reasonably related to any proper governmental objective." *Bolling* v. *Sharpe,* 347 U.S. 497, 500.

Petitioners seek to avoid the impact of the *States Rights* decision by arguing that its rationale is limited to political associations; that it holds only that the protection accorded political associations is restricted to their governmental, or would-be governmental, activities.

But *States Rights* cannot be so re-stricted. Whether or not the First Amendment right is limited to the right of political assembly, see *Yamaguchi* v. *Weinberg,* 370 U.S. 93, 99, we hold that the Amendment does not shield a mere social organization from the Discrimination Act. It would indeed be strange if it were otherwise. No discriminations leave deeper or more lasting scars than do social ones, and it was Congress' particular intention, in creating the Commission, "to forge a weapon capable of dealing with this threat to our democratic society." S.Rep. No. 316, 89th Cong., 1st Sess. 26.

Petitioner's other contentions are equally devoid of merit. It is settled that "the content of the term 'discriminatory' is sufficiently rooted in the common conscience of the American people to constitute a valid standard with ascertainable criteria." *Harrison* v. *United States, supra,* at 16. Thus, the Commission's condemnation of offensive pronunciations of group names, *Harrison* v. *United States, supra;* of printing the word "Negro" without a capital initial, *United States* v. *377 copies of the*

Kreuttner

"It's so difficult to put your finger on the exact point where concessions to unenlightened legislation must give way to Creative Interpretation!"

London Times, 236 F. Supp. 346; of advertising a musical instrument as a "Jew's harp," *Apex Piano Co.* v. *United States,* 44 F. 3d 619, certiorari denied, 399 U. S. 924; and of employing the phrase "dirty Irish trick," *Ng Yang Toy* v. *United States,* 399 U.S. 772, have all been upheld. We have approved, in *Northfield Aircraft Co.* v. *United States,* decided this day, Commission regulations forbidding prospective employers to inquire as to the names of job applicants, since this might reveal the applicants' ancestry or national origin. At any rate, we are not here concerned with the borderlines of the discrimination concept. The flagrantly exclusionary conduct of the petitioners is sufficiently extreme to satisfy any definition.

Petitioners contend, finally, that the fact that no so-called "Negroes" applied for admission to membership absolves them of any responsibility for discrimination. This contention is likewise without merit. Ever since *Barrett* v. *United States,* 380 U.S. 585 —in one sense, indeed, ever since the New York schools case, *Hunt* v. *Board of Education,* 355 U.S. 116—it has been clear that it is no defense to a charge of exclusionary discrimination that no members of the group discriminated against have sought admission. As we pointed out in *Barrett,* "the lack of applications tends to show not apathy but repression; to demonstrate good faith it is necessary that the party charged actively seek out members of other groups." It is urged that this confers irrebuttability on the statutory presumption of discrimination when no member of the minority group is found in the group or organization involved; but that this is not so should be obvious from *Northern Vermont Driving School, Inc.* v. *United States,* 400 U.S. 333.

We hold, therefore, that the Act is constitutional as applied to petitioner; that social organizations cannot discriminate against members of minority groups. There are limits, of course, to the extent to which social alignments can be regulated: see *Gotlieb* v. *New York,* decided this day, holding invalid the New York Compulsory Intermarriage Law. But those limits were not reached in this case. They were not even approached.

Affirmed

The Regime of the South

Key Argument

Why do Liberals attack the South? Because, says the author, its order, based on custom, history and a common faith, challenges their own hollow nihilism

RICHARD M. WEAVER

In the national controversy raging over segregated schooling, we often hear of "the Southern way of life." I suggest that this phrase is used with too little understanding both by those who wield it for defense and those who hurl it in attack. It is true that the South has a "way of life," but the point that is missed is that a "way of life" is a normal social phenomenon. "Way of life" is in fact our everyday translation of the old term, "regime." And "regime" is a word rich in social meaning.

Modern social scientists have a way of finding or coining words which only obscure their discussions. They could communicate better if they dropped a good deal of their special jargon, but now and then they bring forward a term which is really serviceable. One of the most interesting of these is *anomie*. This word comes from two roots which combine to mean "an absence or privation of custom and order." Interpreted more fully, it signifies a condition of society in which the guide lines of belief and behavior have largely disappeared, so that frustration and chaos reach dangerous levels. A society suffering from *anomie* is in a state of disorganization, from the lack of whatever has previously given it the power to unify and cohere. *Anomie* is, in brief, a word for disintegration; and it is the judgment of many students that large parts of the modern world are suffering more or less acutely from *anomie*. If so, the most urgent task of social criticism is to diagnose the condition and find some remedy which will bring the disintegrated parts back into a unity. The remedy will have to be "regime."

It is the nature of a regime to be much more than the sum of the government and the laws. It is these plus beliefs, traditions, customs, habits, and observances, many of which affect the minutiae of daily living. A regime tells the individual from early days, through his nurture and education, what is expected of him, how he stands in regard to this person and that, and what kind of social response he can expect from the choices that are open to him.

Locations and Directions

Regime is, in substance, a complex of law, custom, and idiomatic social behavior, and it fills all the interstices of life. Described thus in outline, it might appear a set of imprisoning forces, but we must be careful to remember that walls support as well as obstruct. In actual fact a regime is a system of sustaining forms, and everyone who has been in contact with a regime recognizes its capacity to give every man, the high and the low, some sense of being at home. It tends, moreover, to diminish the sense of being "low" by sustaining the sense of belonging.

A regime is thus comparable to the rule of a household. There is a place for everybody, though the place cannot be the same for everybody. The the very fact that we speak of "place" means that we envision a social whole, in reference to which there are locations and directions. The principle of the ordering may be more intuited than reasoned out. Yet this sense of inclusive ordering makes the individual feel that his presence is acknowledged in more than a perfunctory way. A regime is thus a powerful check against the sense of lostness, the restlessness, and the aimless competition which plague the modern masses and provoke the fantastic social eruptions of our era.

The idea of regime is thus an antidote to much that is complained of in modern life. It is, to tell the truth, what all of us except the lawless and the nihilistic are looking for. It is the richest and freest form of communal life because it does not depend on top-heavy government, but upon the voluntary preferences of many individuals, acting and interacting out of respect for some basic values.

There is no doubt, on the other hand, that a regime as a "way of life" is also a principle of exclusion. It is a way of rejecting what is inimical or foreign to the group's nature and of retaining what can be assimilated. Social and cultural groups, like organisms, must be able to fend off what they cannot accept without ceasing to live. To say that this is a law of life is almost superficial; it is rather a law of existence. Intolerance of what would be fatal is a necessity for survival. The difficulty of most people who have been conditioned by "modern thinking" is to interpret all exclusiveness as having its root in injustice. But this is so far from being true that one can affirm that some degree of exclusiveness is essential to self-identity and self-preservation.

Those societies which have a way of life have a distinctive culture. A culture is a body of forms organized about certain ideas expressing value, which gives structure to the life of a people. In so doing it satisfies psychic needs which cannot be met in any other way. Culture is inexplicable save through reference to this inner need for beliefs, forms, settled dispositions, rituals, and other defined patterns. If these things are somehow lost by a people or are suddenly taken away from them, the result may be so grave as to produce actual illness. A regime therefore is definitely hygienic, and we should look with suspicion upon those who oppose the very idea of regime.

There are many things compelling us to believe that Liberalism is the death-wish of modern civilization. In its incapacity for commitment, its nihilistic approach, and its almost

— Regime Prefers small govt..

S!//// Explains Refusal to change Survival @ Stake

Necessary for order .. otherwise = Nihilism

pathological fear of settled principle, Liberalism operates to destroy everything and conserve nothing. The reason it hates the idea of regime is therefore not far to seek. A regime is sustained by the kind of self-definition and self-constitution which require a love of life and of the positive arrangements that enrich the enjoyment of life. A regime therefore cannot be liberal about itself any more than a man can be "liberal" about his own existence. A regime can be generous, kindly, humane, even humanitarian, but it cannot be liberal in the sense of perpetually entertaining the question of whether it ought to continue. This does not mean that it cannot accept correction or make the empirical changes that are required by changes in the world. But a regime cannot live exclusively on a diet of self-questioning, to say nothing of self-hate. Liberalism has worked itself into an impasse where the only thing that it can postulate is the necessity for questioning what exists. Liberalism cannot postulate anything positive, because such affirmations will carry with them exclusions, and the only source Liberalism can recognize for exclusion is intolerance or "narrow-mindedness."

Some American Regimes

It follows inevitably that the Liberal is exacerbated by the sight of any independent and healthy growth. Such a growth can only remind him of his own hollowness. A regime holds the mirror up to the Liberal. He hates what he sees there, and strikes out in anger against the bearer of the unpleasing image. Those who know that the struggle of these times is neither sectional nor national but world-wide must be prepared to deal with this hatred of regimes as a struggle within the consciousness of the man afflicted by modernism.

Everyone knows that the regime of the South is under heavy assault by Liberalism. But before taking up this conflict in particular, I wish to call attention to the presence of other regimes in the United States. I am not asserting that the South is the only region which has created this form of cultural life. There is no doubt that New England had a regime during a period of its history, a real and a charming one, with its chaste

ideals. Yet New England, despite the fact that it was on the victorious side in our civil struggle, does not seem to have been successful in preserving its "way of life." That way lingers north of Boston; and the New Hampshire celebrated by Robert Frost clearly has its appeal to the poet as regime. But the New England regime has certainly decayed in the centers of influence. The very idea of attachment to it is caricatured in the novels of John P. Marquand.

One might claim that even the Old West had a regime during the period when it was, more or less, as it is represented by our cowboy films. The rule by the man who was quickest on the draw, the rough and ready classification of people into good and bad, the figure of the cowboy with his horse and saddle, and the clear lines of social approval and disapproval—these probably add up to a regime, though one based on the transient circumstances of a frontier. The Old West had a structure and an ethos, and these are the essentials of social cohesion.

Today it is not uncommon to hear references to "the American way of life." Whether the American way of life is enough of a piece to be reckoned a regime can be argued one way and the other. If the definition is somewhat relaxed, and if the data are taken from certain areas of activity, perhaps it is. But the important thing about the phrase is that we hear it introduced when the object is to contrast the United States with Soviet Russia or, in some cases, with certain forms of Europeanism.

When we want to stress the way in which we are *really* different from the Soviets, we refer not to our government or the Bill of Rights, but quite properly to our regime, which is to say, our ingrained way of doing

things, our habitual preferences, and the rest of what makes up the very fabric of living. This underscores the fact that a regime is not something abstract, like a written constitution, but a multiplicity of matters large and small, which are felt with varying degrees of intensity. It is also a clear warning to those who would attack a regime in the name of some deduced and doctrinaire theory. A regime evokes emotional responses at a thousand and one points. This is the sign of its capacity to make people feel deeply and peculiarly at home with it. When therefore I hear of "the American way of life," I take it as a sign that the Americans have as much natural desire for a regime as does any large group, although some accidents of their history may have kept them from developing more than regional regimes in the full sense intended here.

Three Reasons

Of all the regions of the country, the South has maintained a regime in the clearest and most enduring form. It has a society more unified by imponderables, more conscious of self-definition, more homogenous in outlook than any other region. This is not the place to rehearse the history behind that fact, but I can mention three things which seem to me to explain its persistence. One is the South's adherence to a structural form of society, known odiously in some quarters as "aristocratic." A second is its receptivity to the idea of transcendence, which has been referred to seriously as its religiousness and scornfully as its Bible Beltism. The third is its preservation of history, which by the modern mind is equated with "living in the past." All of these are strong barriers to *anomie*. A stable structural society creates the feeling of permanence because it provides the shelter of an accredited authority which cannot be overturned by tomorrow's vote. The idea of transcendence is the real source of symbolization in life, which persuades men that they have lived and are living for something more than things of the moment. And the preservation of history keeps tradition from seeming arbitrary, endowing it not only with reason but with grace.

It will be recognized that these are

conserving forces. The effect of a regime is to conserve and to stabilize. No one has to believe that every particular thing conserved by them is valuable. No society has met that standard, and it certainly has to be granted that societies, like people, are properly subject to correction through appeals to logic and ethics. The South has had the enormously difficult problem of accommodating a large minority distinct in race and culture. But what I am talking about here is a cohesive social ordering, which the South has had in outstanding measure. The use of the term "Southern culture" is the popular recognition of this fact.

The South is the natural prime target of those who hate the very idea of regime. Anyone who looks beneath appearance to reality must see that the attack upon the Southern school system is but one front of a general attack upon the principle of an independent, self-directing social order, with a set of values proper to itself. It is the one pushed most vigorously now because for a variety of reasons it can draw the most publicity, and it is the kind of action for which the Liberal's sentimentalism makes him most gullible.

The Real Motive

No long memory is needed to recall other fronts on which the attack against the South has formerly been active. Not very long ago the issue was "fundamentalism," and the South was being crucified for holding a religious belief not terribly different from that of respectable contemporary neo-orthodoxy. Later it was the sharecropping system, which certainly brings great wealth neither to owner nor cropper, but which is nothing to get excited over from a distance, unless one starts with a strong initial prejudice. Still later it was the poll tax, again nothing to get excited over unless you believe that adding to the number of votes automatically adds to the amount of wisdom. Thus the attackers have said by their actions, "Any stick to beat a dog!" This is the reason we urgently need to look for the real impulse behind their militancy.

The modern Liberal has confused liberty with power, but the only use he has for power is to destroy. If these fanatical destroyers are allowed to have their way, the next thing to be challenged will be the basis on which the more general "American way of life" is forming. The same charges of inequity levelled against the Southern regime will be levelled against capitalism, private property, the family, and even individuality. The Liberal's rage is directed against all restraints which allow things to grow in their own native character. He has a verdict of guilty against everything that stands in the way of certain ideas which are themselves life-denying.

This issue goes back to ultimate concepts about the right not merely to be free but to live. The right to live in the proper sense of "live" means the right to follow the law of one's being. When doctrinaire liberalism is applied to societies, the choice is between rejecting it in favor of a natural regime, or accepting it in the form of an enforced Utopia sustained by the police state. The first prevents *anomie* through the traditional means of consent and organic growth; the other strives to prevent it through an imposed conformity which is without soul. The attempt is futile because spirit is the final integrating factor of a society.

Most of us readily admit that this nation owes both its independence and its happiness to the principle of self-determination. That principle is now in danger of being suppressed by a blind zeal for standardization and enforced conformity. To oppose that trend, we do not have to become sectionalists. We need only grant the right of distinct groups to exercise some liberty of choice in the ordering of their social and cultural arrangements. If that liberty is denied, there will be no ground left on which to assert any other liberty.

ANTHROPOLOGY '56

THE RACES OF MAN

CAUCASIAN NEGRO MONGOLIAN

Kreuttner

"First of all, I want to pay tribute to the exhaustive research our team of scientists put into the preparation of this chart, thus enabling us to clarify our thinking and eliminate certain misconceptions."

Cyrus Eaton: An Old Man Goes East

Mr. Eaton isn't just a capitalist— he's
a capitalist who made good. Why, then,
his compulsive urge toward Moscow?

JOHN CHAMBERLAIN

Cyrus Stephen Eaton, the 76-year-old Canadian-born Cleveland financier, **railroad man and ironmaster, has** been making news recently on the old man-bites-dog principle. He, the most fearsome living incarnation of the old-time competitive capitalist spirit, has seldom missed an opportunity to embrace Soviet dictator Nikita Khrushchev, who stands for everything in the way of social organization that Mr. Eaton temperamentally abhors.

The facts in the case are plain. Eaton, with his wife, tours the Soviet Union, passing out compliments to the commissars and making extreme statements reflecting on the integrity and even the sanity of the American government. He lends his name, and his ancestral home at Pugwash, Nova Scotia, to gatherings of atomic scientists who urge the West to reach an atomic test accord with the Russians.

At home in the U.S., Eaton entertains Russian journalists, diplomats and traveling members of the Soviet Politburo at his Ohio farm or his Cleveland business suite. Again the compliments flow, along with the undertow of wild derogation of Washington. He sends a prize bull to Moscow and, in return, accepts a troika (three Russian horses and a carriage). He uses an appearance on a Mike Wallace television show to lump the FBI, the Internal Revenue commissioners and the Department of Agriculture together as snoopers (which they are), but he spoils his point by adding the innuendo that they are comparable to Hitler's Gestapo (which is the sort of ridiculous nonsense that one reads in the Communist press). Altogether Cyrus Eaton, who has made "savage poetry" out of his career as a capitalist, boxes the compass of the Communist line from North to South and from East to West, not even missing the standard cracks at Chiang Kai-shek.

How is it that such a strange bedfellowship as Eaton-Khrushchev could come about? How is it that Cyrus Eaton, who used to be pained whenever a municipality in the U.S. took over a power station, can hobnob with a Tartar dictator who would socialize every last cabbage patch inside the USSR, if not the world? Why, indeed, should the last great capitalist adventurer, a man who put together two staggering fortunes in a career that was only momentarily interrupted by the 1929 crash, suddenly emerge in his old age as America's Number One Fellow Traveler and Communophile? And how, above all, can a person with some kindly instincts (Eaton once bought a decrepit steel mill in West Virginia to keep a whole town from going down the drain) be so profoundly callous as to dismiss the Hungarian revolution as a "phony issue"?

The motive could be simple: after all, the late Ernest Weir, head of the National Steel Co., turned pro-Russian before he died merely because he hoped something could be made out of U.S.-Soviet trade. But Mr. Eaton, though he, too, is a trader who would not scorn rubles provided they could be turned into dollars, is a tremendously complex personality. The probability is that this smiling man with the icy-blue eyes, this "capitalist who looks like a cardinal," has a whole complex of reasons for linking arms with the dictator who has said "we will bury you."

Economic Empire Builder

Riffling through Mr. Eaton's stirring past, one is impressed first of all by the vast scale upon which the man has operated. He has always wanted to play with continents the way boys play with toy railroad sets. As a public utilities tycoon in the 1920s he had one ambition: to run an electric power empire bigger than that of Samuel Insull. As a steel man in the twenties Eaton put together the Republic Steel Corporation—and he was busy fighting Bethlehem Steel for Youngstown Sheet and Tube when the 1929 depression sent his best-laid plans agley. He went broke grandiosely, losing $20 million with the failure of his investment trust, Continental Shares, Inc.

Then, instead of jumping out of a hotel window, Eaton came back. He now controls billions in transportation (Chesapeake and Ohio Railroad, Slick Airways), iron ore (Steep Rock in western Ontario, the Ungava deposits in northern Quebec), and in banking and public utilities. Plotting to sell Ungava iron ore to Europe from an ice-free storage depot in Greenland, Eaton has brought Krupp of Germany and a number of allied Rhineland steel companies into his Quebec project on a fifty-fifty basis.

The man is incredibly healthy: he eats well, sleeps well, and never takes aspirins (he suspects they give other men ulcers). If he lives to exploit some still-to-be-discovered iron ore deposits on Baffin Island (he has already had a prospector there) in his nineties or even in his hundredth year, nobody would be less surprised than Cyrus Eaton.

Along with the vast scale of his operations Eaton has developed some proportionate obsessions. In revenge he is as implacable as Orestes or any single-minded tragedian in a drama of blood. Conversely, he likes to play Medici, civic benefactor and kindly old man. He thinks of himself as an intellectual. Finally, echoing William Zeckendorf, he dotes on a latter-day alchemy that changes paper into gold. ("If two and two don't make five," said Zeckendorf, "there's no deal.")

Eaton's obsessions crop up in a number of constantly recurring patterns. To sustain his enmity-motif, Eaton has developed the memory of an elephant for slights and rebuffs; he never lets up on an enemy so long as there is the remotest possibility of giving him one last flick with the back of his hand. These enmities have frequently propelled Eaton into strange alliances, on the principle that "the enemy of my enemy is my friend."

Because of his hatred for "Wall Street," Eaton went against all his competitive capitalist instincts and embraced the New Deal. To stop Newton D. Baker, a Cleveland lawyer and politico with Wall Street connections, Eaton became a "Roosevelt man before Chicago" in 1932. And after Bob Taft had angered him by letting the Taft law firm in Cincinnati serve the eastern investment bankers in a legal capacity in connection with an issue of Cincinnati Terminal bonds, Eaton made a $30,-000 campaign gift in 1950 to Joe Ferguson, Taft's Democratic opponent in the Ohio senatorial race, and to the rest of Joe Ferguson's ticket. It did not matter that Taft, on balance, was far closer to Eaton's own capitalist predilections than Ferguson: revenge was obviously on Eaton's mind. Years later he loaned money to the employees of the *Cincinnati Enquirer* to buy their paper, which kept it from falling into the hands of the Taft family.

On the alchemic side, there is Eaton's compelling relish for an "operation." Mr. Eaton loves to put unlike things together to produce an astonishing result. An example: at the end of World War II Eaton, sensing that even high-cost steel mills would be money-makers during the postwar scramble for goods, bought the Portsmouth, Ohio, subsidiary of the Wheeling Steel Company, incorporated it, and put Harold Ruttenberg, once a business-baiting economist for the United Steelworkers of America, in charge of it. Ruttenberg proved to be a capable steelmaster and an excellent salesman, and Eaton eventually sold a profitable property to the Detroit Steel Corporation, meanwhile preserving the old corporate shell of Portsmouth as a holding company. Then, through his holding company, Eaton bought

control—of Detroit Steel! As a result of this complex maneuver (suggestive of the Squidgicum Squee that swallered itself) Eaton had made a profit, kept his old steel mill and acquired a wholly new steel empire.

As a reaction from the vengefulness and the intricate parlays of his business life, Eaton exhibits a third pattern—the combined Medicean and Faustian motif. Finding his fellow industrialists dull, Eaton seldom plays or relaxes with them; instead, he seeks to be both the peer and the patron of intellectuals. A full half-century before he had conceived the idea of transforming his ancestral home at Pugwash into a summer retreat for authors, historians, university administrators and atomic scientists. Mr. Eaton gloried in his friendship with William Rainey Harper, President of the Rockefeller-endowed University of Chicago; he has always quoted poetry and read the philosophers; he has written six books and many articles, including a review of Supreme Court Justice William O. Douglas' *Democracy and Finance* for the University of Chicago *Law Review*. John Dewey was Eaton's friend and a summer visitor in Nova Scotia (at a second Eaton vacation retreat at Deep Cove) long before there was an Eaton-organized "Pugwash Conference" of intellectuals to deplore the atomic arms race with Soviet Russia.

The recurrent patterns or motifs in Mr. Eaton's life have nothing to do *per se* with Communism. But when one scrambles together Eaton's enmities for Wall Street and Wall Street lawyers, his zest in a complex international market parlay which can bring Krupp into Canada, and his desire to mingle with atomic physicists who have the atom bomb on their collective conscience, the emergence of the Fellow Traveler of Moscow becomes plausible.

Like Eaton, the Communists also hate Wall Street. They also love any and all Western atomic scientists (and allied intellectuals) who wear sackcloth and ashes because of the bomb. And (the final fillip of the Eaton parlay that has brought Krupp of Germany into Quebec iron ore), the Communists have a deal with the Krupp companies to take large amounts of finished steel products for the Soviet Seven Year Plan. It

used to be Tinker to Evers to Chance; now it's Eaton to Krupp to Mikoyan.

Mr. Eaton, it must be said, has some reason for his bitterness. He began by taking the capitalistic system seriously. He thought it a good thing for the steel business to be decentralized. And a competitive system, so he argued, should be competitive all the way: when a railroad or a utility has bonds to float, all underwriters, not merely a favored few, should have a chance to bid for the privilege of marketing them. In all this Mr. Eaton is a more consistent competitor than his enemies.

Tycoon into Operator

If the believer in true competition must throw up his hands in horror at Eaton's career as a Soviet apologist since 1954, the same believer in true competition must grant that Eaton has been a towering figure in American industrial history. He has brought many things to fruition. True, there are those who argue that Eaton's Cleveland investment banking house, Otis and Co., welshed on a promise in 1948 when it failed to go through with the underwriting of a Kaiser-Frazer automobile stock issue of 900,000 shares. But the courts vindicated Eaton, and history subsequently demonstrated that the Kaiser-Frazer prospects were nowhere near as good as the company's prospectus. So Eaton can't be called a liar when he says he would have been faithless to his customers if he had gone through with the Kaiser-Frazer deal.

Many of Eaton's business critics, in fact, sound unctuous and hypocritical; their unadmitted objection would seem to be that Eaton has beaten them at their own game. Certainly the man is admirable for his nervous force, his refusal to curl up and die when, by all the portents, that was what was in store for him. In 1933 Eaton's career lay in ruins; he had kept his Acadia Farm home at Northfield, Ohio, and he had hung on to his share of Otis and Co., but everything else—his utilities, his steel mills, his investment trust, even his first wife, who sued him for divorce —was gone. Eaton's response to failure was to make a quick grasp for new levers of power. Plotting a triumphant return from Elba, he ceased to be a tycoon and became what is known as **an operator.**

The distinction is important. For where a tycoon is superior to his surrounding atmosphere, an operator tries to adapt the prevailing psychological climate to his own uses. The tycoon gives orders to politicos; the operator associates himself with their pet causes. The tycoon watches market forces; the operator tries to anticipate those who interfere with market forces.

As an operator Eaton cultivated Washington personalities—not the elected members of Congress but the young raring-to-go administrative employees of the Reconstruction Finance Corporation and the SEC. With Robert R. Young, who had taken over the Chesapeake and Ohio Railroad as a preliminary to his later onslaught on the New York Central, Eaton forced the New Deal to require competitive bidding for railroad bond flotations, a move which diverted a good percentage of this lucrative business to two bumptious western investment houses, Halsey, Stuart of Chicago and Eaton's own Otis and Co., of Cleveland. Meanwhile, again fighting side by side with Young, Eaton urged the Department of Justice to crack down on the Morgan, the Kuhn, Loeb and other eastern investment interests for "monopolizing" the market in new stock issues.

As an "operator" Eaton had departed from the pure milk of the capitalistic word; here he was depending on government to make opportunity for him. But he remembered all that John D. Rockefeller Sr., his first employer, had taught him about capitalist performance. As a young man from the herring-smelly shores of Pugwash up near the cold Gulf of St. Lawrence, whither an ancestor had gone as a Loyalist refugee from the American Revolution, Eaton had visited his uncle, the Rev. Charles Aubrey Eaton, in Cleveland. Charles Eaton, later destined to fame as head of the House Committee on Foreign Affairs, happened to be the pastor of the "Rockefeller church" on Euclid Avenue. It wasn't long before nephew Cyrus had a job in the Rockefeller household, where he listened to tales of how John D. had picked up the Mesabi iron mines of Minnesota for

virtually nothing during the panic year of 1894, later selling them to the United States Steel Corporation in 1901 for $68 million. Cyrus also heard the elder Rockefeller refer to J. P. Morgan, who had put U. S. Steel together, as a "mere banker." Both the story of the Mesabi and the characterization of Morgan stuck with Eaton.

They were to have their belated echoes in 1943. Eaton's reiterative criticisms of "mere bankers" during the years when he was wailing about the shortage of investment capital in the Midwest had been heard in Canada, where the Canadian investment banking system was not adequate to the development of the more risky mining ventures. For years prospectors had been running across "floating" bodies of ore at the south end of Steep Rock Lake which indicated the presence somewhere of a mother lode. Then, one cold winter, a Port Arthur, Ontario prospector, Julian Cross, had a bright idea; he persuaded Joseph Errington, an adventurous mining man with funds, to set up rigs on the top of Steep Rock Lake ice. The drills bit down through the ice, through 150 feet of water, and through a thick glacial overburden of gravel. At three points of the W-shaped Steep Rock Lake, Cross and Errington struck rich ore.

The only catch was that 120 billion gallons of water covered the iron. A Steep Rock company, headed by Major General D. M. Hogarth, Quartermaster General of the Canadian Army in World War I, tried Wall Street for money to drain the lake and got "no" for an answer. Then Hogarth thought of Eaton, whom he had once met in a hotel elevator in Toronto.

It was at this point (the year was 1943, and John D. Rockefeller's Mesabi range was being eaten up for armaments) that Eaton's memories, his burning ambition to do some-

thing that Wall Street had deemed too big for it, and his two careers as tycoon and operator finally paid off. When Hogarth was talking to him the whole story of his old mentor, John D., and the Mesabi range flashed through his mind. As for the 120 billion gallons of water, he had had experience handling rivers when he was in the utilities business. He told Hogarth he would get him the money to drain Steep Rock Lake, then caught a train for Washington.

His labor leader friend, Phil Murray, got him to Harold Ruttenberg, the steel union's War Production Board representative whom Eaton later hired. Priorities on drills and pumps were quickly arranged, Jesse Jones of the RFC came through with the promised $5 million RFC loan— and the lake was drained. When Eaton was through setting up exploitative companies, taking stock rights, he was again a **fabulously** wealthy man.

Follows Red Line

The man who has accomplished these things is in the great mold of the Rockefellers, the Guggenheims, the Vanderbilts, and all the other builders who were traduced by the pigmies of the Rooseveltian decade as "robber barons." Mr. Eaton is an attractive man in many ways. He is a bird-lover and a man of the open air who lives quietly on 850 well-tended acres at his Northfield, Ohio farm, where he takes a meticulous interest in his piggery, his prize Shorthorn cattle, and the fields of millet, soybeans and sunflower seeds that he grows for visiting goldfinches and whitethroats. He loves cold country and cold weather; ten years ago, at 65, he was still playing pick-up ice hockey, and he still goes skiing every winter at Mont Tremblant with some of his thirteen grandchildren. Recently he married a second time; his wife, the former Mrs. Anne Kinder Jones, was a college classmate of his daughter-in-law. The new Mrs. Eaton is a victim of polio, which she contracted in maturity; she travels about with Eaton in a wheelchair, and she has ambitions to run for the U.S. Senate, preferably for the seat now held by Taft's Democratic friend, Frank Lausche. Clevelanders speak well of her, and deny the gossip that it was she who put Cyrus up to his pro-Soviet tricks.

Canny students of Marxism think it completely inexplicable that Eaton, a man of riches and many blessings, should bite off virtually the entire Communist line for the U.S. from FBI-baiting to recognition-for-Red-China and let's-stop-atomic-tests-right-away. They find it incomprehensible that Eaton should entertain A. Topchiev, the commissar of the Soviet Academy of Sciences, at his Pugwash gatherings of scientific men. After all, Topchiev has called it a "profoundly mistaken conclusion" for scientific workers to believe that there can be a "coexistence of the two ideologies," a "peaceful coexistence of countries with different social-economic systems." If that doesn't sound like a declaration of eternal war, then words mean nothing.

But to Eaton, the words do mean nothing. He thinks Khrushchev's and Topchiev's Marxist imprecations are mere "campaign oratory," the sort of gabble that was once indulged in by Americans in the "Manifest Destiny" epoch. Eaton forgets that "Manifest Destiny" led to the Mexican and Spanish-American wars and the acquisition by the United States of real estate from the Rio Neuces to the Philippines, and—going the other way—from California to Puerto Rico. Marxist "Manifest Destiny" has been no less dynamic.

In short, Eaton, who prides himself on being an intellectual, has apparently never bothered his head to study Marxism. If you ask him how he knows he can trust Khrushchev, he answers, "How do you know you can trust anybody? People can be trusted in material things when it is to their advantage to live up to their bargain." Since it is illogical to suppose that Khrushchev, Mikoyan, Gromyko and Menshikov and Sobelov (all friends of Eaton) could want to see the Soviet Union devastated in an atomic war, Eaton thinks the basis for an agreement with the Russians is there. He cannot see the counterargument, that if Khrushchev is really afraid of atomic war, there is no reason why the West should hurry to deal with him. If we hold the cards, why not wait?

When it is suggested to Eaton that it is the Communists, not the capitalists, who have been knocking off country after country (Czechoslovokia, Poland, Hungary, Red China, Indochina, Tibet) since Yalta, the words roll off his back. He thinks peace is to be had merely by soft words on the part of the West. In business, he says, you don't go around plastering men with epithets.

This is strange doctrine to come from a master of epithet, one who has referred to the "sacred seventeen" of the eastern investment bankers as members of the "colorless fraternity." But Eaton does not submit his own recent behavior to the test of logic. He fell into the business of entertaining Russians by accident. Some three or more years ago Frank Kluckhohn was busy shepherding a group of Soviet journalists into Cleveland to see a football game between the Cleveland Browns and the Pittsburgh Steelers. Although the Steelers were good enough to form a personal guard for the Soviet journalists as they passed through a picket line to their hotel, the Russians said they would be glad to forego the football match if they could meet a live American capitalist. Eaton was in town; and he fell. He liked the Russians—and he has been entertaining them at his Northfield farm ever since.

A Case of Vanity?

The most plausible explanation for his behavior is that his vanity has become involved. Playing host to the Soviets, Eaton knew that he was annoying an old business enemy, John Foster Dulles. He knew he was doing what comes naturally to his intellectual friends who contribute to the *Bulletin of the Atomic Scientists* and that he was pleasing his old friend Bertrand Russell. He knew that he was furthering the Ungava iron ore campaign which he has mapped out with Alfred Krupp, who has no compunctions about selling heavy machinery to Moscow and to Asiatic "neutralist" nations. And if he delights in attacking the FBI, he can recall that Max Lowenthal, his old brother-in-arms of the days when Eaton, Robert R. Young and Senator Burton Wheeler were all fighting the eastern railroads, was the author of the first anti-FBI book.

Eaton is not the first big figure in American industrial history to be trapped by his emotional commitments. Old Henry Ford, for example, had nothing against any particular Jew. But he hated bankers, and, since some bankers had Jewish names, Henry Ford was easily beguiled into accepting the balderdash about a conspiracy of the Elders of Zion. The fact that Henry Ford was a child in some respects does not detract from his genius at his own business of making cars. Similarly with Eaton: the fact that he knows nothing about Marxism does not detract from what he has done as a entrepreneur. Conversely, his ability to swing a business deal, to match capital to the raw materials of the Canadian wilderness, does not make him an authority on foreign affairs.

If there is anything more to Cyrus Eaton's recent behavior than has been here surmised, it rests in the secret places of the heart. But that is a region into which the mere journalist may not enter. The record shows nothing more than has been here disclosed. The picture nevertheless paints itself, and if William of Occam is right in his philosophic contention that there is no use multiplying entities, then the picture is enough.

The truly horrifying and dismaying thing about it all is that Eaton seems blithely unaware that his willingness to break bread with the most bloody-minded gang of murderers in international history involves a spiritual torpor that is doubly inexplicable in the light of Mr. Eaton's earliest career. Long before he became a great capitalist Eaton studied for the ministry; indeed, his youthful interest in ethics was what first commended him to the Baptist in John D. Rockefeller Sr. Eaton has obviously been betrayed by the circumstances of his career as a chronic "ag'iner" into his present lurid eminence as Number One U.S. Fellow Traveler of Moscow's murderous combine. What should be our reaction to this? In some cases it may be permissible to say that "to understand everything is to forgive everything." But hardly in the case of a former student of divinity who once served as lay pastor of a Baptist church. After all, it was not of ethically trained individuals that Christ said: "Father, forgive them, for they know not what they do."

July 4, ~~1984~~ 1959

Ode Written in Newspeak

MORRIE RYSKIND

Ring out, ring out, Security Bell!
    Ring out all over the U.S.A.!
        On this, our sacred Dependence Day,
Proclaim the truths that we know so well:
Toil and thrift are a twin impurity
Scorned by a nation that's come to maturity;
    Self-reliance is out-of-date,
        And a patriot depends on The State—
So down with Freedom and hail Security!

(And to hell, to hell
With the flibberty-gibberty Liberty Bell!)

Tell of the Pilgrims and Plymouth Rock—
And, mind you, none of that poppycock
Of freedom to worship as they chose
But the truth that's as plain as your very nose—
They suffered hardship, they tempted fate
Not for love of God, but the Welfare State;
They faced the tempest, they rode the wave
To be rid of want from cradle to grave.
That was their God and their Holy Spirit—
Ring out, O Bell, that the world may hear it!

Quote Patrick Henry, who rose from obscurity
    All in one breath
By telling the Burgesses, "Give me Security—
    Or give me Death."

Hail Lexington, Concord and Bunker Hill
    And the lessons they teach us with simple
clarity!
(The embattled farmers are with us still—
    Fighting for Parity!)

Let Betsy Ross have an extra chime:
    Who stayed up nights with patches and rags,
    Sewing the first of our country's Flags!
(She could have taken the day-shift, but
She wanted the overtime.)

Ring out, ring out, Security Bell!
Ring out defiance

To self-reliance!
Forget the maxims Poor Richard gave us—
Hail to the glorious chains that enslave us!
For who would stand on his own two feet
When the government will provide a seat
At a festive board that gleams like a star,
Replete with Marxian caviar?

Pitch your tune to the Liberal Line
And tell our progress, superb, divine,
From '76 to '59—
    How the Minute Men's descendants
    Finally achieved Dependence!

Ring out, ring out, Security Bell,
Proclaim the truths we have learned so well:
That there's no such thing as a national debt
(If you owe yourself, you're a fool to fret!);
That all are equal and who would rise
Above the crowd wears a fascist guise;
That a good day's work for a good day's pay
Is the law of the jungle beasts of prey—
And one not fit for the U.S.A.

And warn the tyrant who would undo us
Who treads on Old Glory must answer to us:
We'll seek him out at the Conference Table
    (Square or round, round or square,
    He can be certain that we'll be there!)
And argue as long as we are able!

And if American boys are slain?
We'll gladly discuss it again and again—
And again!

So ring out, ring out, Security Bell!
    Ring out all over the U.S.A.!
        On this, our sacred Dependence Day
Proclaim the truths that we know so well!

(And to hell, to hell
With the flibberty-gibberty Liberty Bell!)

The Meaning of McCarthyism

FRANK S. MEYER

Now, a year after Senator McCarthy's death and three years or more after his political execution by the Watkins Committee, it should be possible to assess with reasonable objectivity the meaning of that movement of thought and action which the Liberals dubbed McCarthyism. It is too soon perhaps to grasp its significance *sub specie aeternitatis*, but we are sufficiently removed from the immediate clamors of those extraordinary years between 1950 and 1954 to abstract from the surface aspects, to see beyond the strengths and weaknesses of Senator McCarthy himself, to begin to delineate what it was that lay beneath those clamors and gave so intense a sense of urgency to those years.

Perhaps one way of approaching the problem is to consider what has changed since Senator McCarthy was eliminated from the political scene. Life is a great deal more tranquil. It was tranquil indeed when he was still alive but no longer heard, when in November 1956 we went about our business while our national honor died and the blood of our friends flooded the streets of Budapest. It is reasonably tranquil today (we are somewhat worried about the recession, of course), as we haggle about the conditions upon which we will meet with murderers on some summit, meanwhile rising at the Metropolitan Opera House to honor the murderers' anthem.

The commanding heights of our society are held by those who preach tranquility. There are problems, of course—out-sputniking Sputnik; out-propagandizing Khrushchev; winning friends and influencing people—Sukarno, Nehru, Nasser. But it is all part of the game, the give-and-take of coexistence. A few voices are raised, but hardly heard, to warn that coexistence with an enemy sworn to the destruction of Western civilization is an impossibility, that it can only lead to the victory of that enemy and to our defeat. But those voices are smothered by the soothing formulas poured down upon us from the heights where the Liberals of both parties sit.

What was it that in the McCarthy period broke through this mist? What was it that penetrated tranquility and brought the country as close as it has ever been to an understanding of the threatening danger? It certainly had nothing to do with Senator McCarthy's "tactics." They were the small change of American politics—nothing that has not been used on every side of every political controversy for scores of years. It was, I submit, an understanding, sometimes crudely expressed, sometimes shrewdly accurate, of the tragic truth of politics in the United States, as in all the West, in the last forty years: *the integral characteristics of the Liberalism which became increasingly predominant during those years are such that our present leadership can neither resist the infiltration of Communists within nor concert an effective strategy against Communists without.*

It was an instinctive realization of this among large sections of the American people which Senator McCarthy activated—a gnawing sense of something wrong, something which they could not define, but of which they were intuitively sure. Senator McCarthy, to be sure, did not contribute much towards definition. What he did was done not by analysis but by courage, pertinacity, and rhetorical expression of the mute and strangled common sense of millions of Americans.

Be it said that such an expression of the instincts of a people is not the best expression intellectually or aesthetically that could be found, nor, in the end, the most effective. Every society needs intellectuals capable of articulating its fundamental instinct in terms of reason and the accumulated wisdom of tradition. But what is to be done when the immense majority of the putative intellectual leaders of society go a-whoring after strange gods, whose blandishments both the traditions of their culture and the discipline of their profession should enable them to resist? Better by far the rough-hewn truth than a sophisticated and articulated apology for error.

Treason of the Intellectuals

It is unfortunate that the "treason of the intellectuals," their desertion of their duty to truth, has created that suspicion of intellectuality *per se* which gave rise to the ambiguous epithet, egghead, with all that word implies. It is unfortunate that a corrupt intellectuality has put intellectuality itself under suspicion. It is unfortunate that, these things being so, the attack of McCarthyism upon ideas which are dangerous errors and upon the intellectuals who hold these ideas could be so easily interpreted as an attack upon ideas and upon intellectuals in general. Although it is cold comfort to a society which desperately needs intellectuals inspired by truth, those who have perverted their role as articulators of the spirit of their society have only themselves to blame.

The attack on McCarthy as an uncouth enemy of ideas and culture was a defensive effort to confuse the issue which he expressed and dramatized. The normal outlet of Americans who disagree with prevailing authority, the Presidential election, had been foreclosed. The critics of established Liberalism, quadrennium after quadrennium, saw the Republican Party come under the sway of ideas only superficially different from those of the New Deal Democrats. A quiet and undramatic revolution had, since the early thirties, occupied the decisive positions of American society—not only in politics, but in mass communications which became daily more powerful, in the schools and universities, even in a large proportion of the pulpits. A civilization founded upon the premise of the inviolate primacy of the individual person was being steadily socialized.

For the solid citizen, well grounded in the tradition of his ancestors but unequipped in intellectual dialectics,

The Lost Tools of Learning

What *are* the tools of learning? Miss Sayers went
after the answer with the zest and skill of a master
sleuth—and pinned her conclusions to the wall

D O R O T H Y   L .   S A Y E R S

For three years NATIONAL REVIEW *has hammered away at the central
weakness of American education: the lack of educational substance
in the curriculum. In doing so, we have inadvertently neglected
the importance of the tools of learning. Just because John Dewey
and his disciples created and maintain an idolatry in the name of
method, it does not follow that techniques of learning are un-
important. One must master the tools of learning—if one would
learn how to learn. We publish here, for the first time in this
country (by special permission of her estate) a brilliant essay on
the subject by the late Miss Dorothy Sayers, delivered in 1947
at Oxford. The analysis casts a light so bright and penetrating
as to illuminate the problems of any parent who worries about the
educational progress of his child—or other people's children.—*ED.*

That I, whose experience of teaching
is extremely limited, should presume
to discuss education is a matter, surely,
that calls for no apology. It is a kind
of behavior to which the present
climate of opinion is wholly favorable.
Bishops air their opinions about economics; biologists, about metaphysics;
inorganic chemists about theology;
the most irrelevant people are appointed to highly-technical ministries;
and plain, blunt men write to the papers to say that Epstein and Picasso
do not know how to draw. Up to a
certain point, and provided that the
criticisms are made with a reasonable
modesty, these activities are com-
mendable. Too much specialization is
not a good thing. There is also one
excellent reason why the veriest
amateur may feel entitled to have an
opinion about education. For if we
are not all professional teachers, we
have all, at some time or other, been
taught. Even if we learnt nothing—
perhaps in particular if we learnt
nothing—our contribution to the discussion may have a potential value.

I propose to deal with the subject
of teaching, properly so-called. It is
in the highest degree improbable that
the reforms I propose will ever be
carried into effect. Neither the parents, nor the training colleges, nor
the examination boards, nor the
boards of governors, nor the ministries of education would countenance

them for a moment. For they amount
to this: that if we are to produce a
society of educated people, fitted to
preserve their intellectual freedom
amid the complex pressures of our
modern society, we must turn back
the wheel of progress some four or
five hundred years, to the point at
which education began to lose sight
of its true object, towards the end of
the Middle Ages.

Before you dismiss me with the
appropriate phrase—reactionary, ro-
mantic, mediaevalist, *laudator tempo-
ris acti*, or whatever tag comes first
to hand—I will ask you to consider
one or two miscellaneous questions
that hang about at the back, perhaps,
of all our minds, and occasionally
pop out to worry us.

Disquieting Questions

When we think about the remark-
ably early age at which the young
men went up to the university in, let
us say, Tudor times, and thereafter
were held fit to assume responsibility
for the conduct of their own affairs,
are we altogether comfortable about
that artificial prolongation of intellectual childhood and adolescence into
the years of physical maturity which
is so marked in our own day? To
postpone the acceptance of responsibility to a late date brings with it a
number of psychological complica-

tions which, while they may interest
the psychiatrist, are scarcely bene-
ficial either to the individual or to
society. The stock argument in favor
of postponing the school leaving-age
and prolonging the period of education generally is that there is now so
much more to learn than there was
in the Middle Ages. This is partly
true, but not wholly. The modern boy
and girl are certainly taught more
subjects—but does that always mean
that they actually know more?

Has it ever struck you as odd, or
unfortunate, that today, when the
proportion of literacy throughout
western Europe is higher than it has
ever been, people should have become susceptible to the influence of
advertisement and mass-propaganda
to an extent hitherto unheard-of and
unimagined? Do you put this down to
the mere mechanical fact that the
press and the radio and so on have
made propaganda much easier to dis-
tribute over a wide area? Or do you
sometimes have an uneasy suspicion
that the product of modern educational methods is less good than he
or she might be at disentangling fact
from opinion and the proven from
the plausible?

Have you ever, in listening to a
debate among adult and presumably
responsible people, been fretted by
the extraordinary inability of the
average debater to speak to the question, or to meet and refute the arguments of speakers on the other side?
Or have you ever pondered upon the
extremely high incidence of irrelevant matter which crops up at com-
mittee-meetings, and upon the very
great rarity of persons capable of
acting as chairmen of committees?
And when you think of this, and think
that most of our public affairs are settled by debates and committees, have
you ever felt a certain sinking of the
heart?

Have you ever followed a discussion in the newspapers or elsewhere and noticed how frequently writers fail to define the terms they use? Or how often, if one man does define his terms, another will assume in his reply that he was using the terms in precisely the opposite sense to that in which he has already defined them?

Have you ever been faintly troubled by the amount of slipshod syntax going about? And if so, are you troubled because it is inelegant or because it may lead to dangerous misunderstanding?

Do you ever find that young people, when they have left school, not only forget most of what they have learnt (that is only to be expected) but forget also, or betray that they have never really known, how to tackle a new subject for themselves? Are you often bothered by coming across grown-up men and women who seem unable to distinguish between a book that is sound, scholarly and properly documented, and one that is to any trained eye, very conspicuously none of these things? Or who cannot handle a library catalogue? Or who, when faced with a book of reference, betray a curious inability to extract from it the passages relevant to the particular question which interests them?

Do you often come across people for whom, all their lives, a "subject" remains a "subject," divided by watertight bulkheads from all other "subjects," so that they experience very great difficulty in making an immediate mental connection between, let us say, algebra and detective fiction, sewage disposal and the price of salmon—or, more generally, between such spheres of knowledge as philosophy and economics, or chemistry and art?

A Few Examples

Are you occasionally perturbed by the things written by adult men and women for adult men and women to read?

We find a well-known biologist writing in a weekly paper to the effect that: "It is an argument against the existence of a Creator" (I think he put it more strongly; but since I have, most unfortunately, mislaid the reference, I will put his claim at its lowest)—"an argument against the existence of a Creator that the

same kind of variations which are produced by natural selection can be produced at will by stock-breeders." One might feel tempted to say that it is rather an argument *for* the existence of a Creator. Actually, of course, it is neither: all it proves is that the same material causes (recombination of the chromosomes by cross-breeding and so forth) are sufficient to account for all observed variations—just as the various combinations of the same thirteen semitones are materially sufficient to account for Beethoven's Moonlight Sonata and the noise the cat makes by walking on the keys. But the cat's performance neither proves nor disproves the existence of Beethoven; and all that is proved by the biologist's argument is that he was unable to distinguish between a material and a final cause.

Here is a sentence from no less academic a source than a front-page article in the [London] *Times Literary Supplement*:

> The Frenchman, Alfred Epinas, pointed out that certain species (*e.g.*, ants and wasps) can only face the horrors of life and death in association.

I do not know what the Frenchman actually did say: what the Englishman says he said is patently meaningless. We cannot know whether life holds any horror for the ant, nor in what sense the isolated wasp which you kill upon the window-pane can be said to "face" or not to "face" the horrors of death. The subject of the article is mass-behavior in *man;* and the human motives have been unobtrusively transferred from the main proposition to the supporting instance. Thus the argument, in effect, assumes what it sets out to prove—a fact which would become immediately apparent if it were presented in a formal syllogism. This is only a small and haphazard example of a vice which pervades whole books—particlarly books written by men of science on metaphysical subjects.

Another quotation from the same issue of the T.L.S. comes in fittingly here to wind up this random collection of disquieting thoughts—this time from a review of Sir Richard Livingstone's *Some Tasks for Education*:

> More than once the reader is reminded of the value of an intensive study of at least one subject, so as to

learn "the meaning of knowledge" and what precision and persistence is needed to attain it. Yet there is elsewhere full recognition of the distressing fact that a man may be master in one field and show no better judgment than his neighbor anywhere else; he remembers what he has learnt, but forgets altogether how he learned it.

I would draw your attention particularly to that last sentence, which offers an explanation of what the writer rightly calls the "distressing fact" that the intellectual skills bestowed upon us by our education are not readily transferable to subjects other than those in which we acquired them: "he remembers what he has learnt, but forgets altogether how he learned it."

The Art of Learning

Is not the great defect of our education today—a defect traceable through all the disquieting symptoms of trouble that I have mentioned—that although we often succeed in teaching our pupils "subjects," we fail lamentably on the whole in teaching them how to think: They learn everything, except the art of learning. It is as though we had taught a child, mechanically and by rule of thumb, to play "The Harmonious Blacksmith" upon the piano, but had never taught him the scale or how to read music; so that, having memorized "The Harmonious Blacksmith," he still had not the faintest notion how to proceed from that to tackle "The Last Rose of Summer." Why do I say, "As though"? In certain of the arts and crafts we sometimes do precisely this—requiring a child to "express himself" in paint before we teach him how to handle the colors and the brush. There is a school of thought which believes this to be the right way to set about the job. But observe —it is not the way in which a trained craftsman will go about to teach himself a new medium. He, having learned by experience the best way to economize labor and take the thing by the right end, will start off by doodling about on an odd piece of material, in order to "give himself the feel of the tool."

Let us now look at the mediaeval scheme of education—the syllabus of the schools. It does not matter, for the moment, whether it was devised

59

for small children or for older students; or how long people were supposed to take over it. What matters is the light it throws upon what the men of the Middle Ages supposed to be the object and the right order of the educative process.

The Mediaeval Syllabus

The syllabus was divided into two parts; the Trivium and Quadrivium. The second part—the Quadrivium—consisted of "subjects," and need not for the moment concern us. The interesting thing for us is the composition of the Trivium, which preceded the Quadrivium and was the preliminary discipline for it. It consisted of three parts: Grammar, Dialectic, and Rhetoric, in that order.

Now the first thing we notice is that two at any rate of these "subjects" are not what we should call "subjects" at all: they are only methods of dealing with subjects. Grammar, indeed, is a "subject" in the sense that it does mean definitely learning a language—at that period it meant learning Latin. But language itself is simply the medium in which thought is expressed. The whole of the Trivium was, in fact, intended to teach the pupil the proper use of the tools of learning, before he began to apply them to "subjects" at all. First, he learned a language; not just how to order a meal in a foreign language, but the structure of language—a language, and hence of language itself—what it was, how it was put together and how it worked. Secondly, he learned how to use language: how to define his terms and make accurate statements; how to construct an argument and how to detect fallacies in argument (his own arguments and other people's). Dialectic, that is to say, embraced Logic and Disputation. Thirdly, he learned to express himself in language; how to say what he had to say elegantly and persuasively.

At the end of his course, he was required to compose a thesis upon some theme set by his masters or chosen by himself, and afterwards to defend his thesis against the criticism of the faculty. By this time he would have learned—or woe betide him—not merely to write an essay on paper, but to speak audibly and intelligibly from a platform, and to use

his wits quickly when heckled. There would also be questions, cogent and shrewd, from those who had already run the gauntlet of debate.

It is, of course, quite true that bits and pieces of the mediaeval tradition still linger, or have been revived, in the ordinary school syllabus of today. Some knowledge of grammar is still required when learning a foreign language—perhaps I should say, "is again required"; for during my own lifetime we passed through a phase when the teaching of declensions and conjugations was considered rather reprehensible, and it was considered better to pick these things up as we went along. School debating societies flourish; essays are written; the necessity for "self-expression" is stressed, and perhaps even overstressed. But these activities are cultivated more or less in detachment, as belonging to the special subjects in which they are pigeon-holed rather than as forming one coherent scheme of mental training to which all "subjects" stand in a subordinate relation. "Grammar" belongs especially to the "subject" of foreign languages, and essay-writing to the "subject" called "English"; while Dialectic has

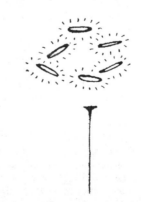

become almost entirely divorced from the rest of the curriculum, and is frequently practiced unsystematically and out of school-hours as a separate exercise, only very loosely related to the main business of learning. Taken by and large, the great difference of emphasis between the two conceptions holds good: modern education concentrates on *teaching subjects,* leaving the method of thinking, arguing and expressing one's conclusions to be picked up by the scholar as he goes along; mediaeval education concentrated on first *forg-*

ing and learning to handle the tools of learning, using whatever subject came handy as a piece of material on which to doodle until the use of the tool became second nature.

"Subjects" of some kind there must be, of course. One cannot learn the theory of grammar without learning an actual language, or learn to argue and orate without speaking about something in particular. The debating subjects of the Middle Ages were drawn largely from Theology, or from the Ethics and History of Antiquity. Often, indeed, they became stereotyped, especially towards the end of the period, and the far-fetched and wire-drawn absurdities of scholastic argument fretted Milton and provide food for merriment even to this day. Whether they were in themselves any more hackneyed and trivial than the usual subjects set nowadays for "essay-writing" I should not like to say: we may ourselves grow a little weary of "A Day in my Holidays," and all the rest of it. But most of the merriment is misplaced, because the aim and object of the debating thesis has by now been lost sight of.

Angels on a Needle

A glib speaker in the Brains Trust once entertained his audience (and reduced the late Charles Williams to helpless rage) by asserting that in the Middle Ages it was a matter of faith to know how many archangels could dance on the point of a needle. I need not say, I hope, that it never was a "matter of faith"; it was simply a debating exercise, whose set subject was the nature of angelic substance: were angels material, and if so, did they occupy space? The answer usually adjudged correct is, I believe, that angels are pure intelligences; not material, but limited, so that they may have location in space but not extension. An analogy might be drawn from human thought, which is similarly non-material and similarly limited. Thus, if your thought is concentrated upon one thing—say, the point of a needle—it is located there in the sense that it is not elsewhere; but although it is "there," it occupies no space there, and there is nothing to prevent an infinite number of different people's thoughts being concentrated upon the same needle-point at the same time. The proper *subject* of the argument is thus seen to be the distinction between location and extension in space; the *matter* on which the argument is exercised happens to be the nature of angels (although, as we have seen, it might equally well have been something else); the practical lesson to be drawn from the argument is not to use words like "there" in a loose and unscientific way, without specifying whether you mean "located there" or "occupying space there."

Scorn in plenty has been poured out upon the mediaeval passion for hair-splitting: but when we look at the shameless abuse made, in print and on the platform, of controversial expressions with shifting and ambiguous connotations, we may feel it in our hearts to wish that every reader and hearer had been so defensively armored by his education as to be able to cry: *Distinguo.*

Unarmed

For we let our young men and women go out unarmed, in a day when armor was never so necessary. By teaching them all to read, we have left them at the mercy of the printed word. By the invention of the film and the radio, we have made certain that no aversion to reading shall secure them from the incessant battery of words, words, words. They do not know what the words mean; they do not know how to ward them off or blunt their edge or fling them back; they are a prey to words in their emotions instead of being the masters of them in their intellects. We who were scandalized in 1940 when men were sent to fight armored tanks with rifles, are not scandalized when young men and women are sent into the world to fight massed propaganda with a smattering of "subjects"; and when whole classes and whole nations become hypnotized by the arts of the spellbinder, we have the impudence to be astonished. We dole out lip-service to the importance of education—lip-service and, just occasionally, a little grant of money; we postpone the school leaving-age, and plan to build bigger and better schools; the teachers slave conscientiously in and out of school-hours; and yet, as I believe,

all this devoted effort is largely frustrated, because we have lost the tools of learning, and in their absence can only make a botched and piecemeal job of it.

What, then, are we to do? We cannot go back to the Middle Ages. That is a cry to which we have become accustomed. We cannot go back—or can we? *Distinguo.* I should like every term in that proposition defined. Does "Go back" mean a retrogression in time, or the revision of an error? The first is clearly impossible *per se;* the second is a thing which wise men do every day. Obviously the twentieth century is not and cannot be the fourteenth; but if "the Middle Ages" is, in this context, simply a picturesque phrase denoting a particular educational theory, there seems to be no *a priori* reason why we should not "go back" to it—with modifications—as we have already "gone back," with modifications, to, let us say, the idea of playing Shakespeare's plays as he wrote them, and not in the "modernized" versions of Cibber and Garrick, which once seemed to be the latest thing in theatrical progress.

Let us amuse ourselves by imagining that such progressive retrogression is possible. Let us make a clean sweep of all educational authorities, and furnish ourselves with a nice little school of boys and girls whom we may experimentally equip for the intellectual conflict along lines chosen by ourselves. We will endow them with exceptionally docile parents; we will staff our school with teachers who are themselves perfectly familiar with the aims and methods of the Trivium; we will have our buildings and staff large enough to allow our classes to be small enough for adequate handling; and we will postulate a Board of Examiners willing and qualified to test the products

we turn out. Thus prepared, we will attempt to sketch out a syllabus—a modern Trivium "with modifications"; and we will see where we get to.

But first: what age shall the children be? Well, if one is to educate them on novel lines, it will be better that they should have nothing to unlearn; besides, one cannot begin a good thing too early, and the Trivium is by its nature not learning, but a preparation for learning. We will, therefore, "catch 'em young," requiring only of our pupils that they shall be able to read, write and cipher.

The Three Ages

My views about child-psychology are, I admit, neither orthodox nor enlightened. Looking back upon myself (since I am the child I know best and the only child I can pretend to know from inside) I recognize three states of development. These, in a rough-and-ready fashion, I will call the Poll-Parrot, the Pert, and the Poetic—the latter coinciding, approximately, with the onset of puberty. The Poll-Parrot stage is the one in which learning by heart is easy and, on the whole, pleasurable; whereas reasoning is difficult and, on the whole, little relished. At this age, one readily memorizes the shapes and appearances of things; one likes to recite the number-plates of cars; one rejoices in the chanting of rhymes and the rumble and thunder of unintelligible polysyllables; one enjoys the mere accumulation of things. The Pert Age, which follows upon this (and, naturally, overlaps it to some extent) is characterized by contradicting, answering-back, liking to "catch people out" (especially one's elders) and in the propounding of conundrums. Its nuisance-value is extremely high. It usually sets in about the eighth grade. The Poetic Age is popularly known as the "difficult" age. It is self-centered; it yearns to express itself; it rather specializes in being misunderstood; it is restless and tries to achieve independence; and, with good luck and good guidance, it should show the beginnings of creativeness, a reaching-out towards a synthesis of what it already knows, and a deliberate eagerness to know and do some one thing in pref-

Propaganda & Truth are key themes, we don't know how to distinguish

erence to all others. Now it seems to me that the layout of the Trivium adapts itself with a singular appropriateness to these three ages: Grammar to the Poll-Parrot, Dialectic to the Pert, and Rhetoric to the Poetic Age.

Let us begin, then, with Grammar. This, in practice, means the grammar of some language in particular; and it must be an inflected language. The grammatical structure of an uninflected language is far too analytical to be tackled by any one without previous practice in Dialectic. Moreover, the inflected languages interpret the uninflected, whereas the uninflected are of little use in interpreting the inflected. I will say at once, quite firmly, that the best grounding for education is the Latin grammar. I say this, not because Latin is traditional and mediaeval, but simply because even a rudimentary knowledge of Latin cuts down the labor and pains of learning almost any other subject by at least fifty per cent. It is the key to the vocabulary and structure of all the Romance

AMO AMAS AMAT

languages and to the structure of all the Teutonic languages, as well as to the technical vocabulary of all the sciences and to the literature of the entire Mediterranean civilization, together with all its historical documents.

Those whose pedantic preference for a living language persuades them to deprive their pupils of all these advantages might substitute Russian, whose grammar is still more primitive. Russian is, of course, helpful with the other Slav dialects. There is something also to be said for Classical Greek. But my own choice is Latin. Having thus pleased the

Classicists among you, I will proceed to horrify them by adding that I do not think it either wise or necessary to cramp the ordinary pupil upon the Procrustean bed of the Augustan Age, with its highly elaborate and artificial verse-forms and oratory.

Latin should be begun as early as possible—at a time when inflected speech seems no more astonishing than any other phenomenon in an astonishing world; and when the chanting of "Amo, Amas, Amat" is as ritually agreeable to the feelings as the chanting of "eeny, meeny, miney, mo."

During this age we must, of course, exercise the mind on other things besides Latin grammar. Observation and memory are the faculties most lively at this period; and if we are to learn a contemporary foreign language we should begin now, before the facial and mental muscles become rebellious to strange intonations. Spoken French or German can be practiced alongside the grammatical discipline of the Latin.

The Use of Memory

In *English*, verse and prose can be learned by heart, and the pupil's memory should be stored with stories of every kind—classical myth, European legend, and so forth. I do not think that the classical stories and masterpieces of ancient literature should be made the vile bodies on which to practice the technics of Grammar—that was a fault of mediaeval education which we need not perpetuate. The stories can be enjoyed and remembered in English, and related to their origin at a subsequent stage. Recitation aloud should be practiced—individually or in chorus; for we must not forget that we are laying the groundwork for Disputation and Rhetoric.

The grammar of *History* should consist, I think, of dates, events, anecdotes and personalities. A set of dates to which one can peg all later historical knowledge is of enormous help later on in establishing the perspective of history. It does not greatly matter which dates: those of the Kings of England will do very nicely, provided that they are accompanied by pictures of costumes, architecture, and other "everyday things," so that the mere mention of a date calls

up a strong visual presentment of the whole period.

Geography will similarly be presented in its factual aspect, with maps, natural features and visual presentment of customs, costumes, flora, fauna and so on; and I believe myself that the discredited and old-fashioned memorizing of a few capital cities, rivers, mountain ranges, etc., does no harm. Stamp-collecting may be encouraged.

Science, in the Poll-Parrot period, arranges itself naturally and easily round collections—the identifying and naming of specimens and, in general, the kind of thing that used to be

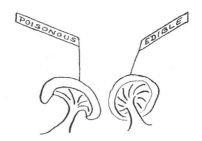

called "natural history," or, still more charmingly, "natural philosophy." To know the names and properties of things is, at this age, a satisfaction in itself; to recognize a devil's coach-horse at sight, and assure one's foolish elders that, in spite of its appearance, it does not sting; to be able to pick out Cassiopeia and the Pleiades; to be aware that a whale is not a fish, and a bat not a bird—all these things give a pleasant sensation of superiority; while to know a ring-snake from an adder or a poisonous from an edible toadstool is a kind of knowledge that has also a practical value.

The grammar of *Mathematics* begins, of course, with the multiplication table, which, if not learnt now will never be learnt with pleasure; and with the recognition of geometrical shapes and the grouping of numbers. These exercises lead naturally to the doing of simple sums in arithmetic; and if the pupil shows a bent that way, a facility acquired at this stage is all to the good. More complicated mathematical processes may, and perhaps should, be postponed, for reasons which will presently appear.

So far (except, of course, for the Latin), our curriculum contains nothing that departs very far from common practice. The difference will be felt rather in the attitude of the teachers, who must look upon all these activities less as "subjects" in themselves than as a gathering-to-gether of *material* for use in the next part of the Trivium. What that material acually is, is only of secondary importance; but it is as well that anything and everything which can usefully be committed to memory should be memorized at this period, whether it is immediately intelligible or not. The modern tendency is to try and force rational explanations on a child's mind at too early an age. Intelligent questions, spontaneously asked, should, of course, receive an immediate and rational answer; but it is a great mistake to suppose that a child cannot readily enjoy and re-member things that are beyond its power to analyze—particularly if those things have a strong imagina-tive appeal, an attractive jingle, or an abundance of rich, resounding polysyllables.

The Mistress-Science

This reminds me of the grammar of *Theology*. I shall add it to the curriculum, because Theology is the mistress-science, without which the whole educational structure will necessarily lack its final synthesis. Those who disagree about this will remain content to leave their pupils' education still full of loose ends. This will matter rather less than it might, since by the time that the tools of learning have been forged the stu-dent will be able to tackle Theology for himself, and will probably insist upon doing so and making sense of it. Still, it is as well to have this mat-ter also handy and ready for the reason to work upon. At the gram-matical age, therefore, we should be-come acquainted with the story of God and Man in outline—i.e., the Old and New Testament presented as parts of a single narrative of Cre-ation, Rebellion and Redemption—and also with "the Creed, the Lord's Prayer and the Ten Commandments." At this stage, it does not matter nearly so much that these things should be fully understood as that they should be known and remem-bered.

It is difficult to say at what age, precisely, we should pass from the first to the second part of the Tri-vium. Generally- speaking, the an-swer is: so soon as the pupil shows himself disposed to pertness and in-terminable argument. For as, in the first part, the master-facilities are Observation and Memory, so in the second, the master-faculty is the Dis-cursive Reason. In the first, the ex-ercise to which the rest of the mate-rial was, as it were, keyed, was the Latin grammar; in the second the key-exercise will be Formal Logic. It is here that our curriculum shows its first sharp divergence from mod-ern standards. The disrepute into which Formal Logic has fallen is en-tirely unjustified; and its neglect is the root cause of nearly all those dis-quieting symptoms which we have noted in the modern intellectual con-stitution.

A secondary cause for the disfavor into which Formal Logic has fallen is the belief that it is entirely based upon universal assumptions that are either unprovable or tautological. This is not true. Not all universal propositions are of this kind. But even if they were, it would make no difference, since every syllogism whose major premise is in the form "All A is B" can be recast in hypo-thetical form. Logic is the art of arguing correctly: "If A, then B": the method is not invalidated by the hypothetical character of A. Indeed, the practical utility of Formal Logic today lies not so much in the estab-lishment of positive conclusions as in the prompt detection and exposure of invalid inference.

Relation to Dialectic

Let us now quickly review our material and see how it is to be re-lated to Dialectic. On the *Language* side, we shall now have our Vocabu-lary and Morphology at our finger-tips; henceforward we can concen-trate more particularly on Syntax and Analysis (*i.e.*, the logical con-struction of speech) and the history of Language (*i.e.*, how we come to arrange our speech as we do in or-der to convey our thoughts).

Our Reading will proceed from narrative and lyric to essays, argu-ment and criticism, and the pupil will learn to try his own hand at writing this kind of thing. Many les-sons—on whatever subject—will take the form of debates; and the place ot individual or choral recitation will be taken by dramatic performances, with special attention to plays in which an argument is stated in dra-matic form.

Mathematics—Algebra, Geometry, and the more advanced kind of Arithmetic—will now enter into the syllabus and take its place as what it really is: not a separate "subject" but a sub-department of Logic. It is neither more nor less than the rule of the syllogism in its particular ap-plication to number and measure-ment, and should be taught as such, instead of being, for some, a dark mystery, and for others, a special revelation, neither illuminating nor illuminated by any other part of knowledge.

History, aided by a simple system of ethics derived from the grammar of Theology, will provide much suit-able material for discussion: Was the behavior of this statesman justified? What was the effect of such an en-actment? What are the arguments for and against this or that form of gov-ernment? We shall thus get an intro-duction to Constitutional History— a subject meaningless to the young child, but of absorbing interest to those who are prepared to argue and debate. *Theology* itself will furnish material for argument about conduct and morals; and should have its scope extended by a simplified course of dogmatic theology (*i.e.*, the ra-tional structure of Christian thought), clarifying the relations between the dogma and the ethics, and lending itself to that application of ethical principles in particular instances which is properly called casuistry. *Geography* and the *Sciences* will all likewise provide material for Dia-lectic.

The World Around Us

But above all, we must not neglect the material which is so abundant in the pupils' own daily life.

There is a delightful passage in Leslie Paul's *The Living Hedge* which tells how a number of small boys enjoyed themselves for days arguing about an extraordinary shower of rain which had fallen in their town—a shower so localized that it left one-half of the main street wet and the other dry. Could one, they argued, properly say that it had rained that day *on* or *over* the town or only *in* the town? How many drops of water were required to constitute rain? and so on. Argument about this led on to a host of similar problems about rest and motion, sleep and waking, *est* and *non est*, and the infinitesimal division of time.

The whole passage is an admirable example of the spontaneous development of the ratiocinative faculty and the natural and proper thirst of the awakening reason for definition of terms and exactness of statement. All events are food for such an appetite.

An umpire's decison; the degree to which one may transgress the spirit of a regulation without being trapped by the letter; on such questions as these, children are born casuists, and their natural propensity only needs to be developed and trained—and, especially, brought into an intelligible relationship with events in the grown-up world. The newspapers are full of good material for such exercises: legal decisions, on the one hand, in cases where the cause at issue is not too abstruse; on the other, fallacious reasoning and muddleheaded argument, with which the correspondence columns of certain papers one could name are abundantly stocked.

"Pert Age" Criticism

Wherever the matter for Dialectic is found, it is, of course, highly important that attention should be focused upon the beauty and economy of a fine demonstration or a well-turned argument, lest veneration should wholly die. Criticism must not be merely destructive; though at the same time both teacher and pupils must be ready to detect fallacy,

slipshod reasoning, ambiguity, irrelevance and redundancy, and to pounce upon them like rats.

This is the moment when precis-writing may be usefully undertaken; together with such exercises as the writing of an essay, and the reduction of it, when written, by 25 or 50 per cent.

It will, doubtless, be objected that to encourage young persons at the Pert Age to browbeat, correct and argue with their elders will render them perfectly intolerable. My answer is that children of that age are intolerable anyhow; and that their natural argumentativeness may just as well be canalised to good purpose as allowed to run away into the sands. It may, indeed, be rather less obtrusive at home if it is disciplined in school; and, anyhow, elders who have abandoned the wholesome principle that children should be seen and *not* heard have no one to blame but themselves.

Once again: the contents of the syllabus at this stage may be anything you like. The "subjects" supply material; but they are all to be regarded as mere grist for the mental mill to work upon. The pupils should be encouraged to go and forage for their own information, and so guided towards the proper use of libraries and books of reference, and shown how to tell which sources are authoritative and which are not.

Imagination

Towards the close of this stage, the pupils will probably be beginning to discover for themselves that their knowledge and experience are insufficient, and that their trained intelligences need a great deal more material to chew upon. The imagination—usually dormant during the Pert Age—will reawaken, and prompt them to suspect the limitations of logic and reason. This means that they are passing into the Poetic Age and are ready to embark on the study of Rhetoric. The doors of the storehouse of knowledge should now be thrown open for them to browse about as they will. The things once learned by rote will be seen in new contexts; the things once coldly analyzed can now be brought together to form a new synthesis; here and there a sudden insight will bring about that

most exciting of all discoveries: the realization that a truism is true.

The Study of Rhetoric

It is difficult to map out any general syllabus for the study of Rhetoric: a certain freedom is demanded. In literature, appreciation should be again allowed to take the lead over destructive criticism; and self-expression in writing can go forward, with its tools now sharpened to cut clean and observe proportion. Any child that already shows a disposition to specialize should be given his head: for, when the use of the tools has been well and truly learned it is available for any study whatever. It would be well, I think, that each pupil should learn to do one, or two, subjects really well, while taking a few classes in subsidiary subjects so as to keep his mind open to the interrelations of all knowledge. Indeed, at this stage, our difficulty will be to keep "subjects" apart; for a Dialectic will have shown all branches of learning to be inter-related, so Rhetoric will tend to show that all knowledge is one. To show this, and show why it is so, is pre-eminently the task of the Mistress-science. But whether Theology is studied or not, we should at least insist that children who seem inclined to specialize on the mathematical and scientific side should be obliged to attend some lessons in the Humanities and *vice versa*. At this stage also, the Latin grammar, having done its work, may be dropped for those who prefer to carry on their language studies on the modern side; while those who are likely never to have any great use or aptitude for mathematics might also be allowed to rest, more or less, upon their oars. Generally speaking: whatsoever is *mere* apparatus may now be allowed to fall into the background, while the trained mind is gradually prepared for specialization in the "subjects" which, when the Trivium is completed, it should be perfectly well equipped to tackle on its own. The final synthesis of the Trivium—the presentation and public defense of the thesis—should be restored in some form; perhaps as a kind of "leaving examination" during the last term at school.

The scope of Rhetoric depends also on whether the pupil is to be turned

Imagination shows
limits of logic

out into the world at the age of 16 or whether he is to proceed to the university. Since, really, Rhetoric should be taken at about 14, the first category of pupil should study Grammar from about 9 to 11, and Dialectic from 12 to 14; his last two school years would then be devoted to Rhetoric, which, in his case, would be of a fairly specialized and vocational kind, suiting him to enter immediately upon some practical career. A pupil of the second category would finish his Dialectical course in his Preparatory School, and take Rhetoric during his first two years at his Public School. At 16, he would be ready to start upon those "subjects" which are proposed for his later study at the university: and this part of his education will correspond to the mediaeval Quadrivium. What this amounts to is that the ordinary pupil, whose formal education ends at 16, will take the Trivium only; whereas scholars will take both Trivium and Quadrivium.

The University at Sixteen?

Is the Trivium, then, a sufficient education for life? Properly taught, I believe that it should be. At the end of the Dialectic, the children will probably seem to be far behind their coevals brought up on old-fashioned "modern" methods, so far as detailed knowledge of specific subjects is concerned. But after the age of 14 they should be able to overhaul the others hand over fist. Indeed, I am not at all sure that a pupil thoroughly proficient in the Trivium would not be fit to proceed immediately to the university at the age of 16, thus proving himself the equal of his mediaeval counterpart, whose precocity astonished us at the beginning of this discussion. This, to be sure, would make hay of the English public-school system, and disconcert the universities very much. It would, for example, make quite a different thing of the Oxford and Cambridge boat-race.

But I am not here to consider the feelings of academic bodies: I am concerned only with the proper training of the mind to encounter and deal with the formidable mass of undigested problems presented to it by the modern world. For the tools of learning are the same, in any and every subject; and the person who knows

how to use them will, at any age, get the mastery of a new subject in half the time and with a quarter of the effort expended by the person who has not the tools at his command. To learn six subjects without remembering how they were learnt does nothing to ease the approach to a seventh; to have learnt and remembered the art of learning makes the approach to every subject an open door.

Educational Capital Depleted

Before concluding these necessarily very sketchy suggestions, I ought to say why I think it necessary, in these days, to go back to a discipline which we had discarded. The truth is that for the last 300 years or so we have been living upon our educational capital. The post-Renaissance world, bewildered and excited by the profusion of new "subjects" offered to

it, broke away from the old discipline (which had, indeed, become sadly dull and stereotyped in its practical application) and imagined that henceforward it could, as it were, disport itself happily in its new and extended Quadrivium without passing through the Trivium. But the scholastic tradition, though broken and maimed, still lingered in the public schools and universities: Milton, however much he protested against it, was formed by it—the debate of the Fallen Angels, and the disputation of Abdiel with Satan have the toolmarks of the Schools upon them, and might, incidentally, profitably figure as set passages for our Dialectical

studies. Right down to the nineteenth century, our public affairs were mostly managed, and our books and journals were for the most part written, by people brought up in homes, and trained in places, where that tradition was still alive in the memory and almost in the blood. Just so, many people today who are atheist or agnostic in religion, are governed in their conduct by a code of Christian ethics which is so rooted in their unconscious assumptions that it never occurs to them to question it.

Forgotten Roots

But one cannot live on capital forever. A tradition, however firmly rooted, if it is never watered, though it dies hard, yet in the end it dies. And today a great number—perhaps the majority—of the men and women who handle our affairs, write our books and our newspapers, carry out research, present our plays and our films, speak from our platforms and pulpits—yes, and who educate our young people, have never, even in a lingering traditional memory, undergone the scholastic discipline. Less and less do the children who come to be educated bring any of that tradition with them. We have lost the tools of learning—the axe and the wedge, the hammer and the saw, the chisel and the plane—that were so adaptable to all tasks. Instead of them, we have merely a set of complicated jigs, each of which will do but one task and no more, and in using which eye and hand receive no training, so that no man ever sees the work as a whole or "looks to the end of the work."

What use is it to pile task on task and prolong the days of labor, if at the close the chief object is left unattained? It is not the fault of the teachers—they work only too hard already. The combined folly of a civilization that has forgotten its own roots is forcing them to shore up the tottering weight of an educational structure that is built upon sand. They are doing for their pupils the work which the pupils themselves ought to do. For the sole true end of education is simply this: to teach men how to learn for themselves; and whatever instruction fails to do this is effort spent in vain.

The Reaction Against John Dewey

The malign role which conservatives assign to John Dewey has been exaggerated, says Max Eastman. Not so, replies Russell Kirk, if we judge his works by his own pragmatic standards

MAX EASTMAN

Theme = Socialism

Strange things happen to a man who has changed his mind in midlife on a vital question. Strictly speaking, I did not change my mind about socialism, for I always thought of it as an experiment; I became convinced during the thirties that the experiment had been sufficiently tried and had failed. The enemy of freedom, I learned, is not capitalistic business but the overgrown State.

This change was profound enough to shift me into a different group of intellectual associates and even, to a certain degree, of friends. I find myself now in the company of a group who call themselves libertarian conservatives. Many of them cherish religious notions which I regard as primitive mythology, and which I think diminish their influence, but their zeal for limited government, individualism, and a free market as the basis of other freedoms, makes our association pleasant and inevitable.

This is a long introduction to an essay on John Dewey, but it is not irrelevant. For one of the strangest things that has befallen me as a result of my changed associations is to find this early friend and wise teacher, whom I always thought of as rather painfully conservative, denounced by my political confrères as the arch-demon of radicalism. There is hardly a name, except possibly that of Karl Marx, that is more strictly anathema in the circles of the new conservatism than that of John Dewey. He is regarded as the fountain-source of every horror from teenage delinquency to the confiscatory taxes of the Welfare State. Indeed I wouldn't be surprised if a good proportion of the younger recruits to this banner think of John Dewey as the man who introduced socialism into the United States.

In my life he functioned as a stubborn and somewhat fatherly *opposition* to my youthful impulse to take up with the socialist idea.

"Society is not divided into two distinct classes, as the socialists assert," he would say.

"Yes, but by acting on the hypothesis that it is, we can *split* society in two," I would answer. "What we need is a working hypothesis, something to act on, instead of a lot of vague ideas about how things might get better."

He was never in a hurry to answer such bright but incautious ideas. He would smile indulgently and rub his chin and not say anything, but I could guess what he was thinking. I was teaching logic out of Stanley Jevons' famous book on *The Principles of Science,* and I was recklessly glib in transferring the conceptual apparatus of the physical sciences to social and psychological problems where the subject-matter is so much more mixed-up and undelimited. Dewey had, it seems to me, an opposite fault: he clung to the flux of fact with so much prudence that his

John Dewey

ideas lacked keen edges and his prose was apt to be vague and hard to remember.

At any rate, he exercised as a teacher a cooling-down influence on my revolutionary ardor. It was not until years later, in the thirties, the Red Decade, when I was traveling toward an opposite conclusion, that he came out for a "socialized economy," and for "organized social control" as a means of supporting "the liberty of individuals." He was then seventy-eight years old, and I think his life-influence, taken as a whole, was in a contrary direction. He cared primarily about the liberty of individuals, and about democracy as conceived by idealistic Americans untouched by the Marxian mystique.

The Meaning of Pragmatism

Another mistake made by many of Dewey's conservative critics is to imagine that his pragmatism, or instrumental philosophy as he preferred to call it, is a glorification of America's tough-minded practicality as against the more subtle values called "spiritual" with which other philosophies have concerned themselves. Pragmatism does, to be sure, regard scientific method as a model of the method of all valid knowledge, and if one's conservatism involves a rejection of the authority of science, Dewey's instrumental interpretation goes by the board with it. But the feat accomplished by his interpretation is not to glorify, but to mitigate, the tough or narrow practicality— above all the materialism—of certain fanatic extroverts of what is called scientism. Pragmatism builds the needs and aspirations of man into the very process of acquiring knowledge, no matter how objective, no matter how "scientific" it may be.

The meaning of an idea, according to pragmatism, is its result in action, and the true idea is the idea that, acted upon, leads to the result indicated in its meaning.

William James, in his famous lectures on *Pragmatism* (which, by the way, I had the good fortune to attend), was naive enough to infer that this justified a belief in God. If the truth is what works, he said in effect, and it works to believe that God exists, then it is true that God exists. Dewey was miles away from this facile notion. He was, moreover, primarily concerned with morals rather than religion. His original motive, as he told me more than once, was not to glorify the authority of material science, but to give moral judgments a similar authority. It was, to employ once more the illuminating terms invented by James, a "tender-minded" rather than a "tough-minded" motive. Broadly enough interpreted, it remained an underlying motive in all his philosophizing, finding its concentrated expression, if anything Dewey wrote can be called concentrated, in a paper on "The Logical Conditions of a Scientific Treatment of Morality," to be found in the Publications of the University of Chicago for 1903.

I do not myself believe in the pragmatist definition of truth, either in the mature and cogent form in which Dewey elaborated it, or in the more naive manner in which William James abandoned himself to it. But I think many of his detractors on the so-called Right are making a total mistake when they dismiss pragmatism as a philosophic attack on the values called "spiritual." It would be truer to say, although the terms are far from technical, that pragmatism in all its forms is an effort to build spirituality into science.

A Liberator of Children

On the subject of education as well as philosophy, I think the reaction against John Dewey's theories has gone beyond reasonable bounds. Undoubtedly there has grown up, under the aegis of "progressive education," a generation of rude and ill-behaved youngsters, to whom a strict training in the amenities of life, a course of implacable instruction in reading, writing and arithmetic, and where

indicated, an occasional sound spanking, would be, or would have been, an unmixed blessing. I think that an error, or a tacit assumption that is erroneous, underlies Dewey's educational theories which is to some extent responsible for this. But his insistence that children can and should be interested in what they do in school, and that discipline should be a demand that they carry through faithfully what they have set out spontaneously to do, rather than that

Max Eastman

they should do what some irrelevant ogre called "teacher" tells them to, was of immense benefit to civilization.

"A person who is trained to consider his actions, to undertake them deliberately, is in so far forth disciplined," Dewey wrote in *Democracy and Education*. "Add to this ability a power to endure in an intelligently chosen course in face of distraction, confusion, and difficulty, and you have the essence of discipline."

As a revolt against the previously prevailing notion that certain "subjects," in themselves "disciplinary," should be rammed into the brains of children at all cost to their own enterprise and adventure of living, this was a grand event. Dewey was really a liberator of children throughout the world, and as the quotation shows, liberating them did not mean letting them run wild. He was profoundly concerned, here as elsewhere, with morals. Just as in his philosophy he wanted to combine moral authority with the authority of science, so here he wanted to combine moral character and conduct with freedom of choice for the individual.

The erroneous assumption underlying his theories, as it seems to me,

is that the spontaneous interests of the human cub are to be regarded, by and large, as acceptable. They are to be taken as the starting point of education. The idea of training or disciplining the *interests,* although it is one of the first things that has to be done with a baby, does not seem to find a place when the baby goes to a Dewey school. One of the things modern biology has taught us, is that none of our distinctively civilized attributes, either voluntary or intellectual, are transmitted in heredity to our children. A certain selective breeding no doubt takes place when men become civilized, but since no one has been able to plot the direction of it, it can be assumed that the babies born today do not differ on a large scale from those born thousands of years ago. Nature is not interested in modern improvements. A civilized human being is an artifact. To make one out of the little savages we are at birth requires a moulding of the impulses, not just of the efforts we make to fulfill them.

Really a Moderate

Probably Dewey has discussed this point somewhere and it has eluded my attention, but he failed, I feel sure, to give it the emphasis I think it needs. He was carried away by the role his philosophy gave to human purposes, not only in the development of knowledge, but in the very constitution of truth. He said to me once, speaking of the Dewey school in Chicago: "I was naive enough in those days to think of the school as an experimental proof of my philosophy." Remembering that surprising remark, I have fallen to wondering whether, without being any more naive, I might not regard the excesses to which the school has led as an experimental demonstration of the error in his philosophy. They both give too high and guiding a function to the offhand volitions of this, alas, very human animal.

I trust this remark does not place me among the reactionary martinets, who want to abandon the definition of education as growth under favorable conditions, who resent the world-rejoicing discovery that children can have fun going to school—it has rejuvenated the whole family from grandpa down—or begrudge John

Dewey his place among the immortal benefactors of the human race. Like most daring innovators, he went to extremes; a period of reaction, a dimming of his world-wide fame, was inevitable; but he will ride clear of that. And meanwhile those who imagine they are dancing at the funeral of another wild radical, will be surprised if they open a book and read a few lines actually written by him, how moderate he was, how cautious, how bent on conserving as well as multiplying the finest values of life in a free society.

John Dewey Pragmatically Tested

Deweism lacks truth, value, Morality

Kirk's critique of Dewey's education

RUSSELL KIRK

It seems to me fair enough to judge a man and his works by that man's own standards. John Dewey's measure of all things was whether or not those things work in practice. So judged, the moral and educational and political philosophy of John Dewey—if, indeed, Instrumentalism is not merely the negation of philosophy —is false to the core. For it has failed catastrophically in this hard world of ours, and we stand perplexed amidst ruins. If practical success is the measure of truth—and so Dewey, in substance, declared—then Deweyism was a delusion through and through.

Mr. Max Eastman's mild defense of his old teacher and friend admits so many impeachments of Dewey's thought that I hesitate to break a butterfly on the wheel. John Dewey aspired to shape the destinies of nations: and shape this country's future he did, after an unpleasant fashion. For a man who intended— and in some sense, succeeded—to break down an order and substitute a new domination, I think a better apology is needed than merely the argument that, though wrongheaded in many matters, he was personally amiable and well-intentioned. We all know what Hell is paved with. If most of the mischief was done by Dewey's disciples, rather than by Dewey himself—well, according to the great Pragmatic Sanction, we must judge the truth of a principle by its consequences; and the worth of a theorist, I suppose, by the actions of his students.

Mr. Eastman's only very clear argument in support of his praise of Dewey as "among the immortal benefactors of the human race" is the implication that it was Dewey who made "the world-rejoicing discovery that children can have fun going to school—[which] has rejuvenated the whole family from grandpa down . . ." It seems to me, however, that this alleged modern discovery was known to good teachers from very early times indeed; all that the Deweyites have done is to carry it to excess. The fiction that all pre-Dewey schools were so many Dotheboys Halls has been widely promulgated by the Progressive Educationists; but nevertheless it is an historical falsehood. I myself went to an old-fashioned Michigan school with an old-fashioned superintendent, almost unaffected by Dewey's doctrines so late as 1936 (those notions have crept in since, sad to say); and the quantity of interest and enjoyment there, I venture to estimate, exceeded that of the average post-Dewey school.

Dr. Dewey and Mr. Eastman themselves went to old-fangled schools, I take it, and do not seem to have been permanently soured and disheartened by the experience. A perceptive friend of mine, a parent, calls the average American child of our time "bird-brained"—not that the average Progressively-schooled child is dim-witted, but that, bird-like, he flits impatiently from flower to flower, subject to subject, never pausing long enough really to understand or enjoy anything. This restless discontent, rather than true "fun," seems to me to be the product of Dewey's doctrine of child-interest. And as for gladdening the heart of grandpa by "fun in school," the grandpas I know seem more alarmed than heartened by the swaggering and bored rising generation.

Wrong on First Principles

For the rest, Mr. Eastman damns Dewey with faint praise—he wasn't a very thoroughgoing socialist, he had some concern for morals, he didn't really mean to abolish all discipline, and the rest. These negative virtues or small failings scarcely are the marks of a great philosopher. Mr. Eastman is willing enough to confess that Dewey's prose is turgid; and, as Mr. T. S. Eliot, Mr. Richard Weaver, and others have suggested, a man's style is a man's nature; and a fuzzy understanding is reflected in fuzzy writing. I do not think anyone is going to read Dewey fifty years from now; and I suspect that his very name, by that time, will be as vague and rather comical to scholars as Benjamin Kidd's, let us say, is to us nowadays.

For John Dewey went wrong on first principles—or rather, by denying the validity of first principles. Serving himself from the wisdom of our ancestors—from revelation, traditions, norms, and great imaginative literature—he was left with nothing better than a vague humanitarianism, which he endeavored to erect into a system of morals and politics—to con-

Russell Kirk

Metaphysical TRUTH

vert into a religion, indeed. The "Religious Humanist Manifesto" got up by Dewey and his friends was neither religious nor humanistic; but it was an attempt, as Mr. Eastman suggests, to make religion and morals "scientific"—by reducing them to the condition of mere social phenomena. In this, as in much else, he borrowed from Bentham and the Utilitarian school: as, indeed did Karl Marx. This Americanized Utilitarianism, which seems to be Mr. Eastman's own present creed (as expounded in *Reflections on the Failure of Socialism*) is, as Newman said, a philosophy of death; there is nothing in it to give men hope or comfort; and whatever ethical content it retains is no more than a vestige of the Christian morals from which it dissents. But the pretense that this utilitarian morality was somehow "practical," "realistic," and "useful" appealed to the American dislike for theory and for the supernatural which Tocqueville observed in the 1830's; and thus Deweyism gained, for the time, a hold which is only now relaxing.

Dullness and Prestige

It is Dewey's very dullness and lack of imagination, indeed, which chiefly has contributed toward his success with the dull and sterile clique of educationists who exert "the stranglehold on education." A real philosopher they could not understand; they could make nothing of a cultivated skeptic like Santayana, let alone a man of genius like Newman. A philosopher or philodoxer, I repeat, generally is justly measured by the quality of his disciples. Socrates attracted Plato; Cicero, the great jurisconsults; Burke, Coleridge; and Dewey—why, the intolerant knot of little-minded high-school principals who would ban from school libraries any popular magazine that ventures to suggest our schools may be imperfect. As madness often brings a temporary success in times of revolution, so dullness often carries with it some prestige in decades of smugness; and Dewey's American generation was wondrously smug, even when it tried to be revolutionary.

The dangerous emptiness of Dewey's system has been sufficiently criticized by Professor Eliseo Vivas. Here I venture only to suggest the

fundamental misconceptions which insured that Dewey's own good-natured doctrines would pass into the keeping of "life adjustment" doctrinaires and "social reconstruction" ideologues. And it seems to me that Mr. Eastman, a man still better natured than his mentor, continues to subscribe to these doctrines: notions which, if generally triumphant in society, would utterly subvert the ideals of individuality, ordered freedom, and variety which Mr. Eastman inconsistently cherishes.

Three Illusions

The first illusion upon which I touch is the conviction of Dewey—and Eastman—that our received "religious notions" are "primitive mythology," to be beneficently supplanted by a new morality with the "authority of science." This is a remnant of what Dr. Eric Voegelin calls "the trauma of the Enlightenment," a vestigial eighteenth-century rationalism that Hume sufficiently undid nearly two centuries ago. St. Paul, St. Augustine, St. Thomas Aquinas, Bossuet, Samuel Johnson and John Henry Newman were not primitives. To presume that the physical and biological sciences, the creations—but the limited creations—of modern ingenuity, can operate in the realm of the transcendent is as shallow as to argue that the frescoes of Michelangelo can be sufficiently described by a chemical analysis of the paints he used. The "authority" of science is only the opinions of certain fallible students of science; and those students have changed their own opinions in their own special fields radically, again and again, within the present century. This is the "authority" of Dr. Alfred Kinsey to transfer taxonomic assumptions to human beings in the civil social order —to argue, with a wonderful naiveté, that law for snake and bee is law for man. There remains, of course, the word "science" in its larger meaning, as all systematic knowledge, of which theology is a part; but this science writ large is not what Dewey and Eastman have in mind. It is not "scientific" authority which endures. The authority of Socrates, a moralist, is valid still; but the authority of Newton, a scientist of genius, is pretty thoroughly shattered in our time. "To

build spirituality into science" is lost endeavor, with the tools now at our disposal—the more so when a philosopher has only the foggiest notion of what "spirituality" means.

A second illusion is the tendency of Dewey, and of Eastman, to erect a mundane condition into an absolute; to seek some secular, immanent makeshift for religious belief; to substitute an institution for a truth. With Dewey, the substitute was Democracy; with Eastman, it now appears to be Capitalism. When the descriptive terms of politics or economics are elevated to the estate of god-terms, political and moral philosophy go out the window. Democracy and Capitalism are not absolutes; they are, at best, means to an end, and means with mingled virtues and vices. To be equal, or to be rich, is not the goal of human life. If means are treated as ends, thought and society fall into confusion. Such a state of affairs breeds the fanaticism of ideology. It is no accident that a collectivist like Professor Theodore Brameld is influenced by Dewey: this is the natural descent, the logical consequence, of "Progressive" educationist doctrines. For those doctrines are founded upon a fallacy. The true purpose of schooling is not to teach young people to "adjust to society" or to "adjust to life" or to "create a better world." The true purpose of formal education is to develop the truly human person, intellectually and ethically, for the private person's own sake.

A third illusion is the eagerness of Dewey—and, to a lesser extent, of Eastman—to cast aside theory, tradition, precedent, and history for the sake of experiment: to trust to a moment-to-moment, year-to-year pressing forward, in the expectation that something good is sure to come of Progress, and that any unpleasant consequences of the experiment may be written off as so many incidental slight errors, easily compensated for. This comes of the ingenuous transfer of laboratory techniques to the vast and unpredictable complex of human society, and entails perils of which, Mr. Eastman signifies, he has become somewhat aware.

Now the educational system of a people is a field in which this "Instrumentalism" is especially dangerous. Education is the formal means

[handwritten annotations:]

[right margin:] 2

[right margin:] 3

[right margin:] 3= Disregarding History for experiment

[bottom margin:] Problems w/ Dewey

[bottom margin:] 1= Thinks Rlgn is myth   2= Substitutes institutions for Truth (Dmocy for Rlgn) = loss of Morality

for transmitting culture. Culture is built up slowly and painfully, over the ages, by an elaborate process; and it is preserved, and extended, by certain subtle disciplines of mind and character, expressed in a people's theology, in their poetry, in their historical literature, in custom and habit and precedent. Disciplines so comparatively simple as reading and writing and figuring are dependent upon a continuity of method and training. When that continuity is snapped by the imprudent reformer, it may be extremely difficult—and sometimes next to impossible—to atone for the blunder. It is terribly hard to revive classical studies, for instance—supposing that classical studies become respectable once more after long neglect—when (as in 1957) only two persons in the whole of the United States are awarded doctorates in Greek. It is no less difficult to revive sound historical studies when the very teachers have lost interest in their vocation; or to revive decent manners in a mannerless generation. For society is not an inanimate substance on a laboratory table. Society is vital, with a spiritual unity; and if it is treated as so much lifeless flesh on the butcher's block, the best intentions of the kindest pragmatic reformer will not restore society's continuity. The reformer, as Santayana writes, never knows how close to the root of the tree he may be hacking. Dewey hacked hard at the roots of our educational system.

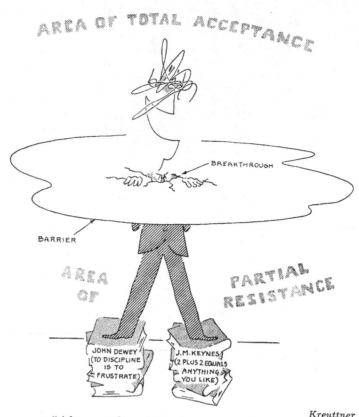

AREA OF TOTAL ACCEPTANCE

BREAKTHROUGH

BARRIER

AREA OF

PARTIAL RESISTANCE

JOHN DEWEY (TO DISCIPLINE IS TO FRUSTRATE)

J.M.KEYNES (2 PLUS 2 EQUALS ANYTHING YOU LIKE)

Kreuttner

"Ask me anything, but make your question complex, so that my answer can be inconclusive. I'm so intellectual I can't understand simple sentences!"

So I do not think that posterity will bless John Dewey. The reaction against his ideas is healthy. As the late Roy Campbell said, the body that cannot react is a corpse. That we still can react against Instrumentalism is some sign that there is sense in this nation yet.

The Dirtiest Word in the Language

If you happen to be a white, Protestant American of Scottish, British, Welsh or even Dutch descent, well then, brother, you've had it

MORRIE RYSKIND

You can't—at any rate, *I* can't—formulate a precise definition of obscenity: there are too many intangibles involved. The saltiness of Chaucer and Rabelais can make me chuckle with delight, while Norman Mailer's use of the same or equivalent expressions sickens me and Tennessee Williams can drive me out of the theater.

This can't be entirely because I'm just a dirty old four-letter-word reactionary, and Chaucer and Rabelais belonged to the horse-and-buggy era whereas Mailer and Williams are the heralds of the Bright New Realism. It has something to do, I insist, with the fact that Chaucer and Rabelais were artists, while Mailer and Williams are merely sensationalists. With

Messrs. C. and R., the words seem not only right but inevitable; with Messrs. M. and W., I have the uneasy feeling that some nasty brats are chalking up the sidewalk.

Similarly, Mae West and Sophie Tucker of the night clubs can make me ill as they describe—with bumps —the kind of men who appeal to them. The impish Joe E. Lewis, on the other hand, can say almost anything —and, come to think of it, he *does*— and make me guffaw. The answer, I suppose, is—if I may venture a bilingual pun that I pray hasn't been used before—*disgustibus non disputandum est.*

But the dirtiest four-letter word of all is rarely to be found on the night club circuit, or even in the pages of *Peyton Place.* You are much more likely to come across it, I regret to say, at a PTA or a League of Women Voters meeting. And this one is so dirty, in fact, that it has *eight* letters in it.

The word, of course, is "minority." Basically a good, sound word, it has been so perverted and debased by the pressure groups and the politicos that I shudder every time I hear it. Its new—and obscene—implications fill me with loathing, and I'd like to root it out of the language once and for all.

You see, I was brought up on Noah Webster and Euclid; and to me a rose is a rose. Though I was progressive enough, when Gertrude Stein came along, to accept a rose is a rose is a rose. So far I will go, but no further. Put up your dukes, because I'm coming out swinging when you tell me a rose is a weed that smells like a skunk in full bloom.

And that's about what they've done with "minority." If you're a member of the minority in this country today, you're one of the largest collection of human beings ever lumped under one banner. You take all the Catholics, Jews, Negroes, Poles, Italians, Hungarians, Mexicans, Puerto Ricans and Nisei in America and what have you got? Any demagogue can tell you: the downtrodden, underprivileged, poorly-housed, underpaid, overworked, segregated two-thirds of a nation, just barely able to keep body and soul and maybe fifty different lobbies alive—that's what you've got. Viewing this sorry spectacle, what candidate for public office can resist mounting a soap-box and promising, as the tears stream down his face, that he will, if elected, do something at the next session to undo man's inhumanity to man? (True, Grover Cleveland might have told the lobbyists to go fly a kite, but there aren't any 'Clevelands around today; no modern Administration would dare make a remark

of that sort unless it had arranged, under the Department of Health, Education and Welfare, for the immediate distribution of free kites to all the needy, kiteless children of the country, with scholarships to Cal. Tech. and MIT for the kids adjudged the best kite-flyers. After all, we need scientists and that's the way Benjamin Franklin started, wasn't it? And you could do the whole thing for only about $25 billion. To start with, that is.)

What makes the situation even worse is that every member of this gigantic minority, except for a mere handful of renegades, is, *ipso facto,* the noblest of all God's creations. You don't have to do anything special to be thus haloed; mere religion or ancestry is enough, and there is ample literature from such authorities as UNESCO, the NAACP, and B'nai Brith to prove it. Not to mention any speech made *any*where before *any*body by Jimmy Roosevelt, Hubert Humphrey, Adam Clayton Powell Jr. or Jacob K. Javits.

These truths have become so self-evident that they have entered our folklore, even to the extent of destroying some of the fun of guessing who dun it. Book or movie or play, if a fellow attends mass or observes Yom Kippur, you can rule him out immediately no matter *what* the circumstantial evidence indicates. Likewise, if he's colored or Mexican, he had nothing to do with the murder of the nice old lady. But if he's a white Baptist · or Presbyterian or Methodist, this is your man. And five will get you ten that his unscrupulous mouthpiece, who uses his shrewd knowledge of the law only to evade it, is an Episcopalian.

But perhaps the most important contribution made by the interlocking directorate of the Minority Lobby—I rank it second only to John Kreuttner's famous cartoon exposing the anthropological "differences" allegedly existing between various ethnic groups—is in the matter of speech patterns. Every Negro, every Irishman, every Jewish refugee—no matter how late he came to our shores—speaks flawless English in the cultivated tones of an Oxford Don. Indeed, if you close your eyes, you are certain it is Churchill talking.

This is all to the good because it means that racist writers like Stephen Foster, Roark Bradford, Finley Peter Dunne and Montague Glass are not only dead but permanently buried —and with them the so-called comics who betrayed their birthright for gold. When I think of the incredible harm that Potash and Perlmutter and Mr. Dooley and Ol' Man Adam did to our international relations: how Africa was revolted by Bert Williams, how East Germany shuddered at Lew Fields and Barney Bernard, how they rioted in Scotland and Indonesia when Harry Lauder sang, "It's a Braw Bricht Moonlicht Nicht" at the Palace, I can only wonder whether the pure joy these performers gave us was worth it.

Only Rochester and the Kingfish— bless them!—survive. And please don't confuse the laughter and applause they get with the real feelings of the audience, which is only demonstrating its superiority complex. Secretly, it wants to lynch them. Indeed, the late Walter White once told me that he was doing everything he could to have Rochester banned from the screen, because of the injury he was doing to the colored race. At that time, I confess, I thought that Rochester, in his own way, was doing more good than Mr. White.

But you learn. For example, I've given up completely the notion of doing a screenplay about my grandfather, whom I adored. He was a tall six-footer with an orthodox beard that was at least five foot seven, and there are a lot of anecdotes about him that might have made an enjoyable hour or so. But—let's face it—he spoke very little English, and, when he did, it didn't sound a bit like Churchill. And who's going to buy *that?*

Nobody, of course. Not while the New Lexicographers rule the roost. The word-changers must be driven out of the temples, and with them must go the compulsory collectivism that has forced the rest of us to pay involuntary tribute to them. On that proud day, an American—white or black, Jew or Gentile, of Mexican or Polish or whatnot descent—can again be an American and an individual, and not a member of a hydra-headed, parasitic and obscene minority.

The Hissiad: A Correction

The author of *Witness* denies saying Alger Hiss 'has paid his penalty.' Far from it: 'The wound is there, and its poisons continue to drain through the system.'

WHITTAKER CHAMBERS

The ever-helpful press has been at it again, this time in the matter of Alger Hiss' decision to go to Europe, and the State Department's decision to issue him a passport for the purpose. Press treatment of this news reached a fine blossom in the paragraph with which *Newsweek* (April 20) wound up its story about the Hissiad: "At the weekend, endorsement of Hiss' travel plans came from an unexpected source. 'Alger Hiss is an American citizen who has paid his penalty for the crime of perjury,' said Whittaker Chambers. 'He has every right to apply for and receive a passport.'"

Whatever the intention, the effect of this paragraph is mischievous. Still, left to myself, I should probably have let it pass without comment. Why single out one item more than another from the quota of distortion that daily passes for news? But good friends insist that this one will deeply puzzle, and even dismay, many people. I am afraid that anybody of whom this may be true is in for a good deal of nervous shock, though for better cause, before this century ends. But I also agree that there are matters about which people have a right not to be puzzled and dismayed unnecessarily. So, for what good it may do, here goes.

Newsweek's paragraph begins with a fumble ("endorsement"), and ends, I am afraid, with a misquotation. Perhaps it can be said of *government* that it "endorsed" "Hiss' travel plans" to the extent that issuance of a passport supposes a considered decision. It cannot possibly be said of me. I have no competence whatever to "endorse" the Hiss plans, no means, no desire; nor, for that matter, any particular interest in a project about which I know nothing beyond the wispy report. I may (and do) speculate that this journey was a predictable next step in that public reorbiting of Mr. Hiss which is so precious a cause to his partisans, among them certain fairly formidable national figures. Beyond that speculation, the report that Alger Hiss is going abroad excites me no more than the news that several thousand other tourists are, even now, poised for the annual pilgrimage ("Ah, Venice—the Leaning Tower!")

Of course, I was aware from the first buzz what fanciful chigger would be inflaming the press just below the skin. For have we, even yet, learned anything that matters about these things, and how they work, and why? I seriously doubt it. Anyway, telephoning newsmen promptly produced the expected chigger in the form of the expected question: "Is *he* going behind 'the Iron Curtain'?" I said: "Of course, *he* isn't going behind 'the Iron Curtain'." Question: "Why do you say that?" Answer: "I must ask you not to press me on the point. You can easily figure it out for yourself." In short, if, for a decade, and in spite of everything, you had been insisting that you never were a Communist, you would scarcely, at first chance, streak for the Communist Empire. Mr. Hiss could find little that would serve his turn in going to Moscow; and neither would Moscow.

My guess would be that Hiss will home on London, to lay a wreath (figurative, at least) on the grave of the late Lord Chief Justice, who, for somewhat cryptic cause, was moved to write a handsomely slanted book in his favor. In Britain, Hiss has long had many partisans, literate, righteous, opinionated, and, in this case, completely muddled, as only clever English minds can sometimes be. There will be an epergne on the luncheon table.

Now to that part of *Newsweek's* paragraph in which I claim to be misquoted. It consists of the words: "[Alger Hiss] has paid his penalty for the crime of perjury." I do not believe that I said this because I do not believe it (except in the shallowest legalistic sense) to be true. So I am as certain as anyone can be, in the absence of transcript, that I could not have said it, even in the haste and annoyance of answering foolish questions. That is not the way the matter presents itself to my mind.

Hiss and the Truth

History and a lengthening lifetime have left me too uncertain on the general subject of society, and the question of debts to it, or penalties, for me to have put the case like that. Society and the least man in it are too bafflingly manifold, the chances of birth and heredity, of time, place, environment and history, too incalculable, for such easy packaging. Moreover, the Scriptural injunction not to judge is not only compassionate; it is almost self-servingly prudent. We never pass judgment on anything or anybody without, by that act, in the same instant, defining our own human limitation. The act of judging always, mercilessly, judges, first of all, ourselves.

Of course, it is true—life does not permit us to live, for the most part, in such terms. We live on the world's terms, and act within their web of reverend compromises. But, in those terms, I can think of few men of whom it seems to me less possible to say that he has paid any effective penalty than Alger Hiss. In his case, a penalty was exacted, and a suffering was incurred. But the horror of it derives only in the last instance (though it sounds heartless to say so). from Hiss' suffering as an individual man. The true horror of it lies in the fact that, on his side, the penalty and the suffering were sheer waste. There is only one main debt, and one possible payment of it, as I see it, in his case. It is to speak the truth. That, to this hour, he has defiantly refused to do. Worse, he has spent much time and contrivance to undo the truth.

If this were a matter touching only him and me, it might be of little moment. Obviously, it goes far beyond any individual man. We are not playing games; we are dealing with the lives of "children's children" in the world we are preparing for them. There are insurrectionists of the 1956 revolt, sitting in Hungarian jails, and in the night that falls when hope fails absolutely, whose fate is touched by Hiss' defiance. And I find it difficult in the extreme to understand how certain of his perfervid partisans can pay lip-service to those resisters and their cause, and not make the basic equation between his defiance and their suffering. Beside it, his own, however immeasurable, loses scale. "With every dawn," Camus tells us of our time, "masked assassins slip into some cell; murder is the question before us." An historic lie on this scale helps turn the key that lets the murderers in.

A Central Lesion

But we do not need to travel so far as Budapest. That celebrated defiance touches much closer home. It divides the minds of some of the best men and women among us at a point on which, in this juncture of the human crisis, they need to be (and we need that they should be) most clear: the point of truth. Hiss' defiance perpetuates and keeps from healing a fracture in the community as a whole. And this is particularly true of that part of the community which is (or should be) the custodian and articulator of its collective virtue, i.e., its mind. For when you accept a lie and call it truth, you have poisoned truth at the source, and everything else is sickened with a little of that poison. If you are looking for its monument, look around you.

You may say that all this is past and tiresome, try to sweep it largely out of sight and mind, and resolve briskly to get on to more pressing things. Your resolution remains chiefly bustle. The least, brushing touch (like this of Hiss' travels) shows that the wound is there, and fresh, and that its poisons continue to drain through the system. That is why the Hiss Case, though it has become modish in certain circles to glance away, though its dimensions in themselves are small among so many greater lesions, remains a central lesion of our time. That is why, ultimately, I cannot say (however differently I should prefer to get at it, at another level) that Alger Hiss has paid any effective penalty. For precisely he can end the lesion at any moment that he chooses, with half a dozen words.

Freedom to Travel

So much for that part of the direct quotation which I claim to be misquoted, and which, in any case, does not reflect my view. The rest of the quotation is fairly reported: "Alger Hiss is an American citizen. He has every right to apply for and receive a passport." This *does* reflect my view, though it was chiefly chance that it was said about Alger Hiss. I suspect that the misleading words were inserted (no doubt, with the best intention) by some newsman, trying to explain, for his own heart's ease, and his readers', how so bizarre a view came to be held by me.

The reason, if dismaying to some, is simpler than the one dreamed up. I am a bug on the question of unrestricted travel, as I am against the obscenities of wire-tapping, mail tampering, and related mischiefs that, in the name of good intention, are helping to pave the road that leads to 1984. I hold strongly that it is a right of man and of the citizen to travel freely where and when he will, and that any extensive restriction of that right is among the usurpations that feed the Total State. Of course, I know the arguments from expediency; here security is "the question before us." I have seen scarcely a shred of evidence, by contrast with the many sweeping arguments, that convinces me on this score. It is not the known Communists whose travels need greatly alarm us. Let them travel where they will, and let us observe their travels. They will take us to their leader, and possibly many NCO's en route. A dozen secret services, not only ours, must exist to watch them. It is the unknown Communist (or sympathizer) whose travels may work us harm; and to him a passport would be issued without question, in any case, because we do not know who or what he is.

So strong has this argument from expediency (or fear) become, that we have all but forgotten how recent travel restriction is. My generation grew up in an almost passportless world. In those days, the Russian Autocracy and the Turkish Sultanate were considered semi-barbarous, in part because almost alone, they inflicted on their nationals the uncivilized indignity of passports. To me, travel restriction seems chiefly to multiply the files behind which bureaucracies always gratefully barricade and entrench their positions, and fiercely defend them.

No doubt, in some quarters on the Right, such views will put me in a lonely minority. I can only urge most careful reflection on the matter. A little shift in the political weather, and it may be the spokesmen of the Right whose freedom of travel is restricted—with a certain smugness. The grounds will be expediency, of course. The precedent will be almost unassailable. Anti-Communists will have promoted it.

I think I can hear a crescent rumble rising: "Why, the man is talking like a Liberal." I have scarcely any interest in invective tags. My concern is not for the political geography of this or that position, but whether or not the position taken makes sense, and is, to that degree, as we say: justified. And of course I know too: Woe to those who grope for reality, and any approximate truth that may be generalized from it, in the No Man's Land between incensed camps. History and certain personal experiences leave me in little doubt about the fate of such seekers. They are fair game to the snipers of both sides, and it is always open season. But while Mr. Hiss hurries to his plane or ship, and the snipers wait for the man to reach, in his groping, the point where the hairlines cross on their sights, I may still have time to sort the dead cats into tidy piles—those from one camp, here; those from the other, there. As one of my great contemporaries put it: "Anybody looking for a quiet life has picked the wrong century to be born in." The remark must be allowed a certain authority, I think, since the century clinched the point by mauling with an axe the brain that framed it.

Roots of the Liberal Complacency

Today's Liberal seems supremely confident.
But beneath his complacency lies moral and
intellectual flabbiness

RICHARD M. WEAVER

That today's Liberal is marked by complacency will appear to some a paradoxical charge. Most Liberals may shrug it off as something which, in the nature of things, cannot be imputed to them. Does not the Liberal creed make criticism of any and all matters a cardinal point? Does it not invite the free competition of ideas in the market place? Has not the Liberal set up a kind of eternal restlessness of the mind as the only enlightened condition?

Until fairly recently one's answer to all of these might have been yes. But the question today is whether the Liberal has not succumbed to certain fallacies of unwarranted assumption, which is the father of complacency. It is not an unknown thing to have the very vices one is opposing slip up on one from the rear in some pleasant disguise. This the Liberal has done, it seems to me, by not being truly circumspect, and by giving in to certain weaknesses which may be in themselves neither liberal nor radical nor conservative, but are human. A fault cutting across all of these is graver than any a mere political *ism* can remove. This means, if true, that the Liberal is now beyond the ministrations of anything save logic and ethics.

To see this complacency, one has only to look at the present generation of academic Liberals. One marks the telltale signs of indifference, of arrogance, of pomposity in their attitudes and their literature. They are very confident of their rightness that nothing is permanently right. This does not keep them, however, from blandly making their dispositions on the theory that the conservative opposition has been permanently routed. Many of them would be surprised to learn that their attitude can be as maddening to the conservative who has found his conservatism the hard way as the incapacity of a Bourbon to learn anything once was to advocates of the rights of man.

The complacency of this new, and often well-heeled, Liberal is fed by a number of roots.

The Liberal has become, to all intents and purposes, a materialist. I do not pretend to use the term "materialism" here in a strict philosophical sense. I mean simply that the Liberal is now inclined to accept wholly the objectives of an efficient material civilization and to judge policies in their relation to the "standard of living." One sees his willingness to carry statism to any length whatever to universalize this standard of living. Writing a few years ago in the *Atlantic Monthly*, Joseph S. Clark, Jr., graduate of Harvard *magna cum laude*, then Mayor of Philadelphia, and now United States Senator, offered this curious definition of the Liberal:

> To lay a ghost at the outset and dismiss semantics, a Liberal is here defined as one who believes in utilizing the full force of government for the advancement of social, political, and economic justice at the municipal, state, national, and international levels.

Nowhere else have I seen so naked a profession of new Liberalism, or one which shows better how far this has gone toward embracing the statism to which nineteenth-century Liberals were, in the name of liberty, most opposed. (The confusion at which Mr. Clark hints is not one of semantics, but one of historical about-face.) The last phrase of the definition leads of course to Point Four thinking, to the materialist illusion that envy, hatred, and violence can be removed from the globe by handouts, by "economic assistance," and by making the "underprivileged" nations of the world urban, industrialized, motorized, and sanitized in an equal degree with Detroit and Los Angeles.

A natural consequence of this is the Liberal's idealization of comfort. He shows a definite antagonism toward all strenuous ideals of life. The code of the warrior, of the priest, and even of the scholar, denying the self for transcendent ends, stands in the new lexicon as anti-Liberal. The working day of a Thomas Jefferson or a Theodore Roosevelt would actually be an affront to the Liberal code. "For they are moderate also even in virtue—because they want comfort," says Nietzsche in *Thus Spake Zarathustra*. He goes on to add that the noble man does not want anything from life gratuitously. But today popularity is substituted for greatness and conformity for heroism. The Liberal preaches an altruism that is sentimental, and he is therefore hostile to all demands that the individual be something more than his natural, indolent, ease-loving, and complacent self.

More damage has resulted from this materialism and its attendant attitudes than from anything else the Liberal has spread. In the first place, is falsifies reality for the masses by leaving out of account the world of ideas and telic concepts which are alone capable of giving to societies a lasting cohesion. In the second place, by setting up comfort as the highest good, it leaves shut up the greatest of all reservoirs of strength, the will to sacrifice for the advancement of some noble good. Thus by its unwarranted assumption it misleads on the one hand, and on the other it stultifies.

Quite likely the Liberal has been betrayed into this by his scientism. Scientism is itself an unwarranted assumption which lends a plausible kind of support to the attitudes described above. Since it is derived from certain propositions about the nature of the world, it requires a little introducing.

Science exists in the form of a set of methods. That the application of these methods has wrought transformations in the outward world is the most ubiquitous fact of our time.

74

What is not so well understood, however, is the effect of this practical success upon the more general theory of reality and knowledge. Until rather recently it was generally held that subject matter is prior to method. But in the last few decades, this position has been reversed, and it is now being said, or assumed, that method is prior to subject matter. This comes from the premise that nothing which cannot be found by the scientific method is real, which is of course the position of modern positivism. What happened in the process of this shift was that methodology became the ontological absolute; things are real in proportion to their capacity for being discovered by the scientific method. Here is a complete victory for instrumentalism whereby, in effect, a methodology makes reality as it proceeds with the act of discovering. So John Dewey could argue that the instruments of inquiry not only inquire, they also determine what can be inquired into. In the old order of knowledge, this latter was a datum provided by God, or at least by the empirical fact of creation.

The effect of this on man's attitude toward the world can be nothing less than revolutionary, and in some quarters it has already been disastrous. For what it does is rule out the given, the contingent, the inscrutable—in sum, all that is greater than or independent of man. The ground for that humility which all the great ethical systems have inculcated is thereby withdrawn. Man, with his Method, leaps into the seat of the Creator, which, in the wisdom of poetry and religion, is the ultimate act of pride.

Hence it comes to be believed that there are no problems which cannot be solved by the methods of science because, in terms of the concept itself, such problems cannot exist. A problem to be conceived at all has to be conceived as something which this ontologically prior set of methods could solve. From this now widely held assumption comes the Liberal's complacent belief that all the situations produced by selfishness, ill will, and violence can be removed once science, with its omnicompetent methodology, gets around to them.

Nowhere has the effect of this belief been more manifest than in "progressive" education, which was the first .practical victim of the heresy. There, as every observer of the movement knows, subject matter, representing the antecedently real, has been virtually retired in favor of methodology. The teacher is not a man who knows facts and ideas but a man trained in method. It is assumed that there is nothing which the method cannot do. When stubborn facts of the given world—such as inequalities of aptitude or the human tendency toward delinquency—stand in the way of the triumph of the method, they are either ignored or misleadingly reported. For these educational positivists there is no nature of man, but only some pliable stuff which can be kneaded into any desired shape by the principles of a materialist psychology.

The Liberals' Alogism

Despite the seeming sophistication of this theory, most Liberals today are not real intellectuals, and their lack of real intellectualism leaves them complacent where wiser men are alert and discerning. When one considers the extent to which they preponderate on college faculties and the extent to which they control the means of publishing ideas, this may appear an audacious statement. But a study of his literature will show that an alogism has turned the Liberal unavoidably down the road toward anti-intellectualism. By alogism I mean a rejection of logical rigor and a complacency in the face of contradiction.

One of the chief directives of Liberalism is to deny the existence of either-or choices. The Liberal insists on substituting the "both-and" choice, which keeps him from ever having to accept or reject flatly. This is why he ends up in the "middle of the road." A desire to squeeze in between two contradictories keeps the Liberal from seeing anything with clarity. At the same time, it leads to a breaking down of categories, so that in the final result he has nothing to think with. It leads to a politics of truces, compromises, and even sellouts. There is a difference between saying that there are no clear-cut principles of right and wrong and saying that a principle cannot always be applied with rigor in a world that is concrete and vari-

ous. The latter is the policy of all men of sense and experience, but it is prudence, or what the Greeks called *sophrosyne,* not "liberalism."

It is the sentimentality of the new Liberal which leaves him incapable of accepting rigid exclusion. He does not like to think that God and the devil are irreconcilable. He thinks that with a little patient explaining and some of his famous tolerance, each could be brought to see some good in the other. In brief, he does not contemplate a right and a wrong.

This propensity to moral and intellectual flabbiness on the part of the Liberal leads to an inordinate fear of a certain type of man, of whom Taft and MacArthur are good examples. Such men reveal, by the very logic of their expression, that they think in terms of inclusion and exclusion. Their mentality rejects cant, snivelling, and double talk. When they speak, one knows that he is listening to a man, in the eulogistic sense in which Emerson and Thoreau used that word. There is, in fact, a great deal to be inferred from the almost hysterical reaction that the man of Plutarchan mold inspires in the Liberals. There must be present a hidden anxiety, born of a knowledge that they will be helpless when the leader of character and conviction comes along, as he must. Hence the voluminous outpouring, from supercilious dismissal to vituperation, whenever an individual of clear mind and strong personality appears on the scene and begins to gather strength. On these occasions, the Liberals' complacency is succeeded by, one might say, a fear for their complacency.

Despite these occasional disturbances of his peace, however, the Liberal feels most of the time that he is protected by an invincible dogma. I use "dogma" here in the etymological sense of "opinion." And the opinion is that today everyone must be a Liberal. This can be seen easily enough in the tone of the popular press, in the philosophy of Progress, and in the cult of scientism. But one finds it entrenched also in sources that are more decisive, in the sense that they furnish the reasoning behind the more popular expressions.

Here it appears in the form of a proposition that liberalism represents a new level of the human consciousness which will never be given up. It is the hidden premise of numberless college textbooks. It is evident in the judicial philosophy of Oliver Wendell Holmes, with its repudiation of "fighting faiths" and its belief that truth is something relative to the demands of the market place. It becomes mandatory, consequently, to oppose all fixed truths and traditional formulations—indeed, all universals—and this on the principle that humanity has found absolutely that they won't work. Even so otherwise discerning a philosopher as Ortega has declared that today all men are Liberals in the sense of sharing this opinion.

One striking result of the dogma in our country today is the complacent assumption that both political parties must be "liberal." It used to be felt that one political party was enough to represent the point of view that is Liberalism; now some of our political leaders say by their acts, if not by their very words, that a party must be Liberal to deserve consideration by the electorate.

Hence the astonishing efforts in the last few years to transform the Republican Party, which in the main has stood for a conservative approach to economic and political questions, into a second "Liberal" party in plain emulation of the Democratic. It is this carbon-copy Liberalism of the "new Republican" leadership which has led candid observers to point out that the American people today do not have a real choice on the major issues confronting them. One alternative is being deliberately withheld. So the American voter is left with the opportunity of voting "ja" for Democratic Liberalism or "ja" for Republican Liberalism. The engineers of this maneuver are assuming that Liberalism, like the Constitution, is antecedent to citizenship; you do not vote for it or against it; you vote only after you have taken a pledge to accept it. This is tantamount to assuming that Liberalism is something no longer within the area of debate, but is rather a part of our organic law. Almost needless to say, recent Supreme Court decisions seem to reflect the assumption.

So successful have the Liberals been in establishing this dogma through education, publishing, and politics that people today are literally unable to understand the language of the conservative point of view. They can conceive neither the meaning of its terms nor the spirit of it. No one has expressed this better, or with more ominous suggestion, than George Santayana.

Modern civilization has an immense momentum, not only physically irresistible but morally and socially dominant in the press, politics, and literature of the Liberal classes; yet the voice of a dispossessed and forlorn orthodoxy, prophesying evil, cannot be silenced, and what renders that voice the more disquieting is that it can no longer be understood. When the prophets or apologists of the modern world attempt to refute those vaticinations, they altogether miss fire, because of their incapacity to conceive what they attack; and even in the exposition of their own case they are terribly confused and divided.

These are faults of the mind and the moral consciousness.

And Then the Bureaucracy

Finally one has to recognize a massive circumstance which has played into the hands of the Liberals. This is the bureaucratization of American life. It is a fact of paramount significance that our contemporary world is dominated by three large, and in some ways comparable, bureaucracies. They are the bureaucracy of government, the bureaucracy of business, and the bureaucracy of education. It is also of paramount significance that these bureaucracies are fed by our educational institutions. This means that most of the members, and certainly nearly all of the upper bureaucrats, will have received the proper indoctrination before they reach their posts. The government bureaucrats will have been taught that the state is destined to grow larger and larger and to gather to itself more and more of the national income. The business managers will have been given a pap which tells them that business is for "service" and not for profit, that owners and managers are only "trustees" of the employees, and so on. And the educational bureaucrats will have been taught that the main concern of education is with democracy and that its immediate task is to speed the evolution of society into a collectivized state. With this formidable apparatus for inculcating and enforcing an orthodoxy, it is little wonder that the Liberals do act as an Establishment. This is why anyone who speaks up in the name of individualism and privacy, and the right of men to win distinction through the exercise of intelligence and energy is likely to find himself solitary and forlorn.

This is a practical circumstance supporting the Liberal complacency, but its effects are far-reaching. The Liberals now operate the training schools for the managerial classes. When it is realized how much the advocates of "progressive" education have been able to do by compulsorily routing all future public school teachers through their highly tendentious curricula, we will not overlook what the Liberals are able to do in their indoctrination centers, which today seem to include most departments in most universities. Here the young person is taught an attitude toward the state which is not Liberal, but servile. He is thereby prepared for the further bureaucratizing of life.

If Liberalism stemmed out of some deeply anchored and coherent philosophy, if it expressed some compelling vision of existence, we could not apply the term "complacency" to the attitude it has engendered. We might speak instead of conviction and tradition and find some satisfaction in the prevalence of settled views. But "conviction" is just the word one must never use in connection with the modern Liberal. His conviction is that there are no convictions—or that convictions are "prejudices"—his belief that there are no enduring beliefs, and his truth a pervasive skepticism. Even his "dogma" has root only in the circumstance that he is now ascendant.

It is this non-committal attitude toward all the positive issues of life that keeps Liberalism from rising to the dignity of a philosophy which might unify an epoch and provide ground for constructive creations. With its lack of attachment to anything except its own relativism and tentative success, it cannot manage, with all its thousand tongues, anything better than superficial and often contradictory observations about its own chaotic world.

Does Not apply at all.
A liberal dream at best

How to Raise Money in the Ivy League

ALOISE HEATH

There Communists in faculty @ university

If you want the old (and young) grads to go over the top for Alma Mater, just present them, as did this Smith alumna, with documented proof that the Best College in the World harbors pink professors

Some morning last month, each of several million Americans refilled his coffee cup, lit his second cigarette and opened, without enthusiasm, a letter from his Alma Mater.

"Dear Fellow-Grad," the letter probably began. "Do you realize that our contributions account for 80 per cent of ALL THE SCHOLARSHIPS our college offers to deserving high school students?" Or perhaps: "Did you know that our Physics Building has long been OVERCROWDED, UNDER-EQUIPPED and in desperate need of a STUDENT SMOKING ROOM?" If the letter came from a woman's college, it almost certainly asked: "Do you remember: the October gold of the elm by College Hall; the faint blue haze from the piles of leaves burning on Appletree Lane? Can you still hear the twilight sound of the college carillon? We hate to intrude Need on Nostalgia but . . . HOW MUCH ARE YOUR MEMORIES WORTH TO YOU?"

Each of several million Americans stopped reading right there, reminding himself to remind himself to send $10 (if a man) or $5 (if a woman) to the Best College in the World. A lot of them even will.

Several thousand Alumni Fund Presidents, who have been hoping, this year at least, for $25 (from a man) or $10 (from a woman) will, upon receipt of Fellow-Grad's check, weep and wail and gnash their teeth and consign to outer darkness this latest of a long series of appeals that failed.

All, however, may not be lost; the Class Goal may yet be met. For to any university—and the chances are doubled in the Ivy League—may come the unbelievable stroke of good luck which smote Smith College in the spring of 1954: the stroke which broke all previous records of alumnae contributions.

The day the gods smiled on Smith was the day a number of her graduates received a letter from me. The letter was three paragraphs long and, even as other fund-raising letters, dealt with conditions at Alma Mater. The response to my letter (and I shall present documented evidence) was not simply electric—it was atomic. According to the Spring 1954 issue of the *Smith Alumnae Quarterly*:

In the ten days following February 25 [the day my letter was received] both the President's Office and the Alumnae House were inundated with letters, telegrams and telephone calls from alumnae. Many of the letters included checks ranging from $1.00 to $1,000. A goodly proportion came from alum-

nae who had already contributed to the Alumnae Fund this year, and a considerable number from alumnae who had never before contributed in any way to the College. Several letters and checks were sent by men whose alumnae wives during their lifetimes had been contributors.

And this was only the beginning. A Hartford newspaper reported that the town of Northampton had had to assign extra postmen to the college, and that students were being pressed into service as clerks in the treasurer's office to handle the deluge of cash, checks and, presumably, old family silver which arrived every quarter hour on the quarter hour from loyal Smith alumnae. In less than three months, the world's largest women's college received more money than had ever been collected in any full year in its history.

The Loyal 28,000

The year 1955 may—God help us all—some day be known as the year of the $64,000 question. Like the television program, the letter I wrote to the alumnae of Smith College revolved around a single question; but my question, even unanswered, turned out to be worth almost four times as much as Hal March's. My question concerned not student scholarships, not faculty salaries, not university equipment, not even Bright College Years. My question concerned the documented Communist-front affiliations of Smith faculty members who help form the opinions of two thousand young minds every year; two thousand young minds which come to college eager, open and, for the most part, blank. "Wine maketh merry, but money answereth all things." The alumnae of Smith College, with or without the influence of wine, answered my letter with two hundred and eighty-four thousand, eight hundred and thirteen dollars, plus twenty-four cents. An answer from the college administration was never given to and, in fact, was never requested nor required by almost 28,000 of the certifiedly educated women of the United States.[1]

To College Treasurers, Alumni Contributions Chairmen, the John Price Jones Company, American Universities, Inc., and all other professional or amateur fund-raising organizations, I offer the secret of my success. The process is simple and the fruits are sweet. The formula: *Point to Pink Professors.* The immediate effect (to write as colorfully as possible) is that the administration turns purple and the alumni see red, but in a matter of days the tumult and the shouting die under the cool green whisper of thousands of dollar bills.

The letter which, to Smith, was worth roughly $2,000 a word was described in its full horror by the *Smith Quarterly*:

> The letter began "Dear Alumna." It suggested that contributions to causes or institutions implied moral responsibility on the part of the donors. It questioned whether contributors to Smith wished to "sponsor the employment of men and women who, through their teaching positions, may be influencing young minds in a direction contrary to the philosophical principles in which most of us believe." The letter then named five members of the Smith faculty who, "together with other members . . . have been or are presently associated with many organizations cited as Communist or Communist-front by the Attorney General of the United States and the Committee on Un-American Activities." The letter concluded with the suggestion that the alumna who could not conscientiously help to make the employment of such teachers possible should withhold contributions "until the Smith Administration explains its educational policy to her personal satisfaction."

In one small matter, the *Quarterly* misquoted me. I began my letter not, "Dear Alumna," but "Dear Fellow Alumna," and the word "fellow"

[1]For some reason, Smith does not include in her take for 1954 the donation referred to by the alumna who wrote me that "to affirm our faith in Smith College, my mother ('22) has just contributed $500,000 for a new dormitory."

was not to be sneered at in terms of its cash value to Smith College. "To be addressed by you as a 'fellow alumna' makes me so ashamed I am doubling my contribution," one of my correspondents informed me. "I had hopefully supposed," hopefully supposed another woman, "that to warrant the title of 'a Smith alumna' one must cherish the principles of intellectual freedom, due process [sic] and individual integrity. I have today forwarded a cheque . . ." Among hundreds of unsolicited donors was one who, referring to my letter, asked reproachfully: "If the graduates of an independent liberal arts college do not know better, who does?" (The question is hazy, but the answer, I think, is clearly people who are not graduates of an independent liberal arts college.)

A spokesman for the sensitive-soul group wrote that she was increasing her contribution though "never again will I hold my head quite so proudly, knowing that you are, indeed, a 'fellow alumna.' " This reference to posture, incidentally, was repeated so frequently and in so many variations that I can only conclude it has become a nation-wide mark of recognition. In any large congregation of women, look around: those with heads unbloody but bowed are Smith graduates. (Except me; I'm the one hemorrhaging in the corner.)

The Disloyal Two

The success of the *Point to Pink Professors* technique in fund-raising is, then, demonstrably enhanced if the Pointer be a graduate of the college in question. To find such a Pointer is of course difficult but, even in the Ivy League, not impossible. President Wright of Smith College openly admitted that among his 28,000 alumnae there were a disloyal two who had asked for the basis of the information I offered.

The "Shame on You" reaction, however, is only one approach to an indignant alumnus' pocketbook. According to my files—and I am sure it is unnecessary to state that my 'phone lines, telegraph operator and postmen were just as busy as Smith's —there is also an inordinately large and vocal minority which belongs to what might be called the Nausea, or Pepto-Bismol School. This group

expresses displeasure not only by bowing its head, but by losing its breakfast in the process. Folding money seems to be used by the sorority as an alkalizing agent. "Your insinuations are nauseous," one woman wrote greenly; "I shall contribute *heavily* to Smith College." Another increased her donation because "your shameful behavior towards Smith College frankly turns my stomach." And again: "Your outrageous letter made me ill—literally ill . . . sending $100 over and above . . ."

Let it not be thought, however, that the *P. to P. P.* technique institutes only an emotional or physical reaction in the average college graduate. Larger by far and even more fluent, though perhaps not quite so rich, was the group which, after reading my letter, contributed to Smith for intellectual reasons. Upon hearing that their money helped to pay teachers who, according to the Government of the United States, had pro-Communist records, the Intellectuals rushed in a body to the bank.

"My loyalty to the College and my faith in its officers are stimulated *as never before;* I am sending today a check doubling my largest previous contribution," wrote one. A 1929 graduate, who described herself as a "student, member of the Administrative staff for three years, and currently member of the Board of Directors of the Alumnae Association," informed me that "your letter has deepened my loyalty to the College *more than any single event I could have imagined.*" (And yet, earthquake, fire and flood are, conceivably, not beyond the scope of her imagination.)

Another intellectual-type note disclosed the fact that "though I know only one of the faculty members you mentioned, I judge [apparently from the information I had offered] that all of them are very good teachers who can stimulate the students at Smith College." One of many "duplicate check" senders owes to me the decision that her Alma Mater is Great. "Because," as she pithily put it, "it is always the great institutions of learning that are attacked first in any police state, for the colleges harbor the 'dangerous' people, the people who know how to think, whose minds are **free.**" (One of the extra little rays of sunshine in my campaign was the fact that I enabled Smith's President to reach the same conclusion. "If I ever had any doubts about the vitality of the liberal tradition in Smith College," he confided to the student body, ". . . they have been resolved. . . . These letters have indicated to me that in the past Smith College has been a very great liberal college."

It was in this same speech that the President announced triumphantly that only two of 28,000 alumnae, trained to search for truth with a Liberal's curiosity, had asked for the basis of what he called "these vague charges and insinuations.")

A Gift for Words

Others of the Bluestocking Group —all of whom have a real gift for words—sent contributions to Smith College in defense of "the American tradition," "the brotherhood of man," "academic freedom," and "the Christian way of life." All of these attributes being clearly embodied in five little professors—four-fifths of an attribute per.

I should like to state at this point that, in the interest of academic accuracy, I have ruthlessly excluded from my Intellectual Group even the most fluent of the one hundred and ten ladies who expressed their "con-*fidance*" in Smith College. I have also excluded a high-minded and wealthy graduate who declared that "Senator McCarthy would have *profitted* from the education I *recieved* at Smith."

Pointing to Pink Professors does not, appearances to the contrary notwithstanding, invariably arouse hostility to the Pointer on the part of the Pointee. In some Pointees (even the one who described herself as "not Catholic or Jewish or anything else subversive") my letter aroused a spirit of Christian charity. Several expressed pity for my "tortured, twisted mind"; several excused me on the ground that I was a frustrated female ("You, madam, are a frustrated female!"); many urged me to place myself and my family in the hands of a good psychiatrist, and one asked if I had "tried God."

And then there were the thank-you notes. "I have doubled my usual contribution . . . thank you for spurring me on," wrote a member of the class of '93. "You have inadvertently done Smith a great favor," admitted an undergraduate. "There has never been so much money contributed as this year," wrote a grateful lady who, in the circumstances, can hardly have been sincere when she added: "Oh, dear, it would have been so nice if only you had gone to Vassar."

Even as mold gave rise to penicillin, one particular letter developed Heath's Law of Fund-Raising. "Dear Mrs. Heath," ran this billet-doux, "Congratulations on your novel (if unethical) method of raising money for our Alumnae Fund. The funds are pouring in, thanks to your letter. Next year you might think up another Smear-Smith stunt to aid the Fund."

Punchdrunk as I was, this letter snapped into focus the whole Smith episode. Derogatory information about Smith equals Smear-Smith equals unprecedented financial support for Smith. If, this year, Smith College were to double its quota of faculty members whose extracurricular activities figured prominently on the Attorney General's Communist-front list, I could, by pointing out these associations, institute another "Smear-Smith" campaign which would double even the 1954 record of alumnae contributions. If Smith tripled its quota, the alumnae would presumably triple theirs.

Although I cannot claim to know what makes the Ivy League graduate tick, I feel I can present incontrovertible evidence as to what makes him give; and my formula, which cannot but constitute a valuable addition to the psychology of merchandising, I here offer without mental or financial reservation. To Point to Pink Professors is to institute an alumni reaction as predictable as pushing the bellybutton of a mama doll—except that in Ivy League alumni, the eructation takes the form of cash.

The late Mrs. Thomas Lamont gave a million dollars to Smith and her son Corliss to Columbia. Any fund-raiser with a keen eye for potentialities can see that Columbia may easily have got the best of the bargain.

Kreuttner

"All the lady said to the gentlemen passing her on the street was, 'Come up and see me some time!' She was merely Advocating an Abstract Doctrine. Case dismissed."

What Would Taft Have Thought?

He would not, in sum, recognize his own party in power, says a journalist who was the friend and collaborator of the late Senator

FORREST DAVIS

The journalistic device which calls for the resurrection of a public figure for the purpose of weighing his known attitudes and bents against the current posture of events is tempting. It affords a certain perspective to the scene. What would the Washington who warned against entangling alliances think of collective security? What would that gifted, iconoclastic son of the eighteenth-century Enlightenment, Jefferson, make of the welfare state? And Lincoln, brooding over the Gettysburg made fortuitously famous by a later President, how would he measure the current disclosures of man's incorrigible inhumanity to man?

In the case of the late Robert Alphonso Taft, austerely entombed on his cherished Indian Hill above the distantly enchanting Ohio, the device is not farfetched. He has not been so long gone. Moreover, he still exists in spirit as the proper foil of that abeyant, timid President who bested him in the faintly disreputable Republican Convention of 1952.

What would "Mr. Republican," that rugged, unsparing, courageous, traditional and nationalistic paladin of the conservative spirit, think of the self-deprecatory "modern Republicanism"? What would he have to say, if happily he were alive, of the irresolute diplomacy which harries our ancient allies over Suez, refusing to demand solutions of the quarrels that produced the incident, while refraining from annoying the enemy of us all over Hungary?

What would Taft, going unillusioned to death's door, objective, capable of a Jovian wrath as well as quiet irony, remark in private concerning the phenomenon of a mythic Eisenhower and the desuetude of the Grand Old Party?

The confrontation of Eisenhower living and Taft dead is appropriate. Actual in 1952, it has an illuminating relevance now. In 1952, Taft stood for responsible, thoughtful, party government in the stable Anglo-Saxon mode. He loomed over his party by virtue of ability, character and principle. His opponent was a personally engaging professional soldier, unused to historical and political generalizations, the nature of his society and the homely practices of civilian politics. Taft lost, Eisenhower won to become in his lifetime (as the November elections manifested) a legend, not Augustan but symbolic of a nation smugly euphoristic and unheroic; a political leader who consciously makes no enemies and whose philosophy, if he has one, may be summed up in the patented inquiry of bandleader Ted Lewis, "Is *everybody* happy?"

Liberal Estimates

Taft, alive, made virulent enemies.

Laid in his crypt, Taft has become the anointed conservative of the Liberal, or Egghead; terms fairly interchangeable. As the Liberal posthumously contemplates the undeniable virtues of Taft he ends by dubbing him Robert the Just. Paul G. Hoffman, an Egghead by adoption who was once, we must assume, a politically unversed motor-car salesman but who now luxuriates his spirit in the Sanhedrin of Robert Maynard Hutchins, expressed the belated judgment of his kind in a pre-election article in *Collier's*. Hoffman described the late Senator as an "honest but rigid conservative," a description no wider of the mark than the usual memorial estimate of Taft by the working Liberal.

Honest Taft was, in all the varied uses of the term. Rigid he was not. It would be accurate to say that he was rigid as to principle, elastic as to method and practice. We cannot expect sensible definition from the Egghead. He prefers to ride clichés.

I can do no more than guess why the Liberal has, in his fashion, exalted Taft. The Liberal, having demolished virtually all the living exponents of individualized, traditional liberty or driven them into an apologetic defensive; having butchered McCarthy to make an Egghead holiday; having employed a sanctimonious, Cromwellian absolutism to lay waste all enemies of the Establishment—the Liberal yearns for an antagonist whom he may indulgently flay. His victory has been too comprehensive, too total, with a pliable instrument at the head of affairs and the Old Guard in the thickets of frustration.

Taft supported Eisenhower's legislative program even to the extent of forcing endorsement of Charles E. (Chip) Bohlen's barren ambassadorship to Moscow on an unwilling Senate majority. That fact alone gives his memory kudos with the Establishment. Under such circumstances a study of Taft and how he would view the current anemic welfare statism and foreign policy nihilism may be counted upon to engage the curiosity of the Liberal as well as that of the libertarian (a brazen term containing a sly connotation of libertinism) remnant.

I begin by asserting that Taft would have entertained a full-bodied dislike for the slack, programmatic intellectualizations that make up "modern Republicanism" as revealed by the President and its literary author, Mr. Arthur Larson. Taft was a stout-hearted controversialist. He believed in the partisan utility of black and white and objected to blurring the edges of what it is now fashionable to call the dialogue between the parties. He disdained the expedient technique of stealing the other fellow's clothes while he is in swimming.

Moreover, unlike Woodrow Wilson who deplored the ideologue perhaps because he so often behaved like one, Taft was no ideologue. A pragmatist perhaps, as when he served the Administration faithfully and powerfully as Senate floor leader, but no Middle-of-the-Roader, no trimmer. The Taft who deliberately incurred the hostility of the trade union hierarchy by sponsoring the Taft-Hartley Act, who denounced the *ex post facto* Nuremberg trials at a time when the fires of detestation of Nazi crimes burned hottest, that Taft would never embrace the ideology of welfare statism and call it virtuous.

A nationalist, he never would have shamed and negated our necessitous and necessary trans-Atlantic friends out of what must be an obsessive fear of organized force and fidelity to a sterile phrase concerning aggression.

On the Welfare State

The President spelled out what he chose to call the "philosophy" of "New Republicanism" at his first press conference after burying his pathetically inept adversary at the polls. As phrased in the President's discursive prose, that "philosophy" called for a clear recognition that it is ". . . the responsibility of the federal government to take the lead in making certain that the productivity of our great economic machine is distributed so that no one will suffer disaster, privation through no fault of his own."

He added, almost as an afterthought:

"Now this covers the wide field of education and health, and so on; but we believe likewise in the free enterprise system. We believe that it is free enterprise that has brought these blessings to America." The "blessings" were not specified.

We may put it down as certain that Taft a) would have thought the President was putting the cart before the horse by mentioning free enterprise after asserting the federal government's obligation to use its manifold powers to shield the citizen from adversity and b) he would, with characteristic flatness, have denied that the federal government has either the right or the obligation to

govern the distribution of this world's goods to that end.

To Taft, the citizen was not the ward of a Utopian, even a Fabian, state, but its master.

He had an all but absolute faith in the right and capacity of the citizen to manage his own affairs, including the extraction of his share of the social product and guarding himself and his from privation. He

likewise thought the sovereign citizen fully competent to pass upon public questions. In that, he was old-fashioned and democratic somewhat in the Jeffersonian mold. His respect for the citizen sometimes seemed excessive, as when, addressing campaign audiences of 50 as well as 5,000, he insisted upon spelling out the complicated issues of the day in all their statistical detail, sometimes pedantically but always out of a dutiful desire fully to communicate.

I recall a colloquy he had with Dorothy Thompson in 1940. The articulate columnist foresaw a Hitler triumphant in Europe, leagued with a Japan on the march in Asia, dominating a helpless British imperial system and a not too reluctant Latin America, and finally isolating the United States in an encircling world. Taft thought that our vital national interests had not yet been infringed. The dispute raged noisily on Taft's part. He sometimes grew vehement. Miss Thompson visualized a United States carried into the Nazi orbit by expedient or frightened politicians.

"But," protested the Senator, "you don't know the American people. You don't know my neighbors, the farmers in Hamilton County. They are,"

he shouted, "as independent as a hog on ice and nobody can fool them."

Taft could not conceive of national policy being forged in the long run anywhere except in the polling place. Nor did he hold with beguiling the voter by deceptive promises, half truths, or the strategems and shenanigans of Madison Avenue. He had a low tolerance for slogans and he wrote his own speeches. His campaign staff consisted of a sort of impromptu bureaucracy at headquarters and a spry and biddable young man to see that he kept his schedule and got into the right car in the procession. He carried his own bulging brief case.

Taft accepted the postulates of welfare statism in one notable instance. To the dismay of certain supporters he voted for federal aid to low cost housing, but he did so not because he had embraced the principle that the government owes the citizen well-being from the cradle to the grave but for a cogent reason. It seemed to him that construction workers at $32 a day had priced housing out of the reach of white collar workers at $32 a week. The Roosevelt-Truman regnum' had, he thought, intervened in behalf of the construction worker's good fortune. He voted to balance the scale.

The Administration's propensity for filling high administrative posts from the ranks of the industrial managerial class, or type, Taft deplored. Taft plainly saw the difference between the art of governing and the profession of profit-making. During the hiatus between election and inauguration in 1952, when his position was for a time equivocal, Taft's recommendations for high office came from the ranks of men acquainted with the business of political persuasion rather than from the field of big business. Big business, it should be interpolated, never cottoned to Presidential candidate Taft. It could be surmised that, while always hospitable to the claims of business in a business society, he had quite palpably a mind of his own.

His suggestions in that tentative period from November 1952, to January 1953, came to little. He had a lively suspicion that they never broke through the "Commodore crowd" to the President-elect.

Although he served Eisenhower

with more loyalty than was bestowed in return, Taft set no great store on the President's grasp of unfamiliar affairs, his understanding of constitutional questions or the experiential range of our history. He related during the interregnum with a certain dry relish an anecdote illustrative of that point.

It seems that Eisenhower, returning from his promised visit to Korea, was importuned at Hawaii to support statehood. The solicitation was baited by the pledge of two additional Republican Senators. According to Taft's version, the President-elect replied: "Why don't you go ahead and elect those Senators? It will make it easier for me."

The Cincinnati Speech

The President's lack of fidelity to Taft was demonstrated somewhat poignantly in the Senator's final weeks. In his last public speech, a legacy to the American public, the Senator took a realistic view of our strategical requirements in the Western Pacific and depicted the divergence of our Atlantic allies from our necessitous policy in that quarter.

The circumstances of this incident bear relating. Taft had gone to Cincinnati to deliver this address at a dinner of the local Conference of Christians and Jews. But when he arrived in his home town, his physicians ordered him to the hospital for tests and forbade his delivering the speech. He therefore revised a final draft and entrusted it to his son, Robert A. Taft, Jr., to be read at the dinner. There was no time to mimeograph copies for the press. Hence, wire reporters present were required to take down the words as spoken. This being a foreign policy speech of some import, the Senator had told the President about it and had sent a copy of the current draft to the White House three days before departing for Cincinnati.

The speech was noteworthy. It suggested that the time might come when the imperialistic pressures of Red China on our advance line of defense in the Far East might compel us to resist without benefit of European allies. The adverse press, notably the *Washington Post*, treated the Taft exposition as a new expression of "isolationism"; erroneously proclaiming that Taft had advocated "going it alone."

Eisenhower, when asked for comment, accepted this hasty hypothesis, speaking without the delivered text before him. The Senator, soon to be put on crutches, was a little grim about this White House repudiation, making, however, no public rejoinder.

Taft, if alive today, would, we can be certain, sternly object to the sacrifice of England and France with the evidence of solidarity with Soviet objectives that our course implies. He was not infatuated with the syllogism that ends in the concept of peace as an absolute good. The last American statesman to embrace that folly with the attendant renunciation of force as a last recourse of statesmanship was William Jennings Bryan. With Bryan Taft had little in common.

In truth, Taft went along with the fetish of Collective Security warily; he reservedly endorsed our involvement in the United Nations. The Senator was a profoundly educated man, although he took care to conceal that fact. His knowledge of the history of international affairs, with its ironies, its betrayals and disappointments, fortified him against illusion. He knew, with Lord Palmerston, that nations put interest above pledges. He understood without resentment, for example, that in the Western Pacific the British supposed their interest to run counter to our own with respect to China, however intimately we might be linked in a common desire to preserve the Atlantic as an Anglo-American lake. Taft mistrusted British guile based on self-interest but he had no disposition to disturb our fundamental community of idealism and interest.

He knew that in the flux of interest today's enemies may become tomorrow's friends (a situation somewhat mockingly exemplified by the Administration's parallelism with Moscow and Cairo over Suez) but he could face that disturbing fact with urbanity.

Taft had the foresight (along with Herbert Hoover) to understand, even during the fury of conflict in World War II, that the Nazi menace was the lesser of the two totalitarian furies; that Nazism was improvised, superficial, dependent on the perverse genius of an individual and,

however revolting to our Western humanitarianism, capable of being put down. The Bolshevik danger seemed to him more monstrous because it sprang from an incalculable and aberrant historical surge such as the drive of the Arabs toward world empire and the westward thrust of the Mongolian khans.

Taft never regarded, as did Franklin D. Roosevelt and Cordell Hull, world Bolshevism as merely another nation similar to England or France. Nor would Taft have misread the intentions of Khrushchev *et al* at Geneva. He would have seen Khrushchev, equally with Stalin, as the expression of a subliminal force, armed with a frenetic will to reduce all mankind to a manageable mass to the greater glory of a demented elite and a false doctrine of man and his destiny.

Taft never would have scrapped the Atlantic alliance in the presence of that danger out of pique with uncommunicative allies, to uphold a stereotyped definition of aggression or through a simple fear of war. Once an "isolationist," or so he was termed, the late Senator would not have been one with what the German Foreign Minister, von Brentano, describes as the "neo-isolationism" of this Administration. Nor would the bluntly realistic Taft ever have publicly renounced war as a recourse of diplomacy, thus enlarging the enemy's field of inimical operations.

Finally, the rigorous Ohioan would not have been taken in by the schematic notion that the Republican Party needs "modernizing" from on high. That he would regard as the invention of an ideologue. To him issues made parties. He would not have found a sound fiscal policy and a tepid, imitative welfare-statism sufficiently salient issues upon which to base party reform.

The voter, he would say as he sometimes did, was entitled to a clearly differentiated choice between the parties. As a stout partisan, he was for party, or corporate, responsibility. He stood for the tripartite balance of powers. He opposed crypto-Socialism as he opposed Communist subversion, backing Senator McCarthy as a means to that end. He would find himself at odds today with many tendencies fashionable in Eisenhower's Washington.

I Acknowledge My Mistakes

A famous writer who once sympathized with the "Soviet experiment" considers his past errors, tells how he came to make them and what—in a free country—he lived to learn from them

MAX EASTMAN

on author's turning away from Marxism

"Acknowledge your mistakes" is one of the ordeals they put a thinking man through in Soviet Russia before shooting him as an enemy of the people. It occurs to me that if the mistakes were not dictated by an external power, and the shooting were also left for the victim to decide upon in case he feels that bad, the ritual might be good for us all. My own big political mistakes, counting from the very beginning, seem to be four in number, although I can be wholly blamed only for the last three.

My first mistake was to be born in a family where kindness and fair-dealing and good logic prevailed to such a degree that when I got out into the public world it looked excessively unjust, cruel, irrational; a subject for indignation and extreme action. It wasn't a bitter or distorted childhood that set me off on a wrong course, but just the opposite. My father was a liberal-minded Christian minister with a passion for farming. The happiest day of his life was when his nervous system broke down and he had to abandon the pulpit and get out on the soil. In consequence I grew up outdoors on a stock farm instead of indoors in a parsonage. My early life was happy and, but for the long summer days I had to spend cultivating the corn or pitching hay or hoeing potatoes, I was free. I loved all kinds of farm work—but I didn't like to do it. I preferred to watch other people do it. This caused a rather sharp difference between me and my father, but it came out all right in the end. I persuaded him that I was by nature a student—an ingenious name I invented for my disinclination toward physical labor—and he finally decided that my case was absolutely hopeless.

I mention this in order to make clear that my further mistakes were not the result of repression or frustration. It was not envy, or privation, or "economic backwardness" that made me into a revolutionist. It is not these age-old things—though both Truman and Eisenhower seem to think so—that have lifted hundreds of millions of people all over the earth into a sacrificial crusade to destroy our relatively free civilization in the cause of what they call a social ownership of the means of production. The reason for that is—the basic and most general reason—that they compare the world as it is, not with something better that might be possible, but with an ideal of perfection.

That is the inner emotional core of the metaphysical mania called Marxism. Marx took the celestial paradise down out of heaven, called it a classless society, and said it was to be achieved on earth by waging war on existing governments and upper classes. Marxism is not a practical or scientific scheme for solving the world's problems, but a religion—a godless religion, but a religion just the same. We are still going to heaven, but the heaven is on earth, and we are to get there, not by being good, but by being bad—by introducing the morals of war into the peacetime relations of men.

That is what the Western world is up against—an armed international religion. And few of our statesmen or diplomats of either party seem able to grasp it. Once you do grasp it, you are not surprised to find converts to this religion in high places. You won't be deceived into thinking that because a man is dressed in a pin-stripe suit, and has good looks and suave manners and a smooth tongue, like Alger Hiss, he can't possibly be a zealot of the new religion. On the other hand you are not deceived into thinking you can stop the crusade by giving dollars to those who can't afford a pin-stripe suit.

How to be Unpopular

Before getting down to my task of humility, I will permit myself a small boast about the mistakes I made. They never got me anywhere personally—nor did my recoveries from them. My timing was always wrong. I was a militant advocate of the Great Experiment in Soviet Russia in the teens and twenties when practically every respected person in the United States was against it. I was defending Bolshevism in my magazine *The Liberator* as the "beginning of a new world where possibilities of Life and freedom for all are now certainly immeasurable," when the American press in general was firm in the opinion that Bolshevism was synonomous with the Nationalization of Women.

Then in the 1930's when the whole American intelligentsia, most especially the literary vanguard to which I belonged, began to whoop it up for the Soviets and the great age of proletarian democracy that was dawning, I was foolhardy enough to discover that the whole thing had been a flop. It was in 1935 and '36, at the height of what has been called the Red Decade in American letters, that I composed my epoch-making work, *The End of Socialism in Russia*, which sold, if I remember rightly, exactly two hundred and eighty-four copies.

Again in 1941 at the tiptop of the fever curve of the Second World War, when Russia as Our Noble Ally was adored as a paragon of freedom in a crusade for democracy, I wrote—and what is more startling, DeWitt Wallace published in the *Reader's Digest*—an article entitled "To Collaborate Successfully We Must Face the Facts

About Russia." The facts I proposed we should face were the facts everybody is facing now: the blood purges, the executions without trial, the war on the peasants, the massacre of enterprising farmers called Kulaks, the slave camps. It was one of the boldest things that a popular American magazine ever did—seventeen pages of it in the lead position at the front of the *Reader's Digest*—and it had, the editors told me, the widest repercussion of anything they ever published. But it did not contribute to my popularity among the raving patriots.

And right now I am under the ban again among those who used to be my friends, because they've all gone in for the Big Brother Welfare State, while I have come to the conclusion that, whatever may have been true in the past, at this hour Big Government and not Big Business is the main enemy of freedom.

To get down to those mistakes: My second was that naive and thoughtless one of comparing reality with perfection, instead of comparing it with something better that might be possible. I believed in the myth of a classless society. I didn't swallow down the whole Marxian religion, I am happy to say. According to that religion history itself is an escalator carrying us all upward, whether we like it or not, toward an earthly paradise. The Communists are walking with history and will get there. The anti-Communists are walking the wrong way, clogging the whole thing and delaying it, and may legitimately be dealt with somewhat as heretics were dealt with in past ages by a more spiritual religion. To be exact about the procedure, they may be taken down the cellar-stairs and shot in the back of the neck on the way down.

I never believed in this so-called "dialectic" escalator. My approach was, in form at least, scientific. I regarded socialism, not as historically inevitable but as an experiment that ought to be tried. That saved me from becoming a fanatic. It prevented my ever joining a Communist party. But it made all the more inexcusable my next big mistake.

With all my skeptical and scientific common sense, I fell absolutely for the Russian Bolshevik Revolution of October 1917. I went all out for the insurrectionary seizure of power by Lenin and Trotsky and the executive

committee of their small minority party. I believed with a haste and eagerness which had little to do with science, that the socialist experiment I had talked about was being made in Russia, and was succeeding. I backed Lenin and Trotsky to the limit.

Pilgrimage to Moscow

After defending them for five years on this side of the ocean, I made the pilgrimage to Moscow in 1922. I told my friends I was going over to find out whether what I had been saying was true, but of course I found it true. Part of it, indeed, was true. Lenin's New Economic Policy, a half step back to capitalism, had just been adopted, and there was food enough, and, compared to what came later, a great deal of freedom. Those who assert that Lenin's regime was "just as bad" as Stalin's are ignorant of the facts. Lenin created the one-party totalitarian state, but he did it reluctantly. He tried to prevent the new gang tyranny implicit in it. He died fighting a losing battle against the growth of a new ruling class, a thing which his theories had never contemplated, and which he called Bureaucratism. Stalin, on the contrary, loved and cherished Bureaucratism. He loved totalitarian gang rule, loved not only the one-party but the one-man state, including the barbaric deification of his own person, any tendency toward which Lenin spat on and laughed to scorn. Lenin's invention made Stalin's tyranny possible. His misguided faith in the Marxian Escalator lies at the bottom of the whole totalitarian tragedy: Stalin, Mussolini, Hitler, Mao Tse-tung—the whole business. But it is a distortion of history to identify Stalin's actual regime with that of Lenin and Trotsky.

Therefore I don't feel too apologetic about my *immediate* reaction to what I found in Russia in 1922. The socialist experiment seemed to be going well. Lenin was already too sick for me to try to see him, but I became good friends with Trotsky. I persuaded him, in the intervals of his task as Secretary of War and Commander-in-Chief of the Red Army, to tell me his life story and let me make a book of it. Working in a foreign language, that was an exacting task, and occupied much of my time during the year and nine months that I stayed in Russia.

Perhaps that's another reason why I didn't have any critical reactions—or any strong ones—to the course that my much-loved "socialist experiment" was taking. I had too much to do. It was all too exciting. It wasn't that I took a wrong turn, but that having started on a wrong course I didn't take any turn at all.

My real emotional blindness came when, six months after Lenin's death, I saw Stalin's steamroller run over Trotsky and with him every man in the party who wanted to continue Lenin's struggle against Bureaucratism. I saw it more closely and intimately, I believe, than any other foreign non-party visitor ever saw any of the inside workings of Communism in Russia. For Trotsky gave me a pass admitting me to the meeting in the Tsar's palace within the Kremlin of the thirteenth congress of the Russian Communist Party, in May 1924. That was the point at which Stalin, as secretary of the Party, having packed the Congress with delegates who owed their jobs to him and would back him through thick and thin, attacked Trotsky and broke him down and destroyed his authority in the party.

It was the climax of a press campaign against Trotsky and the anti-bureaucratic opposition that has few equals in the history of slander and falsification. It was made tense, too, by the fact that all the delegates were thinking about something they dared not mention. The document called "Lenin's Testament," his death-bed letter to the party, warning them against Stalin's excessive power and endorsing Trotsky as the ablest man among them, had on the insistence of Lenin's widow been read privately to the delegates. But it was locked up in the safe and the order issued that no one should mention it on the floor of the congress. The outside world was never to hear of it.

Trotsky himself obeyed that order. He made no allusion to Lenin's warning, no reply to the storm of slanders against him and his following. He made what he considered a diplomatic speech. It was weak. It was almost incredibly submissive. It contained the fantastic statement that the party could not in the nature of things make a mistake. Nobody would have dreamed, hearing him, that he had ever been a great orator, the organizer of a victorious insurrection, commander of an army that had fought five invaders to a standstill on a front seven thousand miles long. Trotsky was a great soldier, a great orator, a great writer, but in the art of practical politics, he was an absolute dud. He could no more have taken Lenin's place as leader of the Bolshevik party than he could have flown over the moon. He knew that. And so did I. But I also knew that in continuing Lenin's struggle against Bureaucratism, against the solidification of a new ruling class of state officials, he was defending the only hope there was left of a Workers and Peasants Republic ultimately emerging out of this seizure of power and confiscation of capital by a party. That was the truth, and I thought the truth ought to be defended.

I had gone up to the platform to shake hands with Trotsky and thank him for my pass before the meeting began—incidentally to say goodbye to him, for I was leaving Russia in just a few days. He had asked me what I was going to do when I got home.

"I'm not going to *do* anything," I said. "I'm going to think and write."

He smiled his disapproval—for it was very un-Marxian, that separation of thought from action. To make it worse, I added: "I believe in the class struggle but I love peace."

"You love peace, you ought to be arrested!" he said, and we parted with a laugh.

But after I heard him give his case away, and give the truth away, in that feeble attempt to make a diplomatic speech, I couldn't sit still. I went up again, during an intermission, and pled with him to take command of the situation.

"In God's name," I said, or words to that effect, "Why don't you peel off your coat and roll up your sleeves and sail in and clean them up? Read Lenin's Testament yourself. Don't *let* them lock it up. Expose the whole conspiracy. Expose it and attack it head on. It isn't your fight, it's the fight for the revolution. If you don't make it now, you'll never make it. It's your last chance."

He looked at me in some surprise. I had been on the whole a respectful biographer. I thought he even weighed my advice a moment—at least he paused for reflection. Then he gave me a quizzical look.

"I thought you said you loved peace," he said.

It was indeed his last chance. It was

the end of his *political* prestige throughout the world. Trotsky will live, I suppose, as one of the greatest revolutionists in history. Spartacus, the Gracchi, Danton, Robespierre—I don't know any that excelled him in will, intellectual force, or actual achievement. But the revolution had already failed. Lenin himself had failed, as his Testament and his death-bed fight against Bureaucratism bear witness. It wasn't Stalin, it was the crass facts of human nature that defeated them. It was the logic of reality refuting that ideal of perfection which had driven them to great deeds—the same that lured me into their following. Stalin, a natural born bureaucrat, not troubled by any ideal of perfection but guided, as Lenin warned, by a commonplace thirst for power, was only a supremely astute and ruthless representative of that logic.

On the Eighth Day

The technician pulled out all the
    comrade's teeth
and dropped them in an ideological
    bucket—
free of charge.
"Non-functional," the bureau said,
"with our predigested sesquipedalian
    pap."
(The smile was a capitalistic snarl.
Laughter a popish superstition.)
COMMUNISM CONQUERS CARIES!
    . . . the manufacture of dentures
    . . . so non-productive
    . . . abolished forever.
Dentists have died with lawyers and
    brokers.
"In one degenerate democracy in its
    last years
8,000,000 manhours were wasted on
7,000,000 upper plates alone
to say nothing of bridges, pivots,
lowers, fillings, bands, caps.
ALL HONOR TO OUR SECRETARY

FOR OUR GUMMY GLORY!"

The old man trembled before he
    spoke
like a clock cocking to strike:
"Please leave the rotten molar in
    the back of my mouth,"
he begged them, "I like to feel it
    ache."
FOR THAT
They took away his ration card for
a week.

HERBERT A. KENNY

My big mistake was that, although I was right there looking on at the very inside essence of this process, this living refutation of socialist theory, I would not allow myself to perceive it. I clung to my belief in the so-called Soviet System. For almost ten years I insisted on regarding Stalin and his totalitarian state as an accidental enemy, not a natural result of the October seizure of power.

This, then, is my fourth and my biggest mistake: the unconscionably long time it took me to acknowledge that I had *made* a mistake. I wasn't a fanatic, but my brains were so stubborn, my emotions so fixed in a revolutionary mould, that I might as well have been. I couldn't change my mind. Every impulse to change my mind I rejected as a weakness in my character. It's hard when in doubt to distinguish these two things. When conviction falters, pride holds you fast.

Pride's action must be particularly strong when one is called before some ominous tribunal and asked to state his convictions. Under less pressure, a good number of those seemingly so obdurate Fifth Amendment Communists would, I suspect, admit that they'd like to back down. I feel like telling them:

Never mind the external circumstances; truth is all that matters; acknowledge your mistake and get it over with.

Having freely confessed my mistakes, I may now mention a certain advantage that accrues to me from having made them. It is the advantage of inside knowledge about something of paramount importance at this moment in history. With distinguished exceptions, it is only those of us who have been, if not inside the Communist movement, at least close enough in to feel and know by experience its passions and purposes and schemes for achieving them, who fully realize what the free world, and its captain the United States, are up against. We are, in a way that others are not, fortified against the vice of self-deception. And for the last fifteen years self-deception has been the essential foreign policy of the United States. Our Western statesmen simply can not get it through their heads that they are fighting an armed international religion with a fixed creed and a fixed purpose to destroy free institutions throughout the world. They can't imagine what it

85

is like to belong to such an organization—to be, in the name of an ideal of perfection, a ruthless enemy of the existing civilization. And so they raise up one fatuous hope after another that, if they behave according to the dictates of reason or justice or the golden rule, these fanatics will yield ground and respond.

They won't, and as committed revolutionists they can't. We know this because we were once in a similar state of mind. To us it seemed absolutely ridiculous to send an airload of statesmen and their retinues over to Geneva, squandering hundreds of thousands of dollars, and enough brain power and oratorical energy to found an empire, in order to find out the perfectly obvious fact that the victorious gang in the Kremlin are not going to hand over their prize European conquest in the cause of a security they don't believe in. I refer, of course, to East Germany, and I am wrong to call it a conquest. It was a gift we gave them in this same fatuous mood of self-deception when we stopped the eastward march of our own conquering armies at the end of the war.

For us, who have been friends of the enemy, this self-deception is impossible. We know what we are up against: a war to the death against our Republic and our free way of life —a cold war, to be sure, but a war nonetheless. There are but three possible outcomes of this conflict:

1. The Communists win it and our nation is destroyed.

2. The Communists drive us back until we recoil with a hot war and the whole nexus of civilization is destroyed.

3. We prosecute the cold war with a will to victory and win it.

The third is the true course open to us—the only course short of a bombing war. We must frustrate and force back world Communism until its center of power in the Red Empire is overthrown by forces arising among its own subjects.

Nobody wants a hot war in the present state of technology. The Communists want it least of all, both because they would surely be destroyed, and because their fanatical aim is to take over the American industrial plant as a going concern, not as a heap of unapproachable ruins. But the Communists take advantage of this universal abhorrence of a hot war to wage the cold war with every means and instrument they can lay hold of or devise. We, on the contrary, cannot make up our mind to face continually and with resolution the fact that we are in a cold war. We can't seem to get it through our heads that the golden rule, although a noble and wise aphorism in its place, has no application to the task of calling the bluff and stopping the depredations of a bully. "Speak softly and carry a big stick," was the maxim applied by Theodore Roosevelt to such exigencies. "Carry a perfectly enormous stick, and announce in a loud voice every morning that no matter what happens you are not going to use it," has been the maxim of our government for the last ten years.

We are fighting this cold war for our life, and we must fight on all fronts and in every field of action. We must employ in a campaign to liberate the enslaved countries and deliver the world from the menace of Communist tyranny all the means employed by the Communists to destroy and enslave us—excepting only that we fight with the truth, adhering to moral principle, while they fight with lies and a deliberate code of treachery. And we must make our aim as clear to the world as the Communists have made theirs. We must never affirm our loyalty to Peace without linking to it the word Freedom.

Kreuttner

"Don't think of it as imbecility. Think of it as dynamic imbecility."

A Conversation with Ezra Pound

The poet who spent twelve years in "St. Liz" proves to be eccentric, often obscure, sane and sometimes acutely wise

JAMES JACKSON KILPATRICK

On April 18, the Department of Justice dismissed a 13-year-old indictment against Ezra Pound, and a week later the authorities at St. Elizabeth's Hospital in Washington placed this aging poet on an outpatient status. On the afternoon of April 30, Pound drove to Richmond in the company of Harry Meacham, president of the Virginia Poetry Society, and for a little more than two hours we talked together in the oddly chaste and dulcet surroundings of the Rotunda Club here.

This account of that causerie—it surely was nothing so formal as an interview—should be qualified at the outset: We did not talk serious politics. It is useless to talk serious politics with Ezra Pound. He is the last statesman of a lost cause—a cause lost a thousand years ago—and most of his enemies are dust. Talking with him, it is difficult to separate his live antagonists from the dead ones, the Rothschilds of 1750 from their counterparts two centuries later; and there is this problem for the ignoramus, meaning me, that when Pound touches a subject he does not so much touch it as embrace it. His mind is a river that holds ten thousand years of sand, but it deposits little sediment in washing over the untutored listener. Coleridge once remarked that the best poetry is that which is only generally, and not precisely, understood; and what I am groping to say is that I do not understand Pound even generally. Acknowledging that he is "anti-Semitic," I venture the positive assertion that Pound's anti-Semitism never will inspire the faintest urge in anyone to put a torch to a synagogue; a less effective rabble-rouser could not be conceived: The rabble would not understand a word that he says.

I offer this impression also: if words have any meaning left, Ezra Pound surely is no lunatic; and if it is true,

as Dr. Overholser says, that Pound's condition has not changed since he entered St. Elizabeth's in 1946, then Pound was not lunatic then. Obscure, yes; eccentric, yes; full of apparent confusion, yes. But crazy, no.

He was twenty minutes late arriving for our appointment. The party had left Washington on time, but had stopped midway for a sandwich, and Pound's dentures had proved inadequate for Howard Johnson's corned beef. They had taken their time to inspect the countryside—Rip Van Winkle absorbed in the neon mountains of Route One—and Pound had found the traffic incredible.

"All the time I was in the bughouse," he remarked, "I kept saying there were 160 million nuts outside, but I didn't realize what the poor devils were up against."

He shakes hands with the hard grip and strong forearm of a man who has played much tennis, and he dominates a room as if his armchair were down-stage center. He wore an open-necked shirt of a particularly god-awful magenta, tails out, and a

pair of outsized slacks with the cuffs rolled up. A black coat, flung cloakwise over his shoulders, completed the costume. If the description sounds theatrical, it is intended to suggest that there is in Pound a good deal of the actor, a good deal, indeed, of

the ham. His bearded face, mobile, is the bust of some morning-after Bacchus; but it is seldom in repose. He sits on the lower part of his spine, head supported on the backrest of the chair, eyes closed; his restless hands are forever searching for glasses, or plucking pencil and notebook from a breast pocket, or shaping ideas in the air. Now and again, he bolts from his chair like some Poseidon from the deep, and his good eye—his right eye—is suddenly shrewd and alive.

On Education

Pound opened the conversation by bringing me a message from a Mrs. Lane in Arlington [NATIONAL REVIEW, April 19] and by commenting sociably upon his pleasure in visiting the South. I inquired, in the same agreeable vein, what he wanted most to do now that his full release was in prospect. The question was intended as no more than an ice-breaker, but Pound took it seriously. He said, leaping up, that God knew there was enough to be done right here. "What about some constitutional government in this country?" What about this filth that passes for education?

He began to talk generally of education. From everything he could read (he hated to read, reading was abominable, nothing but pulp came from publishers anyhow; Bowen's *Coke* was a masterpiece; it was a travesty upon the name of education that he was seventy years old, and in his second kindergarten, before he discovered Coke's *Institutes*)—from everything he could read (he read nothing any more, none of the contemporary poets, how can any contemporary criticism of contemporary works amount to a damn?)—from everything he could read, the schools are full of bilge. College freshmen should be required to know two languages, at least one of them inflected, and should be obliged to take analytics; and they should study U.S. history, not by way of Tocqueville and "Sandbag," or Toynbee (Toynbee is flapdoodle), but rather by way of Adams, Van Buren and Benton. It is nonsense for illiterates to be teaching the future when they know nothing of the past.

I single out these observations from a torrent of conversation, much as one plucks a recognizable rooftop from a flood. Pound no sooner launches one thought than he embarks upon another, and I summarize his critique of today's classrooms as one collects miscellaneous fishes after some volcanic churning on the ocean floor. He was thus, in his own fashion, treating current poetry by commenting upon the Italian foreign office in the days of Mussolini, when he sensed that he had lost me altogether.

"I really do have an orderly mind," he said abruptly. And then in a penetrating sentence: "I only want to make certain my interlocutors know the beginnings." Then he was off again, into the causes of war, the suppression of historic truth (of one historian, banished to obscurity by the educationists, Pound had an epitaph: "Poor fellow, he committed accuracy"), the corruptions of the Federal Reserve Board, the usury rates of Byzantium, the reasons why he had not translated a particular Chinese writer, the enduring characteristics of the Manchu Dynasty, the old days in London with Ford Madox Ford. It was wonderful to eat something hot; he had forgotten what it meant for food to be hot. At Rapallo there are surf rafts, and one floats on a blue sea. Had he mentioned that Hemingway once sent him a shark's jaw, the grave of the unknown sailor?

Again the pause, the bright and searching eye. "I don't have a one-track mind," he apologized. He slumped back; he apologized for slumping: "I cannot hold my head up for long; I have to rest it on something; I offered to be tried *in camera*, lying on a couch, but their reverences thought not; no wonder my head hurts, all of Europe fell on it; when I talk it is like an explosion in an art museum, you have to hunt around for the pieces."

Our small group included Miss Charlotte Kohler, editor of the *Virginia Quarterly Review*. Pound had corresponded with her over a long period of time (his code writing reduces the journal to the Va. ¼-ly Rev.), and she had brought galley proofs of several additional poems in the Pisan Cantos that will appear in the *Review* this summer. Pound observed benignly that all literary quarterlies are mutton, dead from the neck up, and inquired what Miss Kohler might do to improve the situation. She is a brilliant and attractive woman, with a tough, resilient mind, and after a brief defense tossed the question back at him.

On Ideas

He said, responding to one of her comments, that variety alone is not enough. There has to be some excitement, and the only way to get that is to put a couple of good minds in range of each other, and let them go to eye-gouging. This took him back to Wyndham Lewis, and to Ford again, and to Yeats. He was asked how he happened to encourage Yeats, twenty years his senior, when he was in a position to do so in England and Ireland forty years ago. He said he thought Yeats was the greatest poet in the world, discovered he wasn't; Yeats is a gargoyle; Eliot is spoiled by the company he keeps. "Dammit, you've got to examine ideas one at a time; I don't care whether the idea you put in your review comes from a Bolshevik, a Fascist, or a bloody pinko, his idea ought to be examined by itself."

Miss Kohler commented that Pound's Pisan Cantos obviously are still incomplete at the point marked by the manuscript he had sent her, and this led Pound into an extended comparative analysis of *La Divina Commedia*. I am sophomore-ignorant of Dante, and the conversation passed clean over my head; but it was evident that Pound was here speaking with easy sureness and a confident grasp of the complexities of both his work and Dante's. His own parallel characters have now passed through Hell and Purgatory and are somewhere in Paradise. When you paint on a big canvas, he said, gesturing largely, you have to start colors down here, gesturing small, but it all ties in, it all ties in.

As for explicating some of his more obscure passages, he had once spent four pages explaining a two-line poem (and that reminded him of a two-line poem by Hemingway; what is the one big reason for the survival of the Catholic Church? Versatility), and damned if he would add to that. He was asked to explain his work often enough. When the word came that he was coming out of St. Liz, an invitation arrived from some group, he could not remember the name, devoted to pondering the aesthetics of aesthetics, and to making higher criticism of the higher criticism. What an omelet their meeting must be! Yolks of the largest and freshest eggheads only. Winchell was not all bad. Winchell had raised hell when Elliott Roosevelt bumped a civilian off the plane so his damned dog could have a ride. And that reminded him of the story of little Abraham who had to write a sentence using the words "once" and "twice." He wrote: "While I was sleeping in my bed last night, I was bit by a Wuntz, twice." What the Fed is doing to the monetary supply is not new. Once, twice. And back to Byzantium.

On Writing and Reading

It was past five o'clock by this time, and Pound was tiring. As we rose to go, someone, still searching for a brief and useful quote, asked Pound what he would advise young writers to do. Surprisingly, he was terse and to the point: "Get a good dictionary and learn the meaning of words." And as for reading: "Read Linnaeus. Not for botany. Read him because he never used an inexact word." That was the trouble with the whole damned educational system. All this bilge, and the universities can't turn out a college senior who can write a coherent sentence.

Reading this over, I doubt that I have said much of anything new about Ezra Pound. I can remember, as a child, a certain ballroom adorned by a multi-faceted chandelier, formed of a hundred tiny mirrors, which revolved slowly in the glow of colored spotlights. Pound's mind spins and refracts in the same way. Or to shift the simile, his speech is like the focusing of a ground-glass camera:

The subject is always there, but now it is blurred, now sharp, now vaguely defined. He loves talk, and this mistress may yet prove his undoing, for his tongue is unbridled, and sly, deceitful men will ride his improprieties for all the embarrassment that can be drawn from them. And Pound, to recall his criticism of Eliot, also is hurt by the company he keeps; he swims with the grand abandon of an ancient shark, but a host of parasitic pilot fish ride on his back. So far, he is not disposed to shake them off.

That Pound, as an American citizen, made some imprudent broadcasts from Italy during the war years, is plain enough. By nice legal definition, perhaps these exhortations gave enough curious aid and comfort to the enemy to constitute treason to the United States, though two hours with Pound are enough to prompt grave doubts on this score; one envisions Bill Mauldin's Buck and Willy listening to Pound on the short-wave.

Whatever these sins may have been, they are long past; the nation has forgiven worse offenders. Pound now has served twelve years as a political prisoner in a land that prides itself on political freedom, and it seems to me good that at long last, this old Ulysses will go back to Rapallo, there to lie in a raft on the infinite sea, and gaze at the infinite sky.

A Spy for Stalin

An informer who put the finger on many of Stalin's victims stands indicted—but only for perjury

RALPH DE TOLEDANO

Mark Zborowski stands indicted of one count of perjury. The law, in its picayune majesty, accuses him of lying when he denied some fifty meetings with Jack Soble, convicted member of an atomic spy ring, and of association with Vassili Zaroubin, Soviet master of espionage in the United States. But whether or not the courts decide that the grand jury spoke true in its charge, they will not consider Zborowski's admitted apprenticeship as Stalin's spy in the 1930's among those prisoners of frustration, the Trotskyists. Nor will any human judge pass sentence for Zborowski's betrayal of his closest friends—or for the brutal deaths which resulted from that betrayal.

He was a struggling student at Grenoble when the NKVD approached him with an offer of money and future academic kudos in the Soviet Union, from which his parents had fled. The year was 1933, the cellars of the Lubianka had begun to fill with those who would figure in the Great Purge trials, and Stalin dreamed that every footfall on the Kremlin's pavement white was a Trotskyist with serpentine and syenite. He wanted his personal agents to penetrate the Trotskyist movement, to report the names of those still in Russia who maintained a relationship with Communism's Fallen Angel.

Others would be assigned to smash a pickaxe into Trotsky's restless brain. It was Zborowski's job to make himself an intimate of Leon Sedov, Trotsky's ill-fated son and a leader of the Fourth International's European operations. Eventually, Zborowski was told, he would be expected to lure Sedov to a place where he might be kidnapped for transshipment (dead or alive) to the Soviet Union. The NKVD manufactured a "revolutionary" past for Zborowski and gave him a monthly salary of 4,000 francs. This was a munificent sum (at the prewar rate of exchange) and Zborowski explained his affluence to the poverty-ridden Trotskyists as an "inheritance" from a capitalist aunt in Poland.

In the fervid world of Trotskyist intrigue, Mark Zborowski posed as a willing worker against Stalinism. A great show of security was made in the Fourth International, but Zborowski's account of his political antecedent was accepted without any check. He became one of Sedov's trusted lieutenants—and of sufficient importance to the NKVD to be given their secret phone number at the Soviet Embassy in Paris. Alexander Orlov, a high-ranking NKVD official who subsequently defected to the West, read Zborowski's reports to Stalin. And so we know that the Trotsky-Sedov correspondence—"correspondence," says Orlov, that "embraced everything of importance to their movement including secret information from and about Russia"—was regularly digested by Zborowski. The names of secret sympathizers in Russia therefore became the property of the NKVD—and of Stalin, who had ordered that all Zborowski's reports be sent to him. The rubber-tired Soviet equivalent of the tumbril rolled in Russia.

By 1936, the Fourth International was at its busiest and most influential. The rising terror within Russia, the stirrings in Asia, the growing influence of the trade union movement, and the Spanish Civil War found the Trotskyists deeply involved. British Intelligence and the *Deuxième Bureau* had little time for an examination of these activities, but the NKVD was immensely interested. In July of that year, the Fourth International called a secret conclave in Paris. Elaborate plans to keep the Soviets from spying on the meeting were made. The delegates, as they arrived in Paris, were to make rendezvous with a trusted courier, at various Metro stations. The courier would conduct them singly to the meeting place. Sedov looked about him for a man untainted by suspicion to serve as the courier. He chose Zborowski.

Their reports from Russia indicated that there was a serious leak in Trotskyism's leadership. To protect

89

the Trotsky archives, invaluable in rebutting the charges of the Moscow trials, they were packed into fifteen large bundles and moved secretly from a private home to the International Institute of Social History, a center of Marxist studies run by Boris Nicolaevsky. Four people knew of this—Sedov, Nicolaevsky, Mrs. David Dallin, and Zborowski. On the night of November 6, 1936—days after the transfer—the Institute was burglarized. Money and other documents were untouched—but the Trotsky archives were stolen. Zborowski protested the raid to his NKVD superiors. "This will throw suspicion on me," he said. He was told coldly to mind his own business. "Those papers are a present to Stalin on the anniversary of the Revolution," was the explanation.

But Zborowski fingered more than papers. In 1937, Ignace Reiss broke with the Soviet apparatus in Western Europe—and there was consternation in the ranks. Reiss was a veteran of the underground wars, a hero of the German struggles. He knew Richard Sorge, another spy then posing as a Nazi as he built up a fantastically successful espionage ring in China and Japan. Reiss' high rank, moreover, gave him first-hand knowledge of the structure and scope of Soviet operations in the West. It was mandatory that he be murdered before he could talk. Hunted by the NKVD and suspicious of the capitalist police, Reiss turned to Sedov. Three people knew that Reiss had agreed to leave Lausanne for a meeting with Sedov in Rheims—and one of them was Zborowski. When Reiss' bullet-torn body was found in the woods near the French border, a ticket to Rheims was in his pocket.

Trotskyist leaders, en route to Spain, stopped off in Paris to see Sedov—and the NKVD phone at the Soviet Embassy rang loudly. A report that Alexander Barmine, youngest Soviet general and key diplomat, was in flight from Stalin reached the NKVD—via Zborowski. When General Walter G. Krivitsky, chief of Red Army Intelligence in Western Europe and a friend of Reiss, broke with his past in those nights of the long knives, Sedov gave him a bodyguard—Zborowski—and the NKVD moved in. One unsuccessful attempt was made on Krivitsky's life in Paris,

and the French police assigned men to keep an eye on him. Orlov reports that the NKVD decided to bide its time. (Suicide was committed on Krivitsky in a Washington hotel room early in 1941.)

By 1938, Zborowski had promoted himself to a Damon and Pythias relationship with Sedov. When Sedov was suddenly stricken, Zborowski rushed to a phone to summon an ambulance—and alert the NKVD. Friends of the healthy young man felt that he would recover quickly—but they tried to keep his illness and the name of his hospital secret. Yet Sedov died, under circumstances which are considered mysterious. To students of Stalin's secret service, however, they were no more mysterious than the sudden death in Cuba of Tina Modotti, an NKVD *apparatchik*, whose health deteriorated dramatically after she had broken with the Red underground.

When Alexander Orlov could no longer stomach his work in the NKVD, he too broke. Unlike many who had departed before him, he kept his own counsel. Knowing about Zborowski, he stayed away from the Trotskyists. But he wrote a detailed anonymous letter to Trotsky, warning him of the Soviet agent in the Fourth International. Mrs. Dallin was in Mexico at the time, and Trotsky showed her the letter. Anonymous letters were not new to him. The NKVD used them to denounce his most trusted followers, hoping to plant a seed of suspicion, to cause dissension in the Trotskyist movement. He showed Mrs. Dallin another letter, accusing her of being a Stalinist agent. When she returned to Paris, she told Zborowski about it. "Smears," he said. And he laughed.

The collapse of Europe brought Zborowski to the United States in 1941. At first, he earned his living as the foreman for a metal products company in Brooklyn. One summer day in 1943, as he strolled along the Coney Island beach—or so he says—Zborowski was approached by a stranger. "Finally we have found you again," the stranger said. Zborowski swears that he refused to accept an order to return to work for the NKVD. But within days he had quit his job, moved to Manhattan—and to the same house where some of his

former Paris associates lived. In 1945 he turned up at Columbia University, doing anthropological research and being cultivated by such people as Gene Weltfish—later to charge that the U.S. was using germ warfare in Korea. A grant from the United States Mental Health Institute brought Zborowski $24,000 for research.

He seemed free of all suspicion. Then, in 1954, Alexander Orlov came out of hiding. His articles on the NKVD had caused a sensation when they appeared in *Life* magazine. He began to mingle with New York's Russian colony. One day, David Dallin, then gathering material for his book on Soviet espionage, asked Orlov how thoroughly the NKVD had penetrated the Trotskyist movement. "The closest friend of Trotsky's son was an agent," Orlov replied. And then he asked, "Is it true that Sedov cried like a child in 1936 when he read that Zinoviev and Kamenev were executed?" It was a question laying bare that curious sentimentality of the *apparatchik*—an intimate and damning detail from one of Zborowski's reports.

The Dallins confronted Zborowski. He calmly admitted that he had spied for the NKVD. Yes, he had reported on his friend Sedov, he had informed the NKVD that Krivitsky was in Paris. All this was true. But he had always reported "late"—after his information had lost its value—never when it could do harm. And he had been very angry when the NKVD had stolen the Trotsky archives. He had not known they would do such a thing. He was sorry, so sorry that he wrote a "confession" for the Dallins. Two years later, he repeated the same story to the Senate Internal Security Subcommittee. Everything that he admitted had occurred in Paris, beyond the reach of American law. He returned to his anthropological research on the cultural components in responses to pain.

But the wheel was spinning. The Soble-Abel-Albam atomic spy ring was broken up by the FBI. Jack Soble turned State's Evidence. Among those he named was Mark Zborowski. Fifty meetings, said the government. None, said Zborowski. The indictment was handed up. The rest of the story remained untold. But guilty or innocent, the story already on the record could never be expunged.

'The Damage We Have Done to Ourselves'

Remarks by William F. Buckley Jr. at the Khrush-chev Protest Rally at Carnegie Hall on September 17

Ladies and gentlemen:

The damage Khrushchev can do to us on this trip is not comparable to the damage we have done to ourselves. Khrushchev is here. And his being here profanes the nation. But the harm we have done, we have done to ourselves; and for that we cannot hold Khrushchev responsible. There is nothing he is in a position to do, as he passes through our land, that can aggravate the national dishonor. We can only dishonor ourselves. Mr. Eisenhower invited him to come. But that was a transient damage that might have been laid to the vagaries of personal diplomacy. The lasting damage is related to the national acquiescence in Mr. Eisenhower's aberration. That acquiescence required the lapse of our critical and moral faculties. And for so long as they are in suspension, regeneration is not possible.

I deplore the fact that Khrushchev travels about this country—having been met at the frontier by our own prince, who arrived with his first string of dancing girls, and a majestic caravan of jewels and honey and spices; I mind that he will wend his lordly way from city to city, where the Lilliputians will fuss over his needs, weave garlands through the ring in his nose, shiver when he belches out his threats, and labor in panic to sate his imperial appetites. I mind that Khrushchev is here; but I mind more that Eisenhower invited him. I mind that Eisenhower invited him, but I mind much more the defense of that invitation by the *thought-leaders* of the nation. Khrushchev cannot by his presence here permanently damage us, I repeat; and neither can Mr. Eisenhower by inviting him. But we are gravely damaged if it is true that in welcoming Khrushchev, Eisenhower speaks for America; for in that case the people have lost their reason; and we cannot hope to live down the experience until we have recovered our reason, and regained our moral equilibrium.

I mind, in a word, the so-called "reasons" that have been advanced—and accepted—as to why Mr. Eisenhower issued the invitation. I mind first that "reasons" are being put forward, but mostly that they are being accepted. Khrushchev's visit has been successfully transmuted into a "diplomatic necessity"; and many even speak of it as a stroke of diplomatic genius. If the invitation had been rendered by President Eisenhower in his capacity as principal agent of American foreign policy, the deed would have been explosive enough. But the true dimensions of our national crisis became visible upon the appearance of the concentric ripples of assent that followed upon the issuance of the invitation. *A splendid idea,* said the chairman of the Foreign Relations Committee of the Senate, having presumably first consulted the editorial columns of the *New York Times* to make sure his compass was properly oriented.

And in a matter of days, we were being solemnly advised by the majority of the editorial writers of the nation that a) the invitation was bound to meet with the approval of all those who favor peace in the world and good will towards men; and that b) in any event, those who opposed the invitation have no alternative save to abide by the spirit that moved the President—as a matter of loyalty. "If you have to throw something at him," said Mr. Nixon upon touching ground after his visit to Moscow, "throw flowers." And then Mr. Gallup confirmed the popularity of the President's decision—which, it turns out, exceeds even the popularity of the President himself.

I do not recall that six months ago Mr. Gallup canvassed the American people on the question whether Mr. Khrushchev should be invited to this country, but I doubt that anyone would dispute my guess that as emphatic a majority would then have voted *against* the visit.

What happened? The sheer cogency of the invitation evidently struck the people as forcibly as the superiority of round as against square wheels is said one day to have struck our primitive ancestors. *Obviously* the visit is in order, the people seem to have grasped, giving way before the intuitions and analyses of their leaders. How mischievous is the habit of adducing reasons behind everything that is done! I can, happily and unassailably, delight in lobster and despise crabmeat; all my life—as long as I refrain from giving *reasons* why the one food suits and the other sickens. But when I seek rationally to motivate my preferences, I lose my authority. If only the publicists had refrained from shoring up the President's caprice with a Gothic rational structure! But no. We are a rational people. We do nothing without cause. There must be cause behind the invitation; and so the reasons for it are conjured up.

I have not heard a "reason" why Khrushchev should come to this country that is not in fact a reason why he should *not* come to this country. *He will see for himself the health and wealth of the land?* Very well; and having confirmed the fact, what are we to expect? That he will weaken in his adherence to his maniacal course? Because the average American has the use of one and two-thirds toilets? One might as well expect the Bishop of Rome to break the apostolic succession upon being confronted by

NATIONAL REVIEW

40 Cents
September 26, 1959

A JOURNAL OF FACT AND OPINION

One World

the splendid new YMCA in Canton, Ohio. Does Khrushchev really *doubt* that there are 67 million automobiles in this country? What is he to do now that he is here? Count them? And if it is true that he doubts the statistics on American production and the American way of life, statistics that have been corroborated by his own technicians—then what reason is there to believe that he will trust the evidence of his own eyes as more reliable? And what will he do if there is a discrepancy? Fire Alger Hiss?

If Khrushchev were a man to be moved by empirical brushes with reality, how could he continue to believe in Communism? He cannot turn a corner in the Soviet Union without colliding against stark evidence of the fraudulence of Marxist theory. Where is the workers' paradise? In the two-room apartments that house five families? In the frozen reaches where he commits to slavery the millions upon millions who fail to appreciate the fact that under the Marxist prescription they have been elevated to a state of total freedom? In the headquarters of the secret police, where files are kept on every citizen of the Soviet Union on the *presumption* that every citizen is an enemy of the proletarian state?

Any man who is capable of being affected by the evidence of things as they are need not leave Russia to discover that the major premises of Karl Marx are mistaken. Dante cultivated a love of heaven by demonstrating the horrors of hell. It did not occur to him that the devil might be converted by taking him around the glories of the Court of the Medici. What reason have we to believe that a man who knows Russia and *still* has not rejected Marx, will be moved by the sight of Levittown?

But even if Khrushchev fails to readjust his views after witnessing the economic miracles wrought by capitalism—in which connection it is relevant to recall the amazement of American industrial leaders on learning last winter that Mikoyan knew more about American industrial accomplishments than they did—even if Khrushchev finds out that Mikoyan was right all along, will he learn that other great lesson which the President advanced as a principal "reason" why Khrushchev should come? Is he going to encounter that firmness of American resolution which will cause him, when he returns to Russia, to furrow his brow in anxiety on resuming the war against us?

I suggest that this brings us to the major reason why Khrushchev should *not* have been invited. If indeed the nation is united behind Mr. Eisenhower in this invitation, then the nation is united behind an act of diplomatic sentimentality which can only confirm Khrushchev in the contempt he feels for the dissipated morale of a nation far gone, as the theorists of Marxism have all along contended, in decrepitude That he should be invited to visit here as though he were susceptible to a rational engagement! That

"I kees your hand, madam."

COURTSHIP
The Year of Our Lord 1959

he should achieve orthodox diplomatic recognition not three years after shocking history itself by the brutalities of Budapest; months after endorsing the shooting down of an unarmed American plane; only weeks since he last shrieked his intention of demolishing the West should it show any resistance to the march of socialism; only days since publishing in an American magazine his undiluted resolve to enslave the citizens of Free Berlin—that such an introduction should end up constituting his credentials for a visit to America will teach him something about the West some of us wish he might never have known.

What is it stands in the way of Communism's march? The little homilies of American capitalism? A gigantic air force which depends less on gasoline than on the pronouncements of the Committee for a Sane Nuclear Policy to know whether it can ever be airborne? Have we not something more to face Khrushchev with? Is this indeed the nature of the enemy, Khrushchev is entitled to wonder exultantly, after twelve days of giddy American cameraderie—will he not cherish as never before the pronouncements of Marx about the weakness of the capitalist opposition? Will he not return convinced that behind the modulated hubbub at the White House, in the State Department, at the city halls, at the economic clubs, at the industrial banquets, he heard—*with his own ears*—the death rattle of the West? Is there a *reason* why we should voluntarily expose to the enemy the great lesion of the West—our deficient understanding—which saps the will without which we can never save the world for freedom? Will Khrushchev respect us more as, by our deeds, we proclaim and proclaim again and again our hallucinations, in the grinding teeth of the evidence, that we and the Soviet Union can work together for a better world?

It is the imposture of irrationality in the guise of rationality that frightens. The visit is timely, we are told. Why? State one reason. Why was it not timely, if it is timely now, a year ago? If Eisenhower is correct now in welcoming Khrushchev, then was he not wrong yesterday in not welcoming him? But we were all pro-Eisenhower yesterday—when he declared he would not meet with the Soviet leaders while under pressure of blackmail in regard to Berlin. And yet we are pro-Eisenhower today—when he proceeds to meet with Khrushchev, with the threat still hanging over us. If it is so very urgent that we should acquaint Khrushchev with the highways and byways of the United States, why is Eisenhower doing it seven long years after he first had the opportunity? Why has the same nation that implicitly endorsed the social boycott of Soviet leaders changed its mind so abruptly—to harmonize with so dissonant a change in position by our lackadaisical President? (The social history of of the White House under Mr. Eisenhower will, after all, record only one exclusion and one addition during his tenure. Khrushchev was added, Senator McCarthy was ejected. And both times, the thousands cheered.) Is it a mark of loyalty to go along? What if Mr. Eisenhower had announced that, upon reflection, Red China should be invited into the United Nations? Would it be a mark of loyalty for us to assent? Or if he had decided to yield Quemoy and Matsu? A mark of loyalty to go along? And Berlin?

This afternoon Mayor Robert Wagner danced attendance upon Mr. Khrushchev. Did he do so because Premier Khrushchev is head of a foreign state and so entitled, ex officio, to the hospitality of New York's mayor? It isn't that simple, as we pointed out in the *National Review Bulletin* last week. Last year Mayor Wagner ostentatiously announced his refusal to greet Ibn Saud—on the grounds that Ibn Saud discriminates against Jews in Saudi Arabia, and no man who discriminates against Jews in Saudi Arabia is by God going to be handled courteously by Bob Wagner, mayor of New York. Now, as everybody knows, Nikita Khrushchev not only discriminates against Jews, he kills them. On the other hand, he does much the same thing to Catholics and Protestants. Could *that* be why Mr. Wagner consented to honor Khrushchev? Khrushchev murders people without regard to race, color or creed, that is, on straight FEPC lines; and therefore, whatever he is guilty of, he is not guilty of discrimination, and so he is entitled to Robert Wagner's hospitality? Is that the shape of the new rationality?

Ladies and gentlemen, we deem it the central revelation of Western experience that man cannot ineradicably stain himself, for the wells of regeneration are infinitely deep. No temple has ever been so profaned that it cannot be purified; no man is ever truly lost; no nation irrevocably dishonored. Khrushchev cannot take permanent advantage of our temporary disadvantage, for it is the West he is fighting. And in the West there lie, however encysted, the ultimate resources, which are moral in nature. Khrushchev is *not* aware that the gates of hell shall not prevail against us. Even out of the depths of despair, we take heart in the knowledge that it cannot matter how deep we fall, for there is always hope. In the end, we will bury him.

Many criticism of Ike

An Open Letter to Dr. Oppenheimer

Who is Dr. Oppenheimer and Why? Perhaps he doesn't know himself. But Dr. Medford Evans, who is easily the world's greatest authority on the subject of Dr. Oppenheimer, tells him here

MEDFORD EVANS

[handwritten: Concerned about atomic spying]

Dr. J. Robert Oppenheimer
Institute for Advanced Study
Princeton, New Jersey

Dear Dr. Oppenheimer:

This letter is in three parts:

1. Statement of the hypothesis that you are patriotic and humanitarian, in spite of much circumstantial evidence to the contrary.

2. With this hypothesis, an explanation of your determined opposition in 1949-50 to U.S. development of the hydrogen bomb.

3. An exhortation that you now tell what you know of clandestine channels of atomic information and materials.

At this point you may not want to read further, but others may, and as this is an open letter I will continue. For the benefit of the others I will be explicit about several things which are no news to you. At the same time this is not a primer of atomic politics, and a degree of understanding of the great figure you cut in the Cold-War world will be taken for granted. I thought once to introduce myself, but it will be clear to you anyhow that I am some guy with just enough information to ask certain questions which you are the one man in all the world best qualified to answer.

For the curious and the skeptical, documentary notes are attached. [See page 235].

I. HYPOTHESIS

Assume that you are not a dedicated Communist. Since you are, as Edward Teller observed, "complicated,"[1] you may not know yourself whether you are a dedicated Communist or not. Let us assume that you are not.

It is not an easy assumption. William Borden, Yale Law graduate whom the late Senator Brien McMahon picked to be Executive Director of the Congressional Joint Committee on Atomic Energy—*to supplant Fred Rhodes and Dave Teeple, who were considered too hipped on security*—after five years in the political maelstrom created by the atom, emerged with a singular grasp of officially confidential data (AEC, FBI, congressional) and the stark conclusion: "More probably than not, J. Robert Oppenheimer is an agent of the Soviet Union."[2]

From the record now published, it was a prudent inference. Intellectually prudent, that is. Whether Borden was prudent to say it out loud is another matter. But what else is one to make of your conduct? What can be made of regular cash contributions to Communist causes all during the period of the Nazi-Soviet pact? (That you so contributed is your own testimony,[3] not an accusation by enemies.) What do your friends have to say about that? (I will not say much about it here, either.)

On the other hand, if you were a dedicated Communist, would you not have done more damage to the United States than seems yet to have been done? After all, the Soviet Union has not yet cried to us, Checkmate! and if you were a Soviet agent how would it be possible for the Soviet Union to be militarily thwarted in anything? You were for seven years the key man in the American atomic energy project. The particular seven years I have in mind (1946-1952, inclusive) were Stalinist years in the Soviet Union. Beria was Stalin's man on the atom. If you were a Soviet agent you were Beria's man. Is it conceivable that Beria told you what to do? Dean Latimer did not think it conceivable that General Groves told you what to do.[4] I do not think it easily conceivable that Beria told you what to do. I cannot see how he could impose discipline on you, and I cannot see you willingly submitting to his discipline. Or anyone else's, for that matter. After all, you had become the shatterer of worlds.[5] Who was Beria? Who was Stalin?

As Old as Delphi

Let us assume that you are not a Soviet agent, not a dedicated Communist.

At first blush it is a comfortable assumption. But the comfort is short-lived. You are the emancipated new man, master of the new force; yet your characteristic style is as old as Delphi—with this difference: that where the oracle was ambiguous about the future, you are ambiguous about the past and the present.

Mere reticence is natural enough. After all, as you told the Gray Board: "*Look, I have had a lot of secrets in my head a long time. It does not matter who I associate with. I don't talk about those secrets. Only a very skillful guy might pick up a trace of information as to where I had been or what I was up to.*"[6] This kind of sophistication has surely been useful to the United States now and then. We can hardly expect you to tell us, either, the whole truth. For one thing, as P.M.S. Blackett contended,[7] there isn't time for that.

What is tantalizing is that you so often drop clues. Or so it seems. Perhaps they are apples for Atalanta. I think they are clues. For example, in 1947 you made a speech before a committee of the UN, and quite gratuitously you said—the context concerns the difficulties of disseminating scientific information—"*It requires instruction, it requires work to get an under-*

standing of these things abroad. I know this from experience. I know it is not enough to tell someone a secret: it is very hard to give away a secret. You have to work at it week after week after week because these things are complex.[8] Now why in the world would you say a thing like that?

Is Truth a mistress whom you will not marry but cannot leave **alone?**

The Case of Eldred Nelson

Do you remember when, during the 1954 hearings on your AEC security clearance, counsel for the government read to you a transcript of a wartime interview between you and General Groves' security officer? In that interview (September 12, 1943) Colonel Lansdale told you that he had "reason to believe that you yourself [had been] . . . felt out . . . to ascertain how you felt about . . . passing a little information **to the party.**"[9]

If any such attempt was made, you told Lansdale, "it was so gentle I did not know it."

Then Lansdale tried **to** get you to name some acquaintance who might logically have been suspected of making some such attempt.

"There is," you said, *"a girl called Eldred Nelson."* An odd thing for you to say to a Colonel of Military Intelligence in 1943.

In 1954 you emphasized to Roger Robb, counsel for the Government Board, how odd it had been. "Eldred Nelson," you assured Robb, *"is not a girl. He is not a Communist."*[10] Transcripts, of course, are liable **to error,** but stenographers seldom supply a name like "Eldred."

"Is it now clear to you," asked Robb, "who Colonel **Lansdale was** talking about?"

"I don't know," you replied. *"It might well be Steve Nelson."*

"Isn't that pretty plain?"

"Yes."

"Why didn't you mention Steve Nelson?"

"I seem to have mentioned a Nelson."[11]

Bizarre!

Facing down a police officer, you withhold the name of Steve Nelson (you are later to tell Robb: *"I knew he was a Communist and an important Communist"*).[12] Then, gratuitously, you introduce the name of Eldred Nelson (you will tell Robb: *"He was*

Kreuttner

"Be emphatic about Witch Hunts, McCarthyism, Guilt-by-Association, Police State Methods, Climate of Fear, Reign of Terror, Abridgement of Academic Freedom, and Thought Control. Be vague about Hiss, Greenglass, Gold, Fuchs, Remington, Rosenberg, White, Coe, Eisler, Oppenheimer, Lattimore, Sobell, Ware, Silvermaster and Coplon."

a student of mine. . . . He was not a Communist"[13] (It does you little good, it does Eldred Nelson little **harm (so** far as we know), by itself it causes Lansdale little trouble. But it looks like involving the innocent to protect the guilty. Is this what your admirers have in mind when they call you **seer** and saint?[14] Perhaps so. **Loyalty to** Steve (you were to say: *"He and my wife . . . had close affectionate relationships and I was a natural bystander"*[15]) made you furnish Lansdale the wrong given name; compassion for Eldred made you, to throw the police off his track, lie about his gender; but intellectual honesty dictated the correct surname. *Magna est veritas et praevalebit!* "I seem to have mentioned a Nelson."

"I would suppose," George Kennan observes, "that you might just as well have asked Leonardo da Vinci to distort an anatomical drawing as that you should ask Robert Oppenheimer to speak . . . to the **sort of questions** we were talking about and speak dishonestly."[16]

Superficially, Kennan sounds absurd; for the ordinary supposition would be that if you wanted an anatomical **drawing** distorted **no one**

could do it more artfully than Leonardo could have done it. Yet there is an odd felicity in comparing the prodigious and inscrutable painter of Mona Lisa—the military engineer of Caesar Borgia—with the brilliant director of the laboratory where the first atomic bombs were made, and resolute opponent of the manufacture of hydrogen bombs.

Kennan may have been right, too, in thinking that you have an ineradicable streak of **honesty.** Typically, your speech is an elaborate cryptogram. The tissue of lies is shot through with truth. Similarly with your conduct. In the role of Soviet agent you are almost totally convincing. Yet a stubborn loyalty to the United States apparently persists. You have certainly confused us, but it is almost uproarious to think how you must have **baffled the Comrades.** Otto John is a piker. For he is frivolous. You are serious. Or so it seems.

I am going to assume that, complicated as you are, **you are primarily** patriotic and humanitarian.

II. EXPLANATION

Why did you so energetically oppose the hydrogen bomb program in 1949-50? This question was explored in the hearings before the Gray Board with metaphysical thoroughness and inconclusiveness. Your friends have assumed that you were moved by two considerations: 1) that the U.S. was adequately armed without the H-bomb, and 2) that the use of an H-bomb would actually be just too terrible, that the A-bomb, through which you had already "known sin," was at least enough for the consciences of yourself, your fellow scientists, and the rest of us. Your friends have thought you fully justified in holding such views, whether you were objectively correct or not (assuming that there is here any such thing as objective correctness), and they have further thought it unfair to you and dangerous to all concerned that you should in any way be "put on trial" for having expressed **such** views, merely because they turned out to be counter to the official policy eventually adopted.

Your critics, in contrast, have thought that your friends have somehow missed the whole point, for to these critics the point at issue in the *we can't possibly keep them from getting it too; they depend on us that much, they are tied to us that close*—had you said something like that, the debate might have gone a different way. Perhaps you thought, Surely they can see that for themselves, at least with the hints I have given! However, we have been credulous of everything but the obvious.

Hints and Hedging

You have given hints repeatedly. In the post-mortem before the Gray Board in 1954 you said:

> The notion that the thermonuclear arms race was something that was in the interests of this country to avoid if it could was very clear to us [General Advisory Committee] in 1949. . . . We thought it was something to avoid even if we could jump the gun by a couple of years, or even if we could outproduce the enemy, because we were infinitely more vulnerable and infinitely less likely to initiate the use of these weapons. . . . This is an idea which I believe is still right, but I think what was not clear to us then and what is clearer to me now is that it probably lay wholly beyond our power to prevent the Russians somehow from getting ahead with it. I think if we could have taken any action at that time which would have precluded their development of this weapon, it would have been a very good bet to take that. . . . I believe that *their atomic effort was quite imitative* and that made it quite natural for us to think that *their thermonuclear work would be quite imitative* and that we should not set the pace in this development.[21]

Again you said:

> I think we were right in believing that any method available consistent with honor and security for *keeping these objects out of the arsenals of the enemy* would have been a good course to follow.[22]

To me these look like hints. I understand that later in the hearing Gordon Gray picked you up on this very matter, and you hedged a bit. As follows:

> GRAY: Is it your opinion, Doctor, that the Russians would not have sought to develop a hydrogen bomb unless they knew in one way or another . . . that this country was proceeding with it?
> OPPENHEIMER: That was my opinion in 1949. . . .
> GRAY: . . . Would it not have been reasonable to expect . . . that they

---

would do anything to increase their military strength?
> OPPENHEIMER: Right.
> GRAY: Whatever it might be.
> OPPENHEIMER: Oh, sure.
> GRAY: So you don't intend to have this record suggest that you felt that if those who opposed the development of the hydrogen bomb prevailed that would mean that the world would not be confronted with the hydrogen bomb?
> OPPENHEIMER: It would not necessarily mean—we thought on the whole it would make it less likely. That the Russians would attempt and less likely that they would succeed in the undertaking.
> GRAY: . . . That is two things. One, the likelihood of their success would we all hope still be related to their own capabilities and not to information they would receive from our efforts. So what you mean to say is that since they would not attempt it they would not succeed?
> OPPENHEIMER: No. [I believe this the most ambiguous flat *No* I ever read.] I believe what we then thought was that the incentive to do it would be far greater if they knew we were doing it, and we had succeeded. Let me, for instance, take a conjecture. Suppose we had not done anything about the atom during the war. I don't think you could guarantee that the Russians would never have had an atomic bomb. But I believe they would not have one nearly as soon as they have. I think both the fact of our success, the immense amount of publicity, the prestige of the weapon, the espionage they collect, all of this made it an absolutely higher priority thing, and we thought similar circumstances might apply to the hydrogen bomb. We were always clear that there might be a Russian effort whatever we did. We always understood that if we did not do this that an attempt would be made to get the Russians sewed up so that they would not either.[23]

So Gray took the hint just about as I am taking it now, and when he put it to you if that was what you meant, you backed down a bit, but not completely. You would naturally back down some, unless you were ready to go pretty far the other way. It would startle you to have Gray pick you up like that. It startled you enough so that you proceeded to fumble a related question. At least it looks like a fumble:

> GRAY: . . . at what time did your strong moral convictions develop with respect to the hydrogen bomb?
> OPPENHEIMER: When it became clear to me that we would tend to use any weapon we had.[24]

Now you had said, you know (see above), that "we were infinitely more vulnerable and infinitely less likely to initiate the use of these weapons." There is some difficulty in reconciling the two contentions: 1) that the tendency of the U.S. to use any weapon it might acquire created a moral objection to helping it acquire an H-bomb, and 2) that the small likelihood that the U.S. would use such a weapon as an H-bomb ("infinitely less" than the likelihood that the adversary would use it) would put the U.S. at a dangerous military disadvantage if H-bombs were acquired all round.

I will not press that. Nobody expects Euclidean consistency out of the Delphic Oracle.

Patriotic Impulse

I suggest, Doctor Oppenheimer, that you knew 1) that the USSR was technologically incapable of the independent production of nuclear weapons, and 2) that the U.S.A. was psychologically incapable of effective internal security.

I suggest that you sincerely did not want the United States to develop a weapon which you knew the Soviet Union would and could immediately steal (but could get in no other way), but that you were also unwilling to reveal what it was that made you so sure that Soviet Russia was in a position to steal it.

I suggest that you knew a great deal about the channels by which *information and materials* were transferred from the U.S.A. to the USSR. You did not want to reveal those channels to the American government

SUSPICION

we can't possibly keep them from getting it too; they depend on us that much, they are tied to us that close—had you said something like that, the debate might have gone a different way. Perhaps you thought, Surely they can see that for themselves, at least with the hints I have given! However, we have been credulous of everything but the obvious.

Hints and Hedging

You have given hints repeatedly. In the post-mortem before the Gray Board in 1954 you said:

The notion that the thermonuclear arms race was something that was in the interests of this country to avoid if it could was very clear to us [General Advisory Committee] in 1949. . . . We thought it was something to avoid even if we could jump the gun by a couple of years, or even if we could outproduce the enemy, because we were infinitely more vulnerable and infinitely less likely to initiate the use of these weapons. . . . This is an idea which I believe is still right, but I think what was not clear to us then and what is clearer to me now is that it probably lay wholly beyond our power to prevent the Russians somehow from getting ahead with it. I think if we could have taken any action at that time which would have precluded their development of this weapon, it would have been a very good bet to take that. . . . I believe that *their atomic effort was quite imitative* and that made it quite natural for us to think that *their thermonuclear work would be quite imitative* and that we should not set the pace in this development.[21]

Again you said:

I think we were right in believing that any method available consistent with honor and security for *keeping these objects out of the arsenals of the enemy* would have been a good course to follow.[22]

To me these look like hints, I understand that later in the hearing Gordon Gray picked you up on this very matter, and you hedged a bit. As follows:

GRAY: Is it your opinion, Doctor, that the Russians would not have sought to develop a hydrogen bomb unless they knew in one way or another . . . that this country was proceeding with it?
OPPENHEIMER: That was my opinion in 1949. . . .
GRAY: . . . Would it not have been reasonable to expect . . . that they

General Groves said that Russia didn't seem to appreciate the effect of the A-bomb at Hiroshima until after Bikini, when "the Russian observers who were there against my wishes" got ashore again at San Francisco and went to the Russian consulate. And within twenty-four hours the attitude of the Russian delegate at the UN "changed completely." Maybe the great bureaucracy had been simply filing the spies' reports and ignoring them.

ISABEL PATERSON
National Review, May 23, 1956

would do anything to increase their military strength?
OPPENHEIMER: Right.
GRAY: Whatever it might be.
OPPENHEIMER: Oh, sure.
GRAY: So you don't intend to have this record suggest that you felt that if those who opposed the development of the hydrogen bomb prevailed that would mean that the world would not be confronted with the hydrogen bomb?
OPPENHEIMER: It would not necessarily mean—we thought on the whole it would make it less likely. That the Russians would attempt and less likely that they would succeed in the undertaking.
GRAY: . . . That is two things. One, the likelihood of their success would we all hope still be related to their own capabilities and not to information they would receive from our efforts. So what you mean to say is that since they would not attempt it they would not succeed?
OPPENHEIMER: No. [I believe this the most ambiguous flat *No* I ever read.] I believe what we then thought was that the incentive to do it would be far greater if they knew we were doing it, and we had succeeded. Let me, for instance, take a conjecture. Suppose we had not done anything about the atom during the war. I don't think you could guarantee that the Russians would never have had an atomic bomb. But I believe they would not have one nearly as soon as they have now. I think both the fact of our success, the immense amount of publicity, the prestige of the weapon, the espionage they collect, all of this made it an absolutely higher priority thing, and we thought similar circumstances might apply to the hydrogen bomb. We were always clear that there might be a Russian effort whatever we did. We always understood that if we did not do this that an attempt would be made to get the Russians sewed up so that they would not either.[23]

So Gray took the hint just about as I am taking it now, and when he put it to you if that was what you meant, you backed down a bit, but not completely. You would naturally back down some, unless you were ready to go pretty far the other way. It would startle you to have Gray pick you up like that. It startled you enough so that you proceeded to fumble a related question. At least it looks like a fumble:

GRAY: . . . at what time did your strong moral convictions develop with respect to the hydrogen bomb?
OPPENHEIMER: When it became clear to me that we would tend to use any weapon we had.[24]

Now you had said, you know (see above), that "we were infinitely more vulnerable and infinitely less likely to initiate the use of these weapons." There is some difficulty in reconciling the two contentions: 1) that the tendency of the U.S. to use any weapon it might acquire created a moral objection to helping it acquire an H-bomb, and 2) that the small likelihood that the U.S. would use such a weapon as an H-bomb ("infinitely less" than the likelihood that the adversary would use it) would put the U.S. at a dangerous military disadvantage if H-bombs were acquired all round.

I will not press that. Nobody expects Euclidean consistency out of the Delphic Oracle.

Patriotic Impulse

I suggest, Doctor Oppenheimer, that you knew 1) that the USSR was technologically incapable of the independent production of nuclear weapons, and 2) that the U.S.A. was psychologically incapable of effective internal security.

I suggest that you sincerely did not want the United States to develop a weapon which you knew the Soviet Union would and could immediately steal (but could get in no other way), but that you were also unwilling to reveal what it was that made you so sure that Soviet Russia was in a position to steal it.

I suggest that you knew a great deal about the channels by which *information and materials* were transferred from the U.S.A. to the USSR. You did not want to reveal those channels to the American government or the American public—just as you once did not want to give Chevalier's name to General Groves—but you did have the patriotic impulse to prevent, if possible, our ever putting into the channels to Soviet Russia *information and materials of a new order of danger.*

You were like an embezzler's wife who will not denounce her husband to the authorities, but earnestly urges his employer not to enlarge his department.

"Scorpions in a Bottle"

Perhaps you have been misunderstood because of the same interference that jams my own attempts to get through to the public consciousness—a massive public preconception that Soviet Russia has a great atomic energy project of its own. Sure, it will be granted, Fuchs and the Rosenbergs made possible the Russian accomplishment and that was a terrible thing, but it is spilled milk now and we just have to set our jaws, tighten our belts, and pray for peace. Everyone knows that the Soviets have tested many atomic and hydrogen weapons, that while they are probably behind us in total stockpile the numbers on both sides are so great it hardly matters, that in certain respects they may have moved ahead of us (for example, they may have dropped an H-bomb from an airplane before we did), that on the whole the situation can be described as an "atomic stalemate," that the U.S.A. and the USSR are, in your own vivid phrase, like "two scorpions in a bottle, each capable of killing the other, but only at the risk of his own life."[25]

What people do *not* seem to know, however, is that when you used that image you did not say that the U.S.A. and the USSR had arrived at the stage where they *were* like two scorpions in a bottle; you said the time *might come* when they would be. (You said this on February 17, 1953. Perhaps you think that time has now come.)

In 1953 you very carefully estimated that *"the USSR is about four years behind us. . . . the scale of its operations is not as big as ours was four years ago. It may be something like half as big as ours then was."*[26] You, naturally, thought this was bad enough. *"The very least we can con-*clude," you said, *"is that our twenty-thousandth bomb . . . will not in any deep strategic sense offset their two-thousandth."*[27] This suggests that you thought of us as having a ten-to-one superiority in productivity.

What seems to be unknown is that you—who are our chief authority on the meaning of the scientific evidence concerning Soviet nuclear developments—have never said flatly that the Soviet atomic project is independently formidable. Through you, others have been persuaded to believe that it is independently formidable. They have been persuaded to believe much more than you are committed by the record to uphold. The effect is that of an advertisement in which the advantages of, say, the Tucker automobile are strikingly set forth, while some-

where in the fine print is a statement that nothing is actually in production. The majority of readers overlook the fine print.

Forensically, you have left an overwhelming impression of Soviet achievement; academically, you have been explicit in your reservations, have unobtrusively hedged the bet.

In September 1949 it was you who told the Pentagon and the Congressional Joint Committee the meaning of the reported Soviet explosion—quickly dubbed "Operation Joe." You were the principal expert in a panel of four. "We went over [the evidence of the Soviet explosion] very carefully and it was very clear to us that *this was the real thing, and there was not any doubt about it. . . . This was an atomic bomb."*[28]

Yet three and a half years later you were to say of the then much larger volume of scientific evidence concerning Soviet atomic activities: *"We do need one word of warning: This is evidence which could well be evidence of what the government of the USSR wants us to think, rather than evidence of what is true."*[29] Well, of course, what we the American people think—two scorpions and all—is what the Soviet rulers want us to think.

Why do we think as we do on this subject? Largely because of you, it appears. Indeed you tempt one to the great-man theory of history. Dean Latimer said of you, "I have seen him sway audiences. It was just marvelous, the phraseology and the influence is just tremendous."[30]

"I went over to the State Department," you told the Gray Board, "where the question was being discussed . . . should this [reported Soviet atomic explosion] be publicly announced by the President and I *gave some arguments in favor of that.* . . . I was taken up to hearings before the Joint Congressional Committee. . . . They were quite skeptical and I was not allowed to tell them the evidence. . . . All I could do was just *sound as serious and convinced and certain about it as I knew how.* I think by the time we left, the Joint Congressional Committee understood that this event had been real."[31] Evidently the phraseology was sufficiently marvelous.

A Later Reservation

Yet again, three and a half years later you were to qualify your estimate of Soviet atomic achievement with the reservation: "This [estimate] is consistent with the facts known to us. It has not been proven by them, *by any means."*[32] The little phrase which I have italicized seems to me in its own quiet way to be as startling as Harry Truman's declaration,[33] (which you deplored[34]) that he doubted whether the Russians had a workable A-bomb.

You have convinced the United States government and the American people that the Soviet atomic project is independently formidable, but apparently you have not fully convinced yourself.

Why have your reservations and

warnings about the inconclusiveness of the evidence in this area been so largely ignored? I don't suppose you understand that either. Sometimes people believe because they do not want to believe.

Nobody seems to have thought much about the fact that David Lilienthal, AEC Chairman at the time of the H-bomb debate, testified during your 1954 security hearing that, regarding "possible thermonuclear bomb capability of the Russians" . . . *"there were no intelligence reports that I can recall."*[35] This suggests that the Chairman of the U.S. Atomic Energy Commission had no positive information about the Russian plant which might have been supposed to have produced the Russian A-bomb. For if he had known anything about their A-bomb plant, as distinct from the bomb itself, then he would have known something about their H-bomb capability, just as, knowing something about our plant, he knew something of our capability.

A Counsel of Prudence

Excuse my repetitiousness, but what are we to make of the fact that these three men—1) Harry S. Truman, President of the United States, official source of the world news in 1949 that an atomic explosion had occurred in the Soviet Union, 2) David E. Lilienthal, Chairman of the AEC, government agency under which the scientific analysis of the evidence of all such explosions was conducted, and 3) you, J. Robert Oppenheimer, leading scientific adviser to both Truman and Lilienthal—have all made statements since 1949 casting doubt on the validity of what was officially said in 1949?

Is it not true—I think you would know—that for the past seven and a half years top American officials have based their working estimates of Russian nuclear capability, and their public statements about such estimates, on a certain kind of "counsel of prudence" rather than on complete, verified data? And is it not true that to whatever degree you have yourself been responsible for their having such an attitude, you nevertheless could have had, and did have, in your own mind an altogether different picture of the situation in the Soviet Union?

No doubt you were faced, briefly, with the same contradictory thoughts that puzzled others: 1) the improbability that Russia had the industrial capacity required to make an A-bomb —"machine tools . . . production of electronic control equipment, capacity to produce certain chemicals with the desired degree of purity, and things of that sort," the late Karl Compton explained to the Gray Board[36]—versus 2) the evidence that nevertheless an atomic explosion *had* occurred.

The situation, you saw, was not to be explained by the simple disjunctive implied in such arguments as: "You say they can't make an A-bomb, but I know they've got an A-bomb, so you must be wrong."

Or:

"You say they have an A-bomb, but I know they can't make an A-bomb, so you must be wrong."

Your own flexible imagination would quickly see another alternative:

"They can't make an A-bomb, but they've got an A-bomb—so they must have swiped it."

I know it is not easy to swipe an A-bomb. They would have had to work at it week after week after week because these things are complex. But it could be done.

I suggest that when you concluded in September 1949 that the Soviets had indeed exploded an A-bomb, you knew then that they must have

a pipe line—a damned good pipe line —to the American project. This would be consistent with what you knew of Communist methods (ingenious, thorough, unscrupulous) and American habits (careless, optimistic, naive).

Channels of Espionage

As the former director of Los Alamos you knew that nuclear bombs are assembled from components manufactured in every part of the United States. If such components can be transported so far they can be transported farther.

As a former intimate of Communists and a continuing intimate of former Communists, you knew of Communist channels through Mexico to Europe. Isaac Folkoff, a Communist "treasurer of something" you called him, explained to you in 1940 (you told the Gray Board) *"all the business about the refugees, the camps in France, the resettlement problems, and how much it cost and how much it cost to get to Mexico, and all the rest."*[37]

And you knew New Mexico. *"In 1929,"* you said of your brother Frank and yourself, *"we rented a little ranch up in the high mountains in New Mexico which we have had ever since, and we used to spend as much time there as we could in the summer. . . . It was a very primitive sort of establishment. . . . We spent part of the summer of 1941 together at the ranch . . . That was after my marriage. He [Frank] and his wife stayed on a while."*[38] In 1943, you said *"Groves sent an engineer around to look for a place [for a bomb laboratory]. He was around in the Southwest where I knew the country and in New Mexico, and I showed him and showed General Groves the city of Los Alamos."*[39]

With your intimate knowledge of the process, the organization, and the geography, you were in a position to realize, the moment it became clear in September 1949 that the Soviets had exploded an A-bomb years ahead of cautious estimates, not that you and Compton and others had been wrong about the stage at which Soviet development had arrived, *but that you had not given full credit to the Soviet underground.* Now you knew that the Communist underground railway could carry freight as well as passen-

The three wise men assigned to probe the Oppenheimer case were not even commissioned to look into the real scandal: that for eight decisive years our government was turning to nuclear physicists for guidance, not on technical details of atomic science, but on the very essence of grand strategy and national policies. Yet no dereliction Professor Oppenheimer might possibly be found guilty of can compare with the monstrous shame of statesmen who have invited atom-pushers into the highest policy councils of the nation.

WILLIAM S. SCHLAMM
U.S.A., May 17, 1954

gers. (We Americans are preoccupied with the theft of information data. Materials, to the Soviet mentality, are presumably more important. And in this case, almost as compact.) You knew better than anyone else how worthless the Manhattan District-AEC system of materials-accounting had been, so that no one could know by checking the inventory whether anything had been stolen or not.

More sophisticated than bomb physicist Robert Bacher,[40] you probably would not have been, as he said he was, "very deeply shocked to find how few atomic weapons we had at that time [December 1946]."[41]

What *did* happen to all that stuff they made at Oak Ridge in 1946? It was supposed to go into bombs at Los Alamos. According to Dr. Bacher, not much of it did.

Diversion of Material

Well, I suppose we shall never know. For in 1946 nobody was trying very hard to keep track of the stuff. I remember an old Trotskyite at Oak Ridge (I don't mean an aged Trotskyite; just a guy who had formerly passed for a Trotskyite, though actually some of the 4th International boys thought he was a Stalinist spy in their midst)—I remember how in dire tones he warned a group of young scientists (this was at a meeting in one of the Roane-Anderson buildings near the Central Bus Terminal) never to trust the U.S. Army. For *the Army,* he said, was undoubtedly *secreting quantities of U-235 and plutonium* in order to avoid turning them over to the forthcoming civilian agency, as it was supposed to do.

That is not too plausible, is it, that the Army would do that? But the old Trotskyite at least knew that *any such diversion of material by anybody at that time would hardly be detected.* For he was a sharp mathematician, and himself worked on accountability for fissionable materials at the gaseous diffusion plant. You would probably recognize his name if I gave it. He has written for the *Bulletin of the Atomic Scientists.* He left Oak Ridge, later tried to come back, fortunately (I think) didn't make it.

Then I remember one week-end in the spring of 1947 when an AEC ac-

countant from the production division came to my house in Oak Ridge to get advice on how to draw up an organization chart for the *brand-new* materials-accounting branch.

Three years and some months later, when I was working in the Washington AEC office, I remember a "management improvement" report coming in from Los Alamos to the effect that procedures developed by that materials-accounting branch and approved by the Commission in 1948 were being duly installed at Los Alamos—*in July 1950.*

That was about the same time the FBI arrested Dr. Sanford Simons in Denver for illegal possession of plutonium which he had taken out of Los Alamos in 1946.[42] I don't know how they caught him. Probably a confidential informant. Not through the Los Alamos inventory system, I'm sure. As I recall, he got eighteen months.

Of course that fellow who stole the gold from Los Alamos in 1952 got a stiffer sentence. I believe he is still at Leavenworth. If he hadn't run into difficulties trying to fence the stuff—Treasury men and city detectives stumbled on his track in Oklahoma City in 1954—he would have made a clean break. Los Alamos never knew they had been robbed till Treasury caught the guy. He himself had worked in materials-accounting, and when he quit his job in 1952 he walked off with 110 ounces of pure gold bullion which according to his books was an overage, and he was too embarrassed to turn it back in. Nobody missed it.[43] What a joint!

Case of the English Teacher

Flash back to 1948—the AEC materials-accounting representative at Los Alamos then was a former high-school English teacher. Since, as your successor as Laboratory Director, Dr. Norris Bradbury, told the Joint Committee, "the problem of accounting for so-called S.F. [source and fissionable] materials is a very complicated and technical problem,"[44] the young man was clearly over his head. Nor could he turn to the excellent scientific personnel on Dr. Bradbury's own staff, for they were, Dr. Bradbury told the Committee, "doing all in our power to handle this question *to the satisfaction of the Commission,*"[45] i.e., the young English teacher.

Then the young man got a boss—a pretty high-powered accountant who went out to New Mexico from the AEC office in Washington. In Washington this man had distinguished himself by hiring as one of his two main assistants a former understudy in the bureaucracy of—guess who?—Nathan Gregory Silvermaster! Now don't misunderstand me. I am not a guilt-by-association man. As a matter of fact, I had some association with the protégé of Silvermaster myself. And I am not guilty of any kind of pro-Communist activity. But I think all of us ought to be investigated most thoroughly. I had another acquaintance in AEC who went to Colombia to work with Lauchlin Currie. It's a small world.

The reason why personnel is so important is the inherent difficulty of materials control. Your friend Walter Zinn, the great reactor expert, testified during the Hickenlooper Investi-

101

gation, ". . . if you cannot have people who you are confident will not do this filching . . . your inventories cannot control the situation."[46]

A few days later Dr. C. E. Larson and Mr. Jesse Herndon, Oak Ridge Laboratory Director and Electromagnetic Plant Superintendent respectively, testified before the Committee. Dr. Larson spoke of their use at that time of the polygraph (lie detector), and added, ". . . if we agree that the polygraph is not valid and the amount concerned is within our limit of error . . . we would never catch it."[47]

Mr. Herndon said, "This brings us right back to the personal integrity of the individual involved. If you don't have that, you don't have security."[48]

That Famous Article

But you know more about all this than anybody else. That is what gives so much weight to your words in the famous article in *Foreign Affairs*, where you speak of a time when "there will have been . . . a vast accumulation of materials for atomic weapons, and *a troublesome margin of uncertainty with regard to its accounting.*"[49]

Naturally, you were not inclined to discuss these things fully with anyone. You were in large measure to blame—at least as much as any single other person—for the failure in materials-accounting. You knew that some of your friends would be caught up in any complete investigation into such an operation. More poignantly, you did *not* know which friends *might be* involved in something worse than negligence.

Against all this, however, you now knew that if the U.S. developed a new weapon the USSR would get its share of the product, and you knew that if the new weapon were a hydrogen bomb then even a small share could be catastrophic.

Serious as the Russian A-bomb was, it was by no means decisive. In June 1949 Senator McMahon had asked you: "One final question, Doctor. Are you satisfied with our weapon progress since the end of the war?"[50] And you had replied, "*It is my business not to be satisfied, but I am . . . it is far better than I thought it would be.*"[51] Evidently we had a rather large number of A-bombs. And the

Russians—concerning whom the issue was whether they had any at all—certainly did not have many.

Assuming that the Soviets would never have had any A-bombs if we had not made some first, it could be contended that by developing the A-bomb we had actually increased the danger to this country. For that development you shared responsibility. Yet it could also be argued that so long as we retained a runaway numerical superiority in A-bombs, our advantage would remain decisive. The number of A-bombs required to saturate the military objectives of a major power looked larger every day, and unless or until the Soviet Union achieved such a saturation number the power of restraint would remain in American hands.

With H-bombs the situation would be radically altered. The saturation number of these cannot be very large. Assume a U.S. superiority of 10 to 1

in either kind of bomb. Assume further (we observed above that you have implicitly made assumptions like these) that a great power can use many thousands of A-bombs (kiloton range) in a war, but never needs more than 15 or 20 (megaton range) H-bombs. The bottleneck in A-bomb military power is, then, production; the bottleneck with H-bombs is development. You told the Gray Board: "*We could have had the atom bomb as far as ideas went considerably earlier than we could have had it as far as hardware went. . . . With the hydrogen bomb I believe that the pacing factor was good ideas.*"[52]

1949: U. S. Superiority

Now go back to September 1949. Though A-bombs now evidently existed on both sides, yet it was clearly going to be a long time before Soviet Russia would catch up with the

Kreuttner

"It isn't that we scientists think we're better than other people. It's just that we're in a good position to make things pretty uncomfortable for everybody if we don't get the privileges and immunities we're after!"

United States in production, a usefully long time before the Soviet Union would have thousands of A-bombs—and this was true whether they made them or swiped them. Throughout that long time the U.S. numerical superiority (10 to 1 or whatever) would be an effective deterrent. But once the "good ideas" for making an H-bomb jelled and were tested, it would probably not take the U.S. long to produce two or three hundred. If in this comparatively brief interval the USSR produced or swiped even ten or fifteen, then you would find your two scorpions in the bottle.

Your colleague, the late Dr. John von Neumann (subsequently AEC Commissioner), told the Gray Board what he thought your views had been in 1949—"that we practically had the lead in whatever we did, and the Russians would follow, and that we were probably more vulnerable than they were for a variety of reasons, one of which is that we can probably saturate them right now—I meant right then—whereas they could not at that moment. Therefore a large increment on both sides would merely mean that both sides can saturate the other."[53]

And here is the turn of the screw, the fact that in clandestine methods of delivery the Soviet Union would clearly have the advantage.

Clandestine methods of delivery would not only (as E. U. Condon says) "provide the pinpoint accuracy that long-range weapons may possibly lack,"[54] they might even — it seemed in 1949—be the only methods available. As you wrote "Uncle Jim" Conant, "*I am not sure the miserable thing will work, nor that it can be gotten to a target except by ox cart.*"[55] Or, perhaps—to use Condon again—"in the hold of a ship floating idly at the Brooklyn docks."[56]

No wonder you wrote Conant that for the U.S. to become committed to the hydrogen bomb "as the way to save the country and the peace appears to me full of dangers." No wonder you told Teller to keep his shirt on.[57] No wonder you persuaded Rabi and Serber to reconsider their initial enthusiasm for an H-bomb as the answer to "Joe One"[58] (the first atomic explosion in the Soviet Union).

It was precisely "Joe One"—an atomic bomb essentially made in U.S.A., but assembled in, say, Stalinsk by Stalinists—which convinced you that *now* the U.S.A. *must not* make a hydrogen bomb.

You had a lot to answer for in the Communist apparatus so firmly installed at Los Alamos before 1946. One of the known agents of that apparatus — David Greenglass — last April gave the Senate Internal Security Subcommittee a somewhat more detailed account of an incident which he had related five years earlier during the trial of his sister Ethel and her husband:

GREENGLASS: Julius Rosenberg had instructed me to find people who were sympathetic to Communism in this project, and after finding them, he said, "Don't mention them. Just write them down." . . .
ROBERT MORRIS [Chief Counsel for the Committee]: Now, how many recruits had you written down? How many names had you written down, to the best of your recollection?
GREENGLASS: Oh, I would say there were between 20 and 25. . .
MORRIS: Now, did this list of 20 to 25—did that exhaust, do you think, the reservoir of potential scientists who would turn over, who would work for Rosenberg?
GREENGLASS: Let me—I will answer that. I frankly say "No." These people, these 20 or 25, were in my ken . . . there were others who were just as sympathetic who weren't in Los Alamos, that I heard of but I couldn't check of my own accord, and which I didn't put down, you see.[59]

Your own ken, Doctor Oppenheimer, is—to put it mildly—considerably broader than that of David Greenglass. On the other hand, your ability to assess the political inclinations of atomic scientists is probably much more accurate, too. Since you know so many more scientists, but would probably screen them more finely than Greenglass could, perhaps you too would come out with a list of twenty to twenty-five. The detail is speculation.

Later, your judgment of Communism hardened. Not only were you to speak of *"the obvious war between Russia and the United States,"* but speaking of Communism itself you would say, you did say to the Gray Board, *"Today it is a very simple thing. . . . We have a well-defined enemy."*[60]

Yet as late as June 1949 you still felt that there was some inherent indecency in a national military security program. You told the Joint Congressional Committee, when they asked your advice about the foreign distribution of isotopes, that that was "one of the few areas in which we are free to act the way we would like to act, generously, imaginatively and decently; *in the things that involve security we are inhibited from doing that.*"[61]

You said,

I do not think anybody can be happy at the fine-tooth combing that has to be given to every man that has to work on the atomic energy program. But one understands why it is; and as long as it is restricted to those places where there are some secrets to be kept, people will stand for it.
I think the [Atomic Energy] Commission has balanced very carefully, in the few cases I know about, the requirements of security and the requirements of progress and humanity. It has not been easy.[62]

Not easy for you, either, was it? Once you said:

Though we are men of science and we have a loyalty to each other everywhere, we also have a loyalty to our homes and our countries against which we will not work.[63]

The paradox was that from where you sat the very thing which to Teller and Lawrence and Strauss, and later Truman, looked like the logical move for home and country was the thing which seemed to be most enormously against home and country. For that hellish thing you would not work. But you could not tell them why.

III. EXHORTATION

Seems pretty melodramatic, doesn't it? How does it feel now to lecture at Harvard? How does it feel to preside at the Institute? Does it seem that the decorum there is what is real—that *that* is Veritas—and that Steve Nelson is a comic-strip character whom we can safely leave for Daddy Warbucks to handle?

But that won't do, will it? Steve occupies the attention of the Supreme Court, he is real.

And Bernard Peters is real. It has been a long time since he was telling the Executive Board of the Communist-front Federation of Architects, Engineers, Chemists, and Technicians, in Berkeley (on April 14, 1943) "that it is absolutely necessary to get a good foothold on the hill."[64] Now Dr. Peters is in Tata Institute in Bombay, working for Homi Bhabha—the atomic spirit of Geneva?[65]

Joan Hinton—the girl scientist from Los Alamos who has gone over to the Chinese Communists—is real. As a matter of fact she would fit right in at Cambridge, wouldn't she? I don't know her, but doesn't she have a New England background and good egghead connections (Lattimore, yourself) and a lot of that unobtrusive kind of suddenly disturbing feminine intelligence? The Lord knows where she is—somewhere in Suiyuan province of Inner Mongolia, working with Pontecorvo, no doubt.[66]

These people, and so many more that I can't ask you about because I haven't the slightest idea who they are—or else no documentation so far—have not ceased to exist and to operate just because you are campused.

Doctor, why don't you come clean? It might be a novel experience for you. It might do you good. I think the amount of truth that came out in the 1954 hearings before the Gray Board did you a lot of good. In 1953 you said to the Graduate Alumni at Princeton this tortured kind of thing: "It is true that many particulars can be understood and subsumed by a general order. But it is probably no less a great truth that *elements of abstractly irreconcilable general orders can be subsumed by a particular.*"[67] Now that is pretty high-level stuff and I don't necessarily know what you meant by it, but one thing those words might mean is that *a double life is O.K.* Right?

Almost two years later, chastened (I think) by the loss of your Q clearance and all that was involved in that loss, you said over CBS radio, "Never before have we had to understand the complementary, *mutually not compatible ways of life* and recognize *choice between them* as the *only course of freedom.*"[68] This language is still rarefied—much more so in context, by the way—but surely part of its meaning is, *sometimes you have to stand up and be counted.*

Turn on the Lights

Man, this is it. This is one of those times.

Nobody who knows anything about your case, Doctor—nobody I know—doubts that if you really did break and tell all you know, the whole picture of the national defense and security of the United States would light up like a used-car lot.

If you are patriotic and humanitarian, why don't you turn on the lights? We might not like what we saw, but we sure would be better off seeing it than stumbling on it in the dark.

Maybe I'm wasting my time. Maybe I've got you wrong. Maybe Borden was right.

Well, but even if you are a Soviet agent, you could defect. They **do it** all the time. The damned Communist empire is going to hell in a basket, fast. You can see that. A guy that knows as much as you do still has time to switch. You could probably make a deal.

Not with me. I don't know a thing. I'm suggesting it to you. And to those on our side that have something to deal with. I'll bet you could get a call through to J. Edgar Hoover at almost any hour of the day or night. Very few people could, but I'll bet you could.

All right, think of it this way. You are an idealist, and you are a realist. I'm using both those words in the non-technical sense. You know the condition of man, and you know (for you have said it in your book) that we need to love one another. You want peace. You want to avert the destruction of cities.

Now the United States is a funny country. It is rich and fat and scant o' breath, not to mention naive and semiliterate. I think you know this country pretty well. You've been in New Mexico and Tennessee as well as California and New York. If you will think about it you will know that what we may call Jacksonianism is

not dead by a long shot. Ask Arthur Schlesinger, Jr., what he thinks about that, though of course his opinion is probably not as good as your own.

Here's the thing—Old Hickory was a killer, an arrant nationalist killer. He left his imprint. You see, when he thought it was for Rachel or the United States he didn't think he was being selfish or immoral to shoot to kill, or order the troops to fire.

Nemo me impune lacessit. You know about the rattlesnake flag. And you must have noticed the American reaction to Bulganin's boast about rockets against Britain.

On the other hand, if the U.S. can be sure that it has a monopoly or an unrivaled superiority in atomic and hydrogen weapons, then it will probably be in no hurry to use them. We used them against Japan, but that was a sequel to Pearl Harbor. There doesn't have to be another Pearl Harbor, does there? Then perhaps there will not be another Hiroshima.

Speaking of Hiroshima—if you do decide to talk, you had better open your mouth sort of wide and make it real plain. I read in the *New York Times* where you told a graduating class last June that *"the nation's leaders 'lost a certain sense of restraint' when they decided to drop the atomic bomb at Hiroshima."*[69] This is an unfortunate way for a guy to get himself reported who not only "made the bomb," but also helped select the target.

You will remember that before the Gray Board you swore a solemn oath, and subsequently you said, among other things:

> Hiroshima was, of course, very successful, partly for reasons unanticipated by us. We had been over the targets with a committee that was sent out to consult us and to consider them, and *the targets that were bombed* [Hiroshima and Nagasaki] *were among the list that seemed right to us.* . . . We did say that we did *not* think exploding one of these things as a firecracker over a desert was likely to be very impressive.[70]

We need your testimony, Doctor. Let's have an operation candor and end the torment of secrecy. In spite of my probing into your personal affairs and speculating about your individual psychology, I am not anxious to regulate your life. My concern is with U.S. military security. I think that all invasions of your privacy ought to cease just as soon as you quit keeping private, matters of public consequence.

You can help your country. You can end the arms race by cutting off the "imitative" Soviets' source of supply of new information and materials. You can save from their own fanaticism those of your acquaintances who are working compulsively to undermine and sabotage the land that feeds them and the friends who guard them. They will not all hate you for it, for among them are some who want to be caught, being somewhat like the young fellow in Chicago who scribbled on the wall (in lipstick, wasn't it? It was pretty unpleasant), "Catch me, please, before I kill again."

Once you said, "We are gradually coming to a critical awareness of the fact that it is much harder to tell the truth than we like to think."[71]

Let's try again. It gets easier.

When you have done that you may find a new though ancient complementarity, where "Mercy and truth are met together; righteousness and peace have kissed each other."

Documentary Notes

1. See United States Atomic Energy Commission: *In the Matter of J. Robert Oppenheimer, Transcript of Hearing before Personnel Security Board*, Washington, D.C., *April 12, 1954, through May 6, 1954*. p. 710. U.S. Govt. Printing Office, 1954. Hereinafter this work is cited as *JRO Hearing.*

2. *Idem*, p. 837.

3. *Idem*, p. 184.

4. Wendell Latimer, Associate Director of the Radiation Laboratory, sometime Dean of Chemistry of the University of California, and possibly the saltiest witness in the Oppenheimer Hearings, under cross-examination by one of Dr. Oppenheimer's attorneys, was somewhat scornful in his rejection of the suggestion that Oppenheimer, to whom Latimer attributed tremendous personal influence, was himself under the influence of General Leslie R. Groves, Commanding General of the Manhattan Project, responsible for production of the atomic bomb. "Oppenheimer was the leader in science," said Latimer. "Groves was simply an administrator." *JRO Hearing*, p. 663 et seq.

5. According to Lincoln Barnett, "J. Robert Oppenheimer," *Life*, Oct. 10, 1949, p. 133, ". . . when the great ball of fire rolled upward to the blinded stars [in the original atomic bomb test in New Mexico, July 16, 1945] fragments of the *Bhagavad-Gita* flashed into [Dr. Oppenheimer's] mind: 'If the radiance of a thousand suns were to burst at once into the sky, that would be like the splendor of the Mighty One. . . . I am become death, the shatterer of worlds.'"

6. *JRO Hearing*, pp. 116-117. Italics added, as in any other passages hereinafter quoted from these hearings and italicized.

7. *Fear, War, and the Bomb*, Whittlesey House, McGraw-Hill Book Co., 1948, p. 5.

8. In *Atomic Power and Private Enterprise*, Joint Committee Print, Joint Committee on Atomic Energy, 82d Congress, 2d Session, Govt. Printing Office, 1952, p. 188.

9. *JRO Hearing*, p. 204.

10. *Idem*, p. 205.

11. *Ibid.*

12. *Idem*, p. 195.

13. *Idem*, p. 205.

14. Perhaps the most embarrassing of a number of characterizations of this sort is in Charles P. Curtis' *The Oppenheimer Case*, Simon and Schuster, 1955, p. 276, where Curtis compares Dr. Oppenheimer to Joan of Arc. Two of the three members of the Gray Board, and four of the five members of the Atomic Energy Commission, Curtis compares to Joan's judges—*"as honest a lot of poor fools as ever burned their betters."*

15. *JRO Hearing*, p. 196.

16. *Idem*, p. 357.

17. *Idem*, p. 888.

18. *Idem*, p. 785.

19. *Ibid.*

20. *Ibid.*

21. *Idem*, p. 80.

22. *Idem*, p. 87.

23. *Idem*, pp. 249-250.

24. *Idem*, p. 250.

25. *Foreign Affairs*, July 1953, p. 529. Also in J. Robert Oppenheimer, *The Open Mind*, Simon and Schuster, 1955, p. 68.

26. *Foreign Affairs*, July 1953, pp. 526-527. *The Open Mind*, p. 64.

27. *Foreign Affairs*, July 1953, p. 528. *The Open Mind*, p. 66.

28. *JRO Hearing*, p. 75.

29. *Foreign Affairs*, July 1953, p. 526. *The Open Mind*, p. 64.

30. *JRO Hearing*, p. 664.

31. *Idem*, pp. 75-76.

32. *Foreign Affairs*, July 1953, p. 527. *The Open Mind*, p. 64.

33. To an INS reporter. One place to find it is *Newsweek*, Feb. 9, 1953.

34. *Foreign Affairs*, July 1953, p. 531. *The Open Mind*, p. 70.

35. *JRO Hearing*, p. 409.

36. *Idem*, p. 258.

37. *Idem*, p. 185.

38. *Idem*, pp. 101-102.

39. *Idem*, p. 28.

40. Dr. Robert F. Bacher was Dr. Oppenheimer's wartime colleague at Los Alamos, later a member of the original Atomic Energy Commission.

41. *Investigation into the United States Atomic Energy Project, Hearing before the Joint Committee on Atomic Energy*, Govt. Printing Office, 1949, p. 770.

42. *Soviet Atomic Espionage*, Joint Committee on Atomic Energy, Govt. Printing Office, 1951, p. 193.

43. My information is based on a telephone conversation with the U.S. Treasury Department office in Oklahoma City.

44. *Investigation into the United States Atomic Energy Project, etc.*, p. 823.

45. *Idem.*, p. 824.

46. *Idem*, p. 389.

47. *Uranium Inventory at Oak Ridge, Hearing before Joint Committee on Atomic Energy*, Govt. Printing Office, 1949, pp. 14-15.

48. *Ibid.*

49. *Foreign Affairs*, July 1953, p. 534. *The Open Mind*, p. 76.

50. *Investigation into the United States Atomic Energy Project, etc. Hearing before the Joint Committee on Atomic Energy*, p. 310.

51. *Ibid.* See also Rep. (now Senator) Henry Jackson's almost identical question and Oppenheimer's almost identical answer, p. 302.

52. *JRO Hearing*, p. 233.

53. *Idem*, p. 647.

54. "The New Technique of Private War," in D. Masters & K. Way, *One World or None*, Whittlesey House, 1946, p. 41.

55. *JRO Hearing*, p. 242.

56. *Loc.cit.*

57. *JRO Hearing*, p. 714.

58. *Idem*, pp. 785, 805.

59. *Scope of Soviet Activity in the United States. Hearings before the Subcommittee to Investigate the Administration of the Internal Security Act, etc.* April 27, 1956. Part 21, pp. 1100-1101.

60. *JRO Hearing*, pp. 112, 252.

61. *AEC Investigation Hearing*, p. 299.

62. *Idem*, p. 302.

63. J. Robert Oppenheimer, "The Scientific Foundations of World Order," **2nd** of 7 lectures (by various speakers) before the Social Science Foundation of the University of Denver, 1946-7, published in Philip P. Wiener, *Readings in Philosophy of Science*, Scribner's, 1953, p. 432.

64. See *Facts Forum News*, June 1955, pp. 28-29. "The hill" means here the Radiation Laboratory at Berkeley. In AEC circles in New Mexico it means Los Alamos. And of course in Washington it means Capitol Hill.

65. *JRO Hearing*, p. 215.

66. See *Facts Forum News*, March 1955, p. 36ff.

67. *The Open Mind*, p. 124. Italics added.

68. *Idem*, p. 144. Italics added.

69. *New York Times*, June 10, 1956, p. 47. Italics added.

70. *JRO Hearing*, pp. 33-34. Italics added.

71. Lincoln Barnett, "J. Robert Oppenheimer," *Life*, Oct. 10, 1949, p. 136.

Springhead to Springhead

The independent farmer, says one of their number,

is doomed to lose his fight against bureaucracy;

but it was worth making and will not be forgotten

WHITTAKER CHAMBERS

an govt. invading property through Agricltrl controls

After winter's long, cold enemy occupation, spring is back; no longer halting and promissory, but true, irreversible spring. Now the springheads, dried up in last summer's fierce drought and long silent, burst out again, refilled by this spring's plentiful moisture, and rush on their way to the sea with a chance of drowning babble in babble as they pour past Washington (we are in the Potomac watershed). Now the voices of the fertilizer and lime purveyor and the farm implement hucksters are heard louder than the voice of the turtle in the land. "Make five blades of corn grow where one grew before," they coo. "Let 140 bushels an acre (with fertilizers) swell farm surpluses which 40 bushels (without fertilizer) could never swell so prosperously. Let one man do (with machines) the work that three could scarcely do (without). So disemployment thrives." Of course, they do not really say these things; this is only the logic of what they say.

And, as throughout nature in the spring voice answers voice, their voices are answered by others. These are the voices of the Agriculture Department's employees, and other official and semi-official farmers' helpmeets. There are enough of these turtles in the land so that, if there were time at this season to count noses, I suspect that the bureaucratic nose count in almost any farm county would fill you with wonder at how they manage without colliding. In part, they manage by a division of labor. While some (bringing, often, a good deal of expert knowledge and patient solicitude to jobs, in general, poorly paid) are helping you multiply yields—others (the land-bankers and that ilk) are exhorting you to decrease yields. They will pay you for it, too; and so painlessly that some scarcely notice that the hand which

reaches for the payment is thereafter meshed in the controls. Since few seem to mind this, or to notice the gaping paradox—the coos of increase cancelling the coos of decrease —perhaps it hardly matters. Yet history, glancing back, may be struck by another paradox and wonder if, in America, it was not in the countryside that socialism first took firm root and stooled.

The Bureaucrat Tactic

It has been a carefully nurtured growth. The earlier controls (Roosevelt and Wallace *consulibus*) were rather flirtatious things. Bureaucracy was chiefly feeling out the land to see how many inches it could take before reaching for a mile. On this farm, we were always careful to plant less than the official wheat allotment. But the great tactic (it is almost a reflex) of the bureaucrat mind is to keep things unsettled, to keep you off balance, to make you feel unsure. So I was not surprised when, one day years ago, a small character knocked at the door to say that he was the wheat inspector, that he had been looking over our fields (of course, without asking), and that we were overplanted. His thin, sidewise smile tried to hint at least hanging at sunrise. It disturbed my wife. But I knew that we were not overplanted, and I thought I knew what silver cord connects bureaucracy and politics. "Elections are coming up," I said to her. "You can be absolutely sure that nothing more will be heard of this." Nothing was, of course.

But, shortly afterwards, I happened in on a neighbor who is made of sterner stuff. It was hog-feeding time, and he approached with a pail of slop in each hand. I asked: "Did that fellow look over your fields?"

My neighbor set down each pail, somewhat with the air of a President laying a State of the Union message on a lectern; and eyed me for a moment of dense silence. Then he said: "You know he's a black-hearted skunk," adding with immense relish: "I run 'im." I thought I heard the fifes of '76.

You will not hear them now, or, I think, again. Those days, around Pearl Harbor, were a simpler, sweeter time. Besides, the Second World War, with mass armies and half a world to feed, made nonsense of controls. It remained for this Administration to weld them on. I have never known on just what remote, snow-capped Olympus the wheat allotments were alloted. Official notice of how much (or how little) wheat you could henceforth lawfully plant just arrived, one day, in the mail. But, if you had been alloted less than fifteen acres (most of us were), you could not afterwards vote about continuing or discontinuing this control. Voting about that was henceforth the privilege of the bigger planters. Those under fifteen acres were henceforth stripped of a vote in this rather relevant matter. Moreover, if you planted above your official allotment, even if the yield of the overplant was not for sale, was used wholly to feed your own stock or poultry, you still had to pay a penalty for growing it. Moreover, government surveyors could come into your fields at any time, to measure your wheat acreage and determine what penalty you must pay. This, you will see, went considerably beyond controls in the earlier sense, which most farmers had been content to abide by if only, by doing so, they would be let alone; while some, in the vain hope that the surest way to be let alone was not to take even the subsidies to which controls entitled them, refused these.

So it happened, now, that a few such farmers, who held that their land was inviolable, and that the day of the *kolkhoz* had not yet arrived made known their temperatures by running up, at the entrance to their farms, signs which read: "Government agents keep out!" There was a tiny farm revolt hereabouts, with some strong feelings and words between embattled farmers and officials. And these farmers were certainly mistaken; at least about what hour of history it is. The years of bureaucratic feeling-out were over. The day of submission-or-else had come. The Administration moved swiftly against the resisters in a legal action known (ironically enough, it seemed to some) as: *The People* v. *Morelock*.

You can read about this particular Morelock in *Witness*, where I wrote of him and his family: "Names to be written rather high, I think, on the column which is headed: 'And thy neighbor as thyself.'" In sum, the charge was interfering with government agents in pursuit of their duty. Mr. Morelock and his fellow defendants won that action, on a technicality, rather, I suspect, to the relief of the bureaucracy, which wanted no martyrs; and whose chief purpose, after all, was not to harass or penalize farmers. What was wanted was to seal on controls and cut surpluses, and this the resistance threatened over-all.

One Man's Resistance

It was a silly, hot-headed, inconsequential resistance? It did not reflect the feelings of masses of farmers anywhere? There is a point of view—nowadays we tend to exalt it as "reasonable"—from which any spontaneous resistance on principle, and against odds, is seen always to be silly. And such struggles often appear inconsequential enough at the time. Those who make them are few in number if only because those who react fiercely on principle are, in the nature of men, likely to be few. Nor are they, in the nature of themselves, likely to be worldlywise, to have thought out in crisp detail all the implications of their action. If they could do this, presumably they could not act. For their drive to act is organic and instinctive, not neatly cerebral. So their opponent finds it easy to dismiss them as crackpots and extremists; and, in general, his strength is defined by the degree to which he can afford to dismiss them with the derisive smile. The smile mantles power.

Perhaps I should make a point clear: I was not directly concerned by any of this. Some time before, when we saw that controls were coming to stay, we simply stopped planting wheat. But I could not bear to see my friends mauled. So I spoke privately to the wife of one embattled farmer. I went to the wife because I did not wish to sustain the man's hurt or blazing anger at what I had to say. In effect I said: "Urge him to stop. He cannot win. He will only destroy himself, and for nothing. This cause was lost before it began." These people are strong human types of a kind little known among the mystic circles of the intellectuals. They hate a quitter, and they do not make a quick distinction between a faint heart and the coldly measuring glance. I saw dawning in this woman's eyes, first shock that I, of all people, should say this; then a tinge of just-repressed contempt. "That is not what you did in the Hiss Case," she said. I said: "No. That is why I am saying this to you. Do not destroy your lives for nothing."

Then I went away. I did not return until the action was over; all had simmered down, and reality had taught what words seldom can. For these people have a strong grasp of reality, a simple wisdom of the earth, where ten minutes of unseasonable hail will tear to ribbons a year's corn—but you go on from there. By then, they knew (whether or not they would admit the fact in words) that they were the defeated. They were proud to have made the effort; and I think that this pride was about in ratio to their realization that they could only have been defeated; no other issue was possible. It was their pride to have acted, anyway. Into that pride they retreated. This was no retreat from principle. The retreat was into silent conformity to superior force, the force of the way things are, which compels compliance, but convinces no one. In ending their resistance, they yielded to that force, but from their silence they looked out at it with unyielding scorn.

I asked the woman to whom I had first spoken: "What now?" She answered that, when the Republican Party was first organized, her forebears (they had always lived on this same farm) had voted for Fremont. When, just before and during the War Between The States, Maryland was rent, they had twice voted for Lincoln. They were Black Republicans; in the whole history of the line, they had never voted anything but Republican. She said: "We will never vote for a Republican again." I said: "What do you gain by that? Do you suppose those others [the Democrats] will not give you more and tighter controls?" She said: "Then we will never vote again at all." Never is a long word. But, in so far as anything can be certain in an uncertain world, I think it is certain that these people —they are of the breed of those who built the nation from the unpeopled earth—will never vote again. They have silently seceded, not so much from the electorate (that is only the form the gesture takes), but from what they believe to be betrayal of basic principle, without which their world surrenders a part of its meaning. That principle is the inviolability of a man's land from invasion even by the State, the right of a man to grow for his own use (unpenalized by the State) a harvest which his labor and skill wrings from the earth, and which could not otherwise exist. Freedom was at stake, of which the inviolable land and its harvest were symbol and safeguard. The word "indivisible" is not one that these people commonly think or speak with. So they do not think or say: "Freedom is indivisible." But that is what they sensed and that is why they acted. It was not controls, but coercion, they resisted.

Crisis of Abundance

Do not misunderstand me. I do not suppose that wheat allotments, or similar controls, are inherently wicked, or that government's action in enforcing them was wrong—given our reality. I believe them to be inescapable, which is something different. The problem of farm surpluses is, of course, a symptom of a crisis of abundance. It is the gift of science and technology—improved machines, fertilizers, sprays, antibiotic drugs, and a general rising

107

efficiency of know-how. The big farm, constantly swallowing its smaller neighbors, is a logical resultant of those factors (big machines are fully efficient only on big acreages). Surpluses follow. So does the price trend of farm real estate, steadily creeping upward for decades. So does the downtrend of the farm population (it has fallen by a million in about two decades).

If farmers really meant to resist these trends, to be conservative, to conserve "a way of life" (as they often say), they would smash their tractors with sledges, and go back to the horse-drawn plow. Of course, they have no intention of doing anything so prankish, and, moreover, would not be let do it if they tried. Controls would appear at that point, too. For the cities, which dominate this society, are dependent on machine-efficient yields. So the State would have to act to prevent the farmer from preserving "a way of life," just as it has to act by controlling, in the field, an agriculture of anarchic abundance. Both are actions against anarchy. Controls of one kind or another are here to stay so long as science and technology are with us; or, until the ability of farmers to produce and the ability of the rest of us to consume their product is again in some rough balance, thus ending the problem. That balance will be restored, presumably, in the course of a survival of the fittest, in which efficiency determines survival. And efficiency is itself the result of a number of factors, one of which is almost certainly size of operation. In short, the farm unit tends to grow bigger and more efficient, as the farmers, growing more efficient, too, grow drastically fewer in necessary numbers.

This is the only *solution* of the farm problem; one that is obviously impersonal and rather inhuman (and in that it is exactly like any other comparable development in history, for example the development of the factory system). Short of that solution, no man or party can solve the farm problem. They can only contrive palliatives. All that men and parties can do is to try to mitigate and soften, in human terms, the plight of the farmer in the course of heading toward that impersonal solution which science and technology impose. Hence

controls and the incipient socialism of the countryside which controls imply and impose. This is the basic situation, however much incidental factors may disguise, blur, or even arrest it for longer or shorter terms. That is why the mass of farmers go along with controls which, almost without exception, they loathe. Who will say that they are not right?

Yet neither do I believe my neighbors were wrong to resist. I believe they were right, too—and on a plane which lies beyond controls. In my heart, I believe that no resistance on principle, where freedom is the principle involved, is ever meaningless, or ever quite hopeless, even though history has fated it to fail. For it speaks, not to the present reality, but to the generations and the future. And, in so far as it speaks for freedom, it speaks for hope. Freedom and hope—they are the heart of our strength, and what we truly have to offer mankind in the larger conflict with Communism that we are also locked in.

It was not the initial resistance that I was urging my neighbors against in this case, but an unwise persistence in it. I thought that resistance, once enacted, was well done and full of meaning for us all. I thought that, thereafter, swift disengagement was simple common sense, since neither the battle nor the war could be won —not in this season of history. The fewness of the resisters, their summary defeat, the way in which their struggle passed largely unnoticed and was quickly forgotten, seemed to bear out this view.

A Great Continuity

It also chilled me. It seemed to me that, with the defeat of these farmers, a retaining wall had fallen out. And this not only in the sense that hereby the enveloping State had made a new envelopment, and that, to that extent, the whole outwork of individual freedom and its safeguards was weakened. The real portent was the complacent consensus that it scarcely mattered. No one was stirred. No one really cared. No one rose to say that when, at any point, the steadily advancing State retrenches the rights and freedom of any group, however small, however justified the retrenchment is in terms of imper-

sonal reality, every man's security is breached. That tells us what hour of day it is.

That is why, I think, it is not wholly cranky or idle to remember, with each returning spring, this episode. Not that I think it will be forgotten. The land has a long, long memory. Nothing is much more thought-provoking than to listen—in barns where men meet and talk on days too wet to work, in farm kitchens on winter nights—and hear the names of men and women long dead (names which, in life, were scarcely known beyond a radius of 30 miles) come to life in conversation. They live again in most precise detail—tricks of manner, speech, dress, foibles, follies, generosities, integrities, courage, defeats. Often such recollections are laced, in the telling, with much human malice. Yet even this, at its worst, has the effect of brushing the grass on many an otherwise neglected grave. And, by that touch, is restored a great continuity—the same from the beginning of the earth, through the mentioned dead, to those who mention them. A nation is also its dead. As if any of us lived otherwise than on the graves of those who gave us life, who, so long as we conserve them in memory, constitute that generative continuity. Among such memories, surely, will remain, like a germ in a seed, the little farmers' resistance. Perhaps in some more fully socialized spring to come, someone, listening to that recollection, will pause over it long enough to ask himself: "What was the principle of freedom that these farmers stood for? Why was the world in which this happened heedless or wholly unconcerned? Why did they fail?"

Perhaps he will not be able, in that regimented time, to find or frame an answer. Perhaps he will not need to. For perhaps the memory of those men and women will surprise him simply as with an unfamiliar, but arresting sound—the sound of springheads, long dried up and silent in a fierce drought, suddenly burst out and rushing freely to the sea. It may remind him of a continuity that outlives all lives, fears, perplexities, contrivings, hopes, defeats; so that he is moved to reach down and touch again for strength, as if he were its first discoverer, the changeless thing—the undeluding, undenying earth.

→ Acknowledging Reality of Cptlsm on Agrarian farming ideals